Praise for *Contested Lands*

'*Contested Lands* offers a thorough exploration of the historical background behind the enduring territorial dispute between India and China. With a clear-sighted and measured approach, Raza delves into the core of the issue, providing rigorous research and analysis.'

—*The Times of India*

'Maroof Raza's book *Contested Lands* is a timely book, given that the contemporary affairs involving the two neighbours is a continuation and reflection of historical dissonances. The book adopts a linear narrative that covers the genesis, course, contestations and collisions of India-China history in the 20th century. Books covering the arc of modern India-China relations have faced challenges negotiating the complex layers of events, stakeholders and disputes.

'*Contested Lands*, brings a fresh, coherent perspective through a nifty approach, sharp insights and candid analysis written in spare prose … an important addition to the historiography on India-China that ought to be read by policy makers, army officers, scholars and others.'

—Probal Dasgupta, author of *Watershed 1967*, in *The Indian Express*

'As one of India's foremost strategic affairs experts, Maroof Raza stands apart. His latest offering, *Contested Lands* is now firmly in the bestsellers spot, provides details of India's borders with China. The hallmark of his books remains his depth of research and ability to put across the facts in a logical manner connecting all the dots and looking at issues from a different perspective. The book will surely be amongst the most valued books and a necessary addition of literature by those who wish to understand the historical background and its attendant complexities.'

—Maj. Gen. Jagatbir Singh, in *The Week*

'The contentious areas of Aksai Chin in the north-east of Ladakh and the McMahon Line separating India's north-eastern frontier region from Tibet are the two areas of dispute that dominate the relationship between the two. In spite of numerous attempts, why have the two neighbours have not moved beyond talks towards a settlement?

'*Contested Lands* by Maroof Raza is a masterpiece of an impartial and unbiased account of connected events based on authentic facts and figures—to have been published for the first time. It takes the reader through deep and painstaking research spanning over the larger perspectives of geopolitics, geo-economics, diplomatic and military dimensions at global/regional/national levels to the domestic paradoxes on the subject ... the book in its current form is a must-read for all especially personnel from defence services. It deserves a place in the bookshelves of students of military history all over the world, every proud Indian, military & national leadership in the hierarchy and those who are keen to understand the nuances of the LAC and its evolving dynamics. It is a necessary encyclopaedic addition to the literature on Indo-China relations for easy reference.'

—Maj. Gen. Sudhakar Jee, VSM,
in the Army War College journal *Mhow*

'Maroof Raza's *Contested Lands* succeeds where most other recent works on the India-China boundary dispute failed. This is because of the fact that the book underlines the premise that at the end of six decades of disputation there is a need for matter-of-factness in both the countries. Although Raza seems to lay stress that there has to be "political giants" in order to solve a problem of such a magnitude, his showcasing of the need for pragmatism might well have met Trevor-Roper's first dictum in full measure. After all, the India-China boundary dispute is not yet a dead history.'

—Jaideep Saikia, in *Firstpost*

CONTESTED LANDS

Maroof Raza, a former Indian Army officer, was educated in India and the UK. He is now a well-known media commentator on global, military and security issues in India, and has been consulting editor (on strategic affairs) for India's Times TV network, where he has hosted award-winning shows like *Line of Duty* and *Tales of Valour*. Maroof's areas of interest include the Kashmir issue, Sino-Indian relations and insurgencies. His published works include *Kashmir's Untold Story* (co-authored with Iqbal Chand Malhotra), *Shourya Gatha: Bharat ke Veer Senani* (co-authored with Lt Col. Sheodan Singh) and an anthology of essays that he co-edited, *Confronting Terrorism*. He has also lectured in India and abroad on India's security challenges, and on what India should do to become a great power. For more details visit: https://www.maroofraza.com.

Dedicated to those gallant Indian soldiers who stood up to severe odds against the Chinese army in those high Himalayas. For their grit and gallantry, these words of Thomas Babington Macaulay say it all:

'To every man upon this earth
Death cometh soon or late.
And how can man die better
Than facing fearful odds,
For the ashes of his fathers,
And the temples of his gods'

CONTESTED LANDS

INDIA, CHINA AND THE BOUNDARY DISPUTE

MAROOF RAZA

WESTLAND NON-FICTION

First published in hardback by Westland Non-Fiction, an imprint of Westland Publications Private Limited, in 2021

Published in paperback by Westland Non-Fiction, an imprint of Westland Books, a division of Nasadiya Technologies Private Limited, in 2024

No. 269/2B, First Floor, 'Irai Arul', Vimalraj Street, Nethaji Nagar, Alapakkam Main Road, Maduravoyal, Chennai 600095

Westland, the Westland logo, Westland Non-Fiction and the Westland Non-Fiction logo are the trademarks of Nasadiya Technologies Private Limited, or its affiliates.

ISBN: 9789357768412

10 9 8 7 6 5 4 3 2

The views and opinions expressed in this work are the author's own and the facts are as reported by him, and the publisher is in no way liable for the same.

The designations employed and the presentation of the material on the maps featured have been created by a cartographer, based on historical references and representations. The said maps are for representational purposes only, that is, for a better understanding of the political and geographic context contained in the book. While efforts have made to be compliant with the 'Guidelines for acquiring and producing Geospatial Data and Geospatial Data Services including Maps (2021)', in the event of any inadvertent or non-deliberate discrepancy or error in any of the maps featured in the book, the same will forthwith be removed/rectified on being notified.

Typeset by SÜRYA, New Delhi

Printed at Manipal Technologies Limited, Manipal

CONTENTS

LIST OF MAPS

FOREWORD

Contested Lands takes its readers through the history of India's boundary-making with Tibet and China, starting from the colonial period that involved intricate details of geophysical exploration across the Himalayas—primarily driven by the British Empire's strategic consideration of keeping the Russian Empire at bay. In doing so, the British strategic masters astutely used Tibet as a pawn in the delicate balancing act between the various suitors competing for territorial expansion in Inner Asia. The best the British could consider for Tibet was the idea of having Chinese 'suzerainty' instead of 'sovereignty' over it.

The author then analyses the current India–China boundary contestation stemming from varying interpretations of history in the postcolonial era. When China, under Chairman Mao, denounced all the boundary treaties as colonial constructs and decided to redraw its national boundaries based on China's imperial history, it put India in a precarious position.

If Nehru had taken a position on the boundary based on India's past links with Tibet, it would have meant that India lost more territories, especially with the Tibetans reclaiming territories from post-Independence India that they had lost to British India back in the day. As a result, Nehru had no other option but to base India's post-Independence boundary claims as per the treaties signed by the British.

The author correctly explains that there could be many reasons for recurring military stand-offs between India and

China, and the latter's assertive position vis-à-vis India, but the overwhelming impression among people that an unsettled boundary is caused by what was 'Tibet's border' is being perpetuated as an illusionary fact—something India has never come to terms with.

While tracing the critical factors, one finds that the notion of 'red fear' originally permeated in Indian politics, security, culture and society from the late 1950s, during the initial phases of the Cold War, and has lasted longer than the Cold War itself. In fact, the prolonged politico-military rivalry between India and China has even become more pervasive than the confrontation between the East and the West, which was confined to their ideological differences. If at all, the congruence of values and interests between the two great Asian nations has been replaced by a relationship of antagonism and distrust at all levels through the last six decades.

The author dwells on the efforts being made since 1962 to respect the boundaries through bilaterally evolved agreements and mechanisms. But, far from the countries coming to a binding boundary settlement, the more the two sides tried to change, the more they remained the same, if not become more complicated.

The recent Sino-Indian military Ladakh stand-off—and the Galwan incident as a consequence—is reminiscent of a cyclical crisis initially invented by the Americans in 1959 that continues to erupt from time to time with no end in sight. If the Indians continue to remain guided by American interests and do not apply their own historical sense of judgment and wisdom, the Chinese are likely to have the upper hand, including nibbling on lands perceived by India as its territory.

Ambassador Phunchok Stobdan

Author of *The Great Game in the Buddhist Himalayas: India and China's Quest for Strategic Dominance*

INTRODUCTION

My great-great grandfather, Rai Bahadur Dr Gokul Chand Malhotra, FRCS, a civil surgeon from Punjab, was born in 1845 in the twilight of the Sikh Empire founded by Maharaja Ranjit Singh. This empire was the greatest impediment to the consolidation of British rule in India and the British used every trick in the book to bring about its destruction by allying with Raja (later Maharaja) Gulab Singh, one of the pillars of this empire. Raja Gulab Singh was, however, a strategic visionary who expanded the writ of the Sikh Empire to Gilgit, Shahidullah, Ladakh, Aksai Chin and Minsar at the foothills of Mount Kailash, the holiest pilgrimage for Hindus and Tibetans.

Post 1846, when the British hived off the area of Jammu & Kashmir and bestowed it to the newly crowned Maharaja Gulab Singh, both he and his son, Maharaja Ranbir Singh, would in all probability have extended and consolidated the remit of their kingdom of Jammu & Kashmir to the annexation of Khotan in southern Sinkiang and Gartok in western Tibet. The latter had been conquered by General Zorawar Singh but lost to a Sino-Tibetan counter-attack in December 1841, when the failure of Sikh logistics led to the death of Zorawar Singh in the battle of To-Yo.

Both Gulab Singh and Ranbir Singh were reined in by British policy towards Czarist Russia and Qing China. The British were unwilling to squeeze the Chinese too much lest it, in any way, impede or obstruct the highly lucrative opium trade that was bringing in millions of ounces of silver into India every year. Further, paranoia about Russian intentions in India and Tibet drew the British into propping up the beaten and humiliated Qing Empire as a proxy suzerain in Tibet against the Russians. Therefore, on the one hand, the British actively degraded both the political and sovereign authority of the Qing Empire, while on the other hand, they used their beaten, exhausted and opium-ridden adversary to stand as their proxy against Czarist Russia. In all of these moves, the British liberally used their Indian troops to enforce their writ all over coastal China and Tibet. This policy pursued against China from 1839 to 1939 earned the wrath of the Chinese elite against India.

Therefore, the Indo-Sinkiang border and the two parts of the Indo-Tibetan border, namely the Aksai Chin region and the North East Frontier Region (NEFA), unwittingly became a casualty of this contradictory British policy, which wanted to define and consolidate India's borders, but was willing to remain ambivalent and deliberately slow in this process because China was being milked by the British in many ways from loans, infrastructure development, trade, railways and, above all else, opium. To further this latter end, the British constantly encouraged the Chinese to claim a chimeric sovereignty in Tibet, not realising that one day this would become a fatal sore for the Indian state.

Lord Curzon, the then viceroy of India, provided an opportunity in 1904 to blow aside the constitutional fiction of Chinese suzerainty when his expeditionary force under Col. Francis Younghusband invaded Tibet in December 1903 and forced the dazed and defeated Tibetans to sign the Treaty of Lhasa in August 1904. This treaty gave the Government of India extra-territorial rights in Tibet, including the stationing of small detachments of the Indian Army at the three designated Indo-Tibetan trade marts of Gartok, Shigatse and Yatung. This choice of three locations effectively placed a company of Indian troops at each of the three key centres of Tibet.

The first company was stationed at Gartok, which was at the crossroads en route to Tibet from Sinkiang and Ladakh. This was the initial last stop of Mao's famous highway G219 that linked Pulu in Sinkiang to Gartok in Tibet.

Shigatse was the location of the ancient and powerful Tashilunpo Monastery that, as the seat of the Panchen Lama, was a direct and countervailing power centre to Lhasa. The Panchen Lama is the reincarnation of Amitabha the Buddha of Boundless Light, while the Dalai Lama is the reincarnation of Avalokitesvara the Buddha of Compassion. One mentors the other. Stationing troops in Shigatse provided the Government of India the power in practice to checkmate any potentially hostile moves by the Dalai Lama.

Yatung near the Chumbi Valley was the third location where Indian troops were stationed. This gave the troops the opportunity to provide intelligence on possible Tibetan designs on Sikkim, Bhutan, Siliguri chicken's neck and Tawang.

However, within the space of two years, in the run up to the signing of the Anglo-Russian Convention of 1907, the British watered down the Treaty of Lhasa and signed the Anglo-Chinese Convention of 1906 by which they, for a fee from the Qing court, also agreed 'not to annex Tibetan territory or to interfere in the administration of Tibet', while China engaged 'not to *permit* any other foreign state to interfere with the territory or internal administration of Tibet'. The British brought the Chinese back into Tibet as their proxy.

Curiously, Indian troops were to remain in Tibet till 1954 when Prime Minister Jawaharlal Nehru went several steps ahead of the British and surrendered these three outposts to the Chinese. Nevertheless, from 1904, Tibet became an Indian protectorate in all but name and the constitutional fiction of the

Chinese suzerainty over Tibet itself remained ambivalent until a pushy Stalin and a welcoming Nehru emboldened the Chinese to start the process of the annexation of Tibet and Aksai Chin in January 1950.

Why was Stalin pushy?

He was pushy because he wanted to indiscriminately exploit the nuclear, mineral, petroleum, gold and river resources of Sinkiang's Tarim Basin and its umbilically linked geographical construct of Aksai Chin. For this, he wanted to use the Chinese as a proxy. He also wanted Indian troops as far away from Sinkiang as possible because he did not want the world to know or confirm even by accident how critical Sinkiang was to the Chinese nuclear programme. He also wanted a valid excuse to feed Mao's desire for weapons so as to permanently block off any Chinese move to sound out the Americans.

Why was Nehru welcoming?

Nehru was obsessed with the desire and motivation to both promote the concept of non-alignment on a global scale and to be anointed as the patron saint of this political philosophy. To achieve this end, he needed China's endorsement and support. In order to get their support, he was eager and willing to offer any manner of goodies to Mao. For the British, bringing the Chinese into Tibet was essential to protect the opium trade and also to keep the Russians out. For Nehru, the bet was to offer Aksai Chin, Minsar and Tibet on a platter to the Chinese and secure their support for non-alignment, so that he could then become the leader and elder statesman of this alternate global order.

In order to woo Stalin, Nehru first sacrificed Gilgit and the vassal states to the Anglo-Pakistan alliance, so that the three British nuclear monitoring stations in the Gilgit region would not land in Indian territory and India would not carry the stigma of being a British ally.

In order to woo Mao, Nehru reversed the Indian policy of selling arms to Tibet. The last consignment of arms was supplied to the Tibetans in March 1950, when the People's Liberation Army (PLA) was busy building a road through Aksai Chin. Thereafter, not only did Nehru stop all arms sale and withdraw military advisers and training help, he also pulled the plug on diplomatic support to the besieged and floundering Tibetans. Despite China having completed the famous highway to Gartok in western Tibet by 1952 and the confirmation of this provided to Nehru by the Indian Army, Nehru worked feverishly to ignore the encroachment into, and occupation of, Aksai Chin, close India's consulate in Sinkiang at Kashgar, surrender the Indian enclave of Minsar near Mount Kailash, pull the Indian Army out of its three strategic Tibetan outposts of Gartok, Shigatse and Yatung, and sign away for ever India's hard-won extra-territorial rights in Tibet by signing the disastrous and utterly shameful Panchsheel Treaty of 1954.

In hindsight, every incursion into Aksai Chin, Bara Hoti, Bhutan or Arunachal Pradesh after 1954 is based on the fig leaf of legitimacy provided by this wretched document.

When the Dalai Lama escaped to India in 1959, Mao was enraged. His paranoia about a US–India alliance and the possibility of the Central Intelligence Agency (CIA)-inspired insurrection in Tibet succeeding in throwing out the PLA, thereby transforming itself from a nightmare into reality, greatly bedeviled him. He was also paranoid about the possibility of attacks on Lop Nor. In fact, as the Indian Air Foce (IAF) reconnaissance flights over Tibet and Sinkiang commenced in January 1960, the Chinese were rendered impotent in their ability to thwart them. The intensification of border clashes and Nehru's forward policy inadvertently put Lop Nor into potential jeopardy. Khrushchev, who was playing a balancing game between India and China, also did not want the Chinese to lose their potential nuclear advantage over India. In fact, he brokered the Nehru–Chou summit in April 1960, when Chou made his famous proposal for swapping Aksai Chin for Chinese claims in the eastern sector.

Mao's paranoia, Nehru's turning down of Chou's ill-fated proposals for territory swap and the IAF's continued reconnaissance flights over Tibet and Sinkiang pushed Mao into the Sino-Indian border war of October–November 1962. The war had only one objective, and that was to break Indian morale to such an extent that the IAF flights stop altogether. In this objective, Mao found solid support, for different reasons, from the defence minister of India, Krishna Menon, the Intelligence Bureau (IB) chief, B.N. Mullik, and US ambassador to India, J.K. Galbraith.

Following the ceasefire in November 1962, the Chinese intensified efforts to conclude a territory swap with Pakistan to gain control of the Shaksgam Valley. This swap, executed in early 1963, prevented the establishment of a fourth Anglo-US nuclear monitoring station at Raskam in the Shaksgam Valley. Such a station, if it had come up, would have provided the observers based in it untrammelled and unimpeded geographic, geologic and acoustic access to Lop Nor, which lay across the barren wastes of the Taklamakan Desert. Mao was thus able to insulate Lop Nor and proceed in secrecy with preparations for the Chinese nuclear test of 1964.

After Deng succeeded Mao, China opened its doors to the West. At the same time, a confident and well-armed Indian military under Prime Minister Rajiv Gandhi began to be noticed in Asia. The Chinese feared that Rajiv Gandhi might tilt towards the US and that would not only jeopardise the prevailing Sino-US thaw but might also upset China's strategic position in Asia. It was time to take a crack at breaking this confidence. This started with Chinese troops intruding into the area around the Sumdorong Chu Valley that lay in the shadow of the Thag La Ridge, which was the feature where the Indian Army was routed in 1962. Over the next 18 months, the situation escalated into a massive stand-off as General K. Sundarji, the chief of Indian Army, demonstrated his excellence as a General by sending a clear signal to both China and Pakistan that the Indian Army could simultaneously take on both of them. The Chinese had to back down.

The Chinese decided to change tack as their military bluff had been called and they were unwilling to militarily engage a resurgent India. The approach to undermine India now required deception and a long-term strategy of wearing India down. The wily Deng immediately offered an olive branch to Rajiv Gandhi and invited him to visit China in 1988. Following Rajiv Gandhi's visit, a Joint Working Group (JWG) was set up to discuss, among other things, the alignment of the Line of Actual Control (LAC), the line on the ground separating Indian and Chinese troops.

In September 1991, Chinese premier Li Peng visited New Delhi. The new prime minister of India, P.V. Narasimha Rao and Li resolved to revisit the findings of the JWG set up in 1988 and reach an understanding on the ground position in Ladakh and Arunachal Pradesh. The mandarins in the Ministry of External Affairs (MEA) re-floated the clichéd concept of the LAC, which had first been suggested by Chou to Nehru way back in 1959. To his credit, Nehru had rejected it. This was Chou's way of first legitimising the land grab initiated by the People's Republic of China (PRC) in 1950, which continued unabated till 1959, considering the repeated discoveries of minerals in Aksai Chin and the ever-increasing importance of River Karakash to the PRC.

What is unacceptable is that the then mandarins in the MEA

were both willing to legitimise the de facto transgressions by the PRC into Indian territory and were also willing to leave the Indian position on the ground unrecognised by the PRC. The Chinese were, in effect, saying that you recognise our transgressions and you also accept that your current positions are not accepted by us! This bizarre state of affairs was reduced into the Sino-Indian Border Peace and Tranquility Agreement (BPTA) signed in Beijing in September 1993, when Rao visited China.

In February 1994, a few months after returning from Beijing, Rao piloted a unanimous resolution in both houses of parliament, declaring that the entire state of Jammu & Kashmir is an inalienable and integral part of India. He seemed to have forgotten that only a few months earlier, he had legally recognised the occupation of Aksai Chin by China. Nothing could have been more delusional than this. How could the integrity of Jammu & Kashmir be respected without throwing out China from Aksai Chin?

Following the signing of the BPTA, it was decided to pull back from all of the respective forward checkposts in the Sumdorong Chu Valley from a situation of 'close confrontation'. In 1994, the MEA of India described the situation as one of 'close proximity', where the respective posts were 50 to 100 yards apart. Following the JWG meeting in April 1995, the two sides agreed to a simultaneous withdrawal of their troops from the four border posts—two Indian and two Chinese—in the Sumdorong Chu Valley. As of June 1999, the valley was unoccupied by both armies and their respective posts in the area were close to a kilometre apart.

The folly of 1993 was successively repeated and a continuous stream of deeply flawed agreements were signed in November 1996, April 2005 and October 2013. All of these agreements were a strategic illusion. In fact, this should have become abundantly clear when, in 2003, Kanwal Sibal, then India's foreign secretary, met with Wang Yi, the head of the Chinese delegation, in New Delhi. It was logically proposed that both sides would exchange maps to an agreed scale on each side's perceptions of the location of the LAC in Ladakh. Mind you, here they were willingly discussing the constantly shifting Chinese perception of how much more Indian territory the Chinese were laying claim to. The intention was to superimpose the two sets of maps to assess the convergence and divergence of perceptions.

Both sides exchanged maps. The story goes that Wang opened the Indian map, took a long and detailed look at it, folded it and returned it to Sibal. He provided no explanation and the substance of the meeting ended there and then. By disregarding the Indian map, Wang freed China of being bound to it and, by extension, also freed China from India's perception of the LAC. What this meant was that the PLA did not need to limit or temper its freedom of military action in Ladakh.

Even then, Atal Bihari Vajpayee, the then prime minister of India, never got the message and nor did his successor, Manmohan Singh. Narendra Modi, who succeeded Manmohan Singh, first got a taste of the Chinese medicine when, in September 2014, he was perched on a swing with Xi on the bank of River Sabarmati. Soon news came in that substantial numbers of PLA troops had intruded into the Chumar area in Ladakh. This was perhaps the lowest form of crude disrespect that Xi could hand Modi at the start of their relationship. Hard bargaining resulted in the PLA withdrawing from their intrusions a few days later. To his credit, Modi paid a return visit to China in 2015 and floated a proposal to clarify the LAC. This was rejected by the Chinese.

Thanks to the grandiose magnanimity of the mandarins in the MEA in 1993, the 3,488 kilometre undemarcated India–

China border camouflages a disconcertingly tactical situation along select portions of the LAC. Here the two countries do not have agreement on the location of the LAC, either on the ground or on the map. As a result, hundreds of transgressions by Chinese border patrols occur annually. While China doesn't publicly track Indian transgressions, estimates of nearly 2,500 Chinese transgressions have been recorded by India on the LAC since 2010. On some occasions, accompanied by sabre-rattling political statements, these have devolved into more serious intrusions. In 2013 and 2014, the PLA spent several weeks camped across the LAC in the western sector: Depsang plains (April and May 2013), Chumar (2014 and 2015) and in the Barahoti area of the middle sector in mid-2016. The 2017 Doklam stand-off refers to the military border stand-off between the Indian Army and the PLA over Chinese construction of a road at Doklam near the India–China–Bhutan tri-junction border area, known as Donglang, or Donglang Caochang (meaning Donglang pasture or grazing field, in Mandarin).

On 16 June 2017, Chinese troops with construction vehicles and road-building equipment began extending an existing road southward in Doklam, a territory that is claimed by both China and Bhutan. On 18 June 2017, as part of Operation Juniper, about 270 Indian troops armed with weapons and two bulldozers crossed the Sikkim border into Doklam to stop the Chinese troops from constructing the road. On 28 August, both India and China announced that they had withdrawn all their troops from the face-off site in Doklam.

China may have backed down, because local PLA units were caught off-guard by India's rapid response ordered by the Indian Army chief, General Bipin Rawat, who religiously upheld the traditions left by Lt Gen. Sagat Singh in 1967 and General Sundarji in 1987.

It appears that Xi Jinping did not wish to face a diplomatic fiasco months before his leadership tenure was to be renewed at the Nineteenth Party Congress. Nevertheless, since the crisis ended, China has quietly maintained, and in some ways deepened, its presence in and around Doklam. In late August 2017, just after the stand-off was resolved, a Chinese defence ministry spokesman stated that the PLA would increase patrols in Doklam to 'resolutely safeguard' the country's sovereignty claims. In December, Indian media reported that China had continued to deploy roughly 1,600 troops, about the size of an army regiment, in the contested area. These were reportedly supplemented by an increase in the number of advanced PLA fixed-wing and rotary aircraft based across the border in Tibet at Lhasa and Shigatse. The US geopolitical intelligence company Stratfor's satellite images focus on the accompanying build-up in air power to support these units. The Stratfor analysis looked at four critical air bases—two Chinese and two Indian—that are within range of the Doklam plateau. It revealed that satellite imagery confirmed that both China and India were pursuing wide-ranging strategic build-up that had only accelerated in the wake of the 27 August 2017 agreement. On the Indian side of the border, the imagery of the Siliguri Bagdogra airbase and the Hasimara Air Force Station shows how India has moved to reinforce its air power by deploying front line Su-30MKI fighters close to the Doklam plateau.

What makes the Doklam crisis a unique event is that it does not fall into the traditional category of India–China territorial dispute but instead in a third country which has acted as a 'buffer'. The stand-off was near the India–China–Bhutan tri-junction, and in an area where both China and Bhutan hold competing territorial claims. The stand-off, therefore, was technically related to the Sino-Bhutan border dispute. Nevertheless, Indian involvement was a function of its special relationship with Bhutan and the proximity of the stand-off to its strategically vulnerable 'Chicken's Neck', the narrow sliver of territory (21 kilometres) connecting the Indian mainland to the strategically important north-eastern region. Although the Border Defence Co-operation Agreement of 2013 does not stipulate specifically regarding the tri-junction boundary points between India, China and the third country, New Delhi viewed this incident as an attempt to unilaterally determine a tri-junction point. For all practical considerations, the stand-off, therefore, turned out to be an extension of the India–China border dispute.

Despite Modi and Xi's post-Doklam summit meetings in Wuhan in April 2018 and in Mamallapuram in October 2019, it appears that China not only wishes India to acquiesce to vacating more territory in Ladakh but it also wants India to sit down with both China and Pakistan in a trilateral setting and resolve the issue of Jammu & Kashmir to their advantage and satisfaction. In fact, the joint statement issued after the Mamallapuram summit relegated the border issues to paragraph 16 of the 17-paragraph long joint statement. Ironically, both Xi and Modi designated the year 2020 as the year of people-to-people as well as cultural exchanges.

Did Xi deliver a message to Modi at Mamallapuram which, though couched in a velvet glove, was time bound? What was that message? Did Modi reject that message by not going forward to fulfil it? It is now being speculated that Chinese troop movements towards the Tibet–Ladakh frontier started in February 2020, somewhere after the formal declaration of the COVID-19 pandemic by the World Health Organization (WHO) and around the time of President Trump's visit to India later that month. Was Trump's India visit and Modi's lack of response to Xi's mysterious message interpreted by Xi as a rejection of his proposition by Modi? Did Modi remain silent because he interpreted COVID-19 as a 'weapon of opportunity' as much against India as it was against the rest of China's opponents?

It is clear that by no stretch of imagination could Indian or Israeli or US spy satellites NOT have detected Chinese troop movements in Tibet towards the Ladakh–Tibet frontier that ostensibly began in February 2020. Then why did some important functionary in the Government of India choose to only ask the Russians about this in April 2020 as is being speculated? Was this Russian reassurance of Chinese troop movements only being part of a routine exercise the reason that the XIV Corps remained in its barracks on the official grounds that there was a pandemic and did not mobilise itself for its annual summer exercises near the LAC? These are very important questions that need honest and authentic answers.

On 27 April 2020, a PLA military vehicle intruded into the Indian sector near the rivulet close to the 'Finger Five' area along the northern bank of Lake Pangong Tso in Ladakh. The northern bank has eight mountains, numbered one to eight, and ridges rolling towards the lake. When the vehicle's trespass was challenged by the Indian Army, matters began to escalate. The PLA then calculatedly ratcheted up tension till it manifested itself into physical scuffles involving about 250 troops from both sides. In the face-off that took place on the night of 5–6 May, many soldiers from both sides were hurt.

The second phase of the Chinese strategy unfolded on 9 May 2020, over 2,000 kilometres away from Lake Pangong Tso in a place called Naku La in the Muguthang sub-sector in Sikkim. Naku La is located at a height of 17,000 feet. Again, around 150 soldiers from both sides were involved in physical brawls. It is quite incredible that apart from iron rods no other weapons were used. The iron rod represents primeval hatred towards other cultures and civilisations embedded in the Chinese psyche.

On 6 June 2020, talks to wind down the face-offs commenced at Maldo in China-occupied Ladakh between Lt Gen. Harinder Singh of the Indian Army and Major General Lin Liu of the PLA. On 15 June 2020, an unarmed Indian verification patrol that discovered some newly erected structures on Indian territory was ambushed by the PLA. The commanding officer, who himself led the verification patrol, and his men were brutally murdered by the PLA using primitive clubs and other medieval-era weapons. Twenty Indian soldiers from the 16 Bihar Regiment, including their commanding officer who was a colonel, were brutally murdered. Thereafter, Indian troops retaliated in a frenzy of vengeance and similarly finished off anywhere between 34 to 105 PLA troops. The foreign ministry of China has not disclosed the number of Chinese killed.

The second round of disengagement talks that resumed on 22 June 2020 was also inconclusive. The third round of talks that started on 30 June 2020 also threw up no results. On 7 July 2020, Ajit Doval, India's National Security Advisor (NSA), and Wang Yi, China's foreign affairs minister, thrashed out a combined disengagement and de-escalation deal. While Chinese troops withdrew 2 kilometres from Patrolling Point (PP 14), the Galwan heights Indian troops also had to withdraw 2 kilometres into their own territory onto the river-valley floor. The PLA remain on the heights, which gives them tremendous tactical advantage as they can drive up to PP 14 in a matter of minutes as opposed to the long uphill trudge for the Indian Army.

Further disengagement and/or de-escalation in other contentious sectors never happened. Thereafter, in a bold move that occurred on the night of 29/30 August, the Indian Army took charge of the heights on the Kailash range of mountains which overlook the Spanggur Gap and beyond in the Chushul sector. The PLA formations on the valley floor were suddenly very vulnerable to the Indian Army.

The eighth round of disengagement talks between the Indian Army and the PLA ended on 10 November 2020 with no agreement on disengagement. Both armies have dug in for the long and hard winter. The PLA has no intention of withdrawing and nor does the Indian Army.

In the 175 years since the birth of my great-great grandfather in the twilight of the Sikh Empire, China is still the enemy and both the Indian Army and the PLA are poised for a bitter confrontation. Without decisive military action, the border issue is likely to remain unsatisfactorily unresolved as diplomacy and appeasement have clearly failed. India will have to find the strength and means to do so if it wishes to settle this issue.

Iqbal Chand Malhotra
Author of *Red Fear: The China Threat*

AUTHOR'S NOTE

This book is essentially about the long-standing territorial dispute between China and India, along the Himalayan frontiers, over two geographically separate regions, with different historical origins. One part of the dispute is about the Sino-Indian boundary north-east of Ladakh—essentially about who does Aksai Chin belong to. The other part of the dispute is about the McMahon Line that separates India's north-eastern frontier regions (now primarily Arunachal Pradesh) from Tibet. Could this be India's boundary with China? The dispute over the eastern boundaries of Ladakh (and the question of the rightful territorial ownership of Aksai Chin) can be traced back to the military expeditions of General Zorawar Singh of the Sikh Empire into north Baltistan and then Tibet in the east 1841–42, and the Treaty of Chushul in 1842, the creation of the kingdom of Jammu & Kashmir after the Anglo-Sikh War in 1846, and the military expeditions that were launched north-east onto the Kunlun mountain ranges. The McMahon Line, on the other hand, came into being after the long-drawn-out boundary conference in Simla in 1913–14. The conference was organised by the British Government of India, to define the boundaries of Tibet, with China and India. However, China, which at that point was devastated by the impact of opium on its people and its economy, a consequence of British rule and their trading practices, was a reluctant participant. With no agreement in sight after months of negotiation, in the absence of Chinese cooperation, Sir Henry McMahon, the organiser of the Simla Conference, eventually drew a line to define the southern boundary of Tibet with British India. That came to be known as the McMahon Line. As the British Empire was then at its prime, like other empires of that era, it could define its outer reaches, more so when it concerned its weaker neighbours. But, in the case of India, with the exception of its border with Nepal, the British left a lot of boundaries unsettled, following the messy partition of India. The north-eastern boundary with Tibet wasn't settled, nor was the boundary with Bhutan.

Imperial China and later Communist China refused to accept these boundary alignments. It saw it as a legacy of the British Empire that the Communist elite had come to abhor for several reasons (which is explained in greater detail later in the book). Whereas independent India's leadership, led by Jawaharlal Nehru, had evolved in its role with considerable engagement with the British establishment well after India's independence, and thus understood the historical circumstances and the British explanations for them. Moreover, with its partition, India was busy settling its new borders with the newly created state of Pakistan in its east and west. It was assumed by Nehru that the boundaries to the north with Tibet (now with China) were settled, based on his implicit assumptions that the maps handed over by the British administration were final. However, the Communist leadership of China, though keen to settle its boundaries with its dozen neighbours, put the settlement with India on hold. Instead, China chose to first seek a settlement with the Soviet Union (now Russia) over tracts of Chinese territories that had been annexed by Tsarist Russia. Moreover, Chairman Mao of China was eager to please Stalin and the Soviet leadership and extract strategic benefits, as is also explained in this book.

Thus, the settlement of its boundaries with India—especially the McMahon Line—was lower in the order of priority for the Communist leadership of the People's Republic of China (PRC). And a Sino-Indian boundary line in Ladakh, even less so. Considering the fact that the Soviet Chinese boundary settlement took half a century, it is argued by some that China would have legitimised at least the McMahon Line in due course of time. What perhaps tipped the scales for a confrontation was Nehru's eagerness to put an end to ambiguity about India's boundaries by publishing new maps in 1954 that showed India's whole northern frontier as an international boundary. For good measure, he stated that 'this frontier should be regarded as a firm and definite one which is not open to discussion with anybody', and that it must be held on the ground, 'especially in such places' which may be claimed by China.[1] These newly published maps, based on the lines drawn by the British Empire, became the basis of India's claims, and it included the area of Aksai Chin. Since China was initially slow to react, it was assumed that India's claims had Peking's (now Beijing) acceptance. But then, in 1959 and later in 1960, China put forward its own claims over east Ladakh, including Aksai Chin.

The Chinese had in fact begun their occupation of Aksai Chin from the early 1950s, building what is now their vital highway (G219) that connects Kashgar in Xinjiang to Lhasa in Tibet. This had apparently become known to Nehru's administration by 1954, but it wasn't brought into the public domain until much later. Even the Lonju incident of 1959 hadn't served as a warning. While some, like Neville Maxwell, have argued that Nehru's tough stance on the boundary alignment and his dismissal of the offer by the Chinese premier, Chou En-Lai, on his 1960 visit to India, that, 'you keep what you hold, you take too anything that is in dispute and occupied by neither, and we keep what we hold', had set the scene for the border war,[2] there were several other reasons too.

America had used Indian territory to engage with and

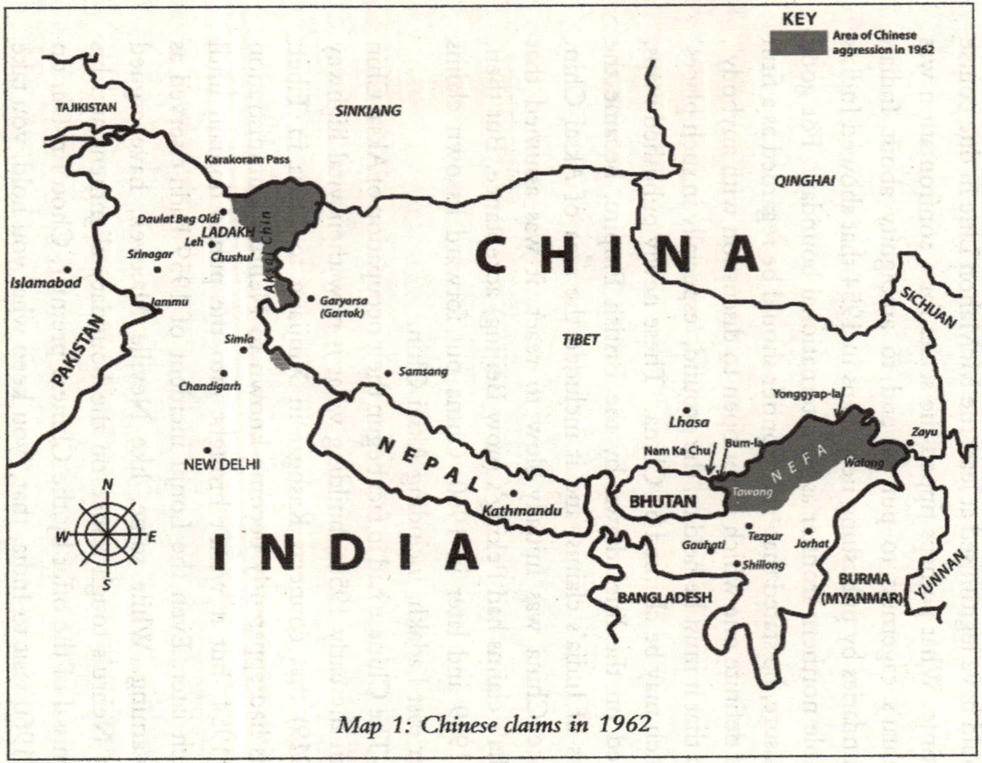

Map 1: Chinese claims in 1962

Source: Kunal Verma, *1962: The War that Wasn't*, p. 60

support Tibetan rebels and guerrillas. The Dalai Lama had fled to India in 1959 and the Indian government had provided him and his followers refuge. The Soviet–China military and nuclear alliance saw India as being in the American camp. Moreover, China felt that the aerial reconnaissance missions of the Indian Air Force (IAF) over Sinkiang and Tibet in 1960 could expose Chinese nuclear facilities in Lop Nor in Tibet, which made it imperative for Mao to restrict India's aggressive postures. Above all, India's 'forward policy' of positioning troops along and beyond the McMahon Line and the assumed boundary lines in Ladakh was the final straw in upsetting the Chinese leadership about the boundary contestations.

Thus, by 1962, Mao and China had decided to not only put an end to Nehru's boundary assertions, but also to give a damaging blow to Nehru's growing international stature and his overconfidence. Nehru and his immediate establishment had, however, deluded themselves into believing that all was well on the Sino-Indian front, despite the ominous signs of China's intent. For instance, Nehru had even chosen to ignore the forcible occupation of Tibet by China from 1950. Instead, in 1954, Nehru's government entered into the Panchsheel Treaty with China. The treaty recognised Tibet 'as a part of China'. Chairman Mao, however, wasn't willing to rest with control over the resource-rich Tibet. He wanted more territory along the Himalayas and was waiting for the right opportunity to 'teach India a lesson'. He and his Communist colleagues had grown up to see India as an extension of the colonial British empire, that had wreaked havoc on China.[3] This opportunity came when the world's attention was focused on the Cuban Missile Crisis. In that precise window, Chairman Mao initiated his Himalayan military campaign from 19 October and it lasted a month, until 20 November 1962, after which the Chinese unilaterally declared a cease-fire. What led China to pull back its troops without holding onto much of their territorial gains? Was their intention only to deliver a psychological blow to Nehru and India?

This book discusses the many factors that led to the conflict of 1962, and why it has become the defining chapter in Sino-Indian relations. It is said that Nehru never quite recovered from the shock of the Chinese invasion. The Chinese 'betrayal', as Nehru and his loyalists were to call it, shattered the myth of 'Hindi-Chini bhai bhai' that was the much-trumpeted slogan, at least amongst those who believed that all matters between China and India would be amicably settled. Nehru and his immediate circle of advisors, like his defence minister, Krishna Menon, Intelligence Bureau chief, B.N. Mullik, and Lt Gen. Bijji Kaul, three men who were primarily responsible for the military disaster of 1962, refused to take the Chinese threat seriously, until the Indian Army was thrown into the high Himalayas, ill-equipped for battles in freezing temperatures. But its frontline units fought with exceptional courage, and when they were routed, like they were in North East Frontier Region (NEFA), it was because of those Indian generals, who allowed the ill-informed civilian leadership to micromanage their battles. The IAF was not used, despite advice despite the many advantages that it could offer. It could really have turned the tide in India's favour.

'1962 was a national failure of which every Indian is guilty.... for the Government of India, it was a Himalayan blunder at all levels ...,' wrote Brig. John Dalvi in his blunt and scathing criticism of India's military debacle following the Chinese invasion in his book titled *Himalayan Blunder*, which some regard as a military classic.[4] Brig. Dalvi and his men faced the first of the many Chinese assaults in NEFA, as his brigade was deployed—against every sane advice—in tactically indefensible positions along the Namka Chu. It was run over by the Chinese on the first night of the attack, and Brig. Dalvi was taken a prisoner along with those who survived the attacks. In Ladakh, however, Indian troops fared better, thanks to a few good generals. But how and why India slithered into such a humiliating defeat is explained in this book. However, the lessons of 1962 were learnt by the Indian Army and this was only too evident in 1967 in the showdown that took place at Nathu La and Cho La, when the Indian troops give the Chinese enough dead bodies to take home, following a brutal confrontation. And then there was the bloody Chinese ambush of an Indian patrol in Tulung La in 1975. These incidents were all on the Sino-Indian frontline in Sikkim, which had acceded to India in 1975, but China regards that as contestable. And then in 1986–87, the Chinese attempt to once again intrude into Arunachal Pradesh (earlier NEFA) was met by a swift military response that checkmated their designs, and eventually led to India's prime minister Rajiv Gandhi to be invited by Beijing for talks in 1988, by Deng Xiaoping, thereby breaking the logjam in Sino-Indian relations. Deng wanted a peaceful periphery to facilitate the economic development of China.

A series of bilateral initiatives followed, like the annual meetings of special representatives and the agreement over claim lines in Ladakh, by renaming it as Line of Actual Control (LAC). It led some observers to assert that the Asian giants were onto a path of peace. But the more astute commentators didn't rule out more confrontations, as there remains a deep distrust between both countries. Many in China saw India as a troublemaker, especially so for New Delhi's support for Tibet, while in India, the Chinese support for Pakistan at various levels was a big hindrance in India's attempts to get Pakistan to abandon terrorism as a tool of influence against India. Moreover, despite many rounds of talks, Chinese delegations have yet to accept India's map markings or exchange detailed maps with boundary markings of their claims, either for eastern Ladakh or about the McMahon Line. In effect, we are where we were in the 1950s! Thus, both sides continue to patrol along their claim lines, while carefully avoiding a confrontation, though they did come close to a major confrontation in 2017 and then again in 2020.

From 2013 onwards, the Chinese focus has essentially been on strengthening their claims beyond the LAC in Ladakh, by occupying areas that fall within the boundary spelt out by China in 1960 that India had refused to accept. But it was the 73-day stand-off at Doklam in 2017, between the Indian Army and the People's Liberation Army (PLA), over China's road and camp constructions on the India–China–Bhutan tri-junction border area, that first sent out a message that India was now willing to stand up to Chinese intrusions. It eventually ended peacefully. The deep-seated differences over boundary perimeters, and Tibet, remain. And despite the boasts of diplomats that both sides had settled down to 'bullet-less' border management, the hopes of this becoming the norm crashed in the summer of 2020, when disputes over territorial claims on the LAC in Ladakh led Indian and Chinese troops into brutal medieval-style skirmishes in June 2020. It led to the death of many soldiers and became another defining moment in Sino-Indian relations. With all the media coverage that followed the death of 20 Indian soldiers and an unspecified number of Chinese troops—the PLA never admits to accurate numbers—there was considerable global concern that Asia's two largest and most militarily powerful neighbours could head into another conflict. Enhanced military deployments of about 50,000 additional troops and round-the-clock aerial deployment conveyed India's resolve. And even though there exists a large military power gap between China and India, especially China's comprehensive national power, the size of its economy and military capabilities being several times more than India's, but unlike 1962, India wasn't a pushover now.[5]

Not only the Himalayan mountain ranges would limit China's ability to enforce its will on India, but also the Indian Ocean, where a strong maritime presence led by the US could draw in other western countries too, as part of an alliance (the QUAD is one), to limit China's territorial ambitions. Even then, China's leaders aren't going to rest until they accomplish the vision that Mao, who saw Tibet as the palm of China's hand and Ladakh, Nepal, Sikkim, Bhutan and Arunachal Pradesh as its five fingers, that China has to 'liberate' these areas. For India, any exchange of territory to settle boundary claims would amount to 'horse trading' as Nehru had put it, following Chou En-Lai's 1960 proposal, which involved accepting all the Chinese territorial claims on 'whether Arunachal Pradesh in the east or Aksai Chin in the west', which Nehru insisted 'were Indian'. For many years even after Nehru had passed away, Indian diplomats were loyally hanging on to this legacy. In due course, this stand has become an Indian article of faith, just like the vision of Mao is for the Chinese. Nehru had argued that the boundaries inherited from the colonial era were legitimate, but Mao had disagreed then and so do the Chinese now!

No wonder, then, that these boundary issues are unresolved and aren't going to go away for a long, long time. Even meetings of the current leaders of these two nations, Narendra Modi and Xi Jinping, have come nowhere near a resolution, despite them having visited each other's countries and having engaged in 18 meetings from the time Modi first became India's prime minister in 2014 until the Galwan Valley clash in June 2020. In fact, even as Modi and Xi undertook their first major bilateral engagement in India (in Gujarat) in 2014, Chinese troops had begun intrusions across north-east Ladakh. Later, following the stand-off over Doklam in 2017, which had become an embarrassment for Beijing, the two leaders met over structured summits at Wuhan in China in 2018 and then in India at Mahabalipuram, near Chennai, in 2019. Yet, despite them having issued 'strategic guidance' to their respective militaries to have better and more frequent communication and strengthen the existing confidence-building measures (CBMs) so that the special representatives could 'seek a fair, reasonable and mutually acceptable settlement to the border question', there seems to be little room for optimism.

Finally, a word about what led me to write this book. While there is considerable amount of existing literature on the subject of Sino-Indian ties, and more so, there's been a spate of publications on the subject in the aftermath of the Chinese intrusions in Ladakh from April 2020 and the military stand-off that has followed, why another book, some might ask. For one, the focus of this book is the boundary disputes per se, put together in a chronological order, as a researched study that should hopefully help the reader to understand the nub of the problems between China and India, and more importantly, to answer the question as to why China and India were unable to move beyond 'talks' to a settlement. Was it because they simply distrust each other, specially so, as their perceptions of each other's intent are so different that confrontations would be inevitable? Historically, the Chinese have held India in disdain, and recent surveys show that Indians continue to see China as a threat to India's security, as a challenge for the Indian economy and now as responsible for the COVID-19 pandemic.[6] However, for me, as a student of warfare, it was the possibility of another Himalayan conflict that drew me towards the subject of this book. As the British soldier-scholar, Captain Sir Basil Liddell Hart had once famously said: 'If you want peace, understand war.' It is in that very spirit that I set out to understand the causes of the 1962 conflict, and I discovered there was a lot more to it than what we've all grown up to believe in India, even though much of the material that was available to me was written objectively by eminent Indian scholars and personalities. I have thus quoted extensively from their works to weave the narrative into an account that would, I believe, be easily absorbed by a reasonably informed reader.

The research for this book, in fact, began after my friend Iqbal Malhotra suggested we should co-author a book on China, since our book on the *Untold Story of Kashmir* was well received. Eventually, I chose to write a book on the 'boundary dispute' and not on the theme of Iqbal's book on China. Thus, once the subject of this book was approved by the publisher of Westland Publications, Karthika V.K., to whom I was connected to by Sudha Sadanand, and after Karthika read my chapter on the 1962 conflict and gave me the go-ahead, I got down to work. This book was, however, written entirely during the lockdowns that were enforced across India due to the COVID-19 pandemic. It led me to make good use of my time, which I did in a disciplined manner. In all these months, my biggest pillar of support was my wife, Anis, who despite her several commitments ensured that we all were very well taken care of, and I could work in my study, without being disturbed. Finally, my gratitude goes to Sonia Madan of Westland Publications and her team, who have taken great pains over this final product, with their superb editing skills. If it wasn't for Sonia and her team, this book would have looked quite different. However, I take full responsibility for the assumptions that I have made in this book, even though these are all backed by information that is in the public domain, as is reflected in the endnotes of this book. The aim, above all, is for this book to serve as an accurate guide on the Sino-Indian boundary dispute. I would be delighted if it serves this purpose.

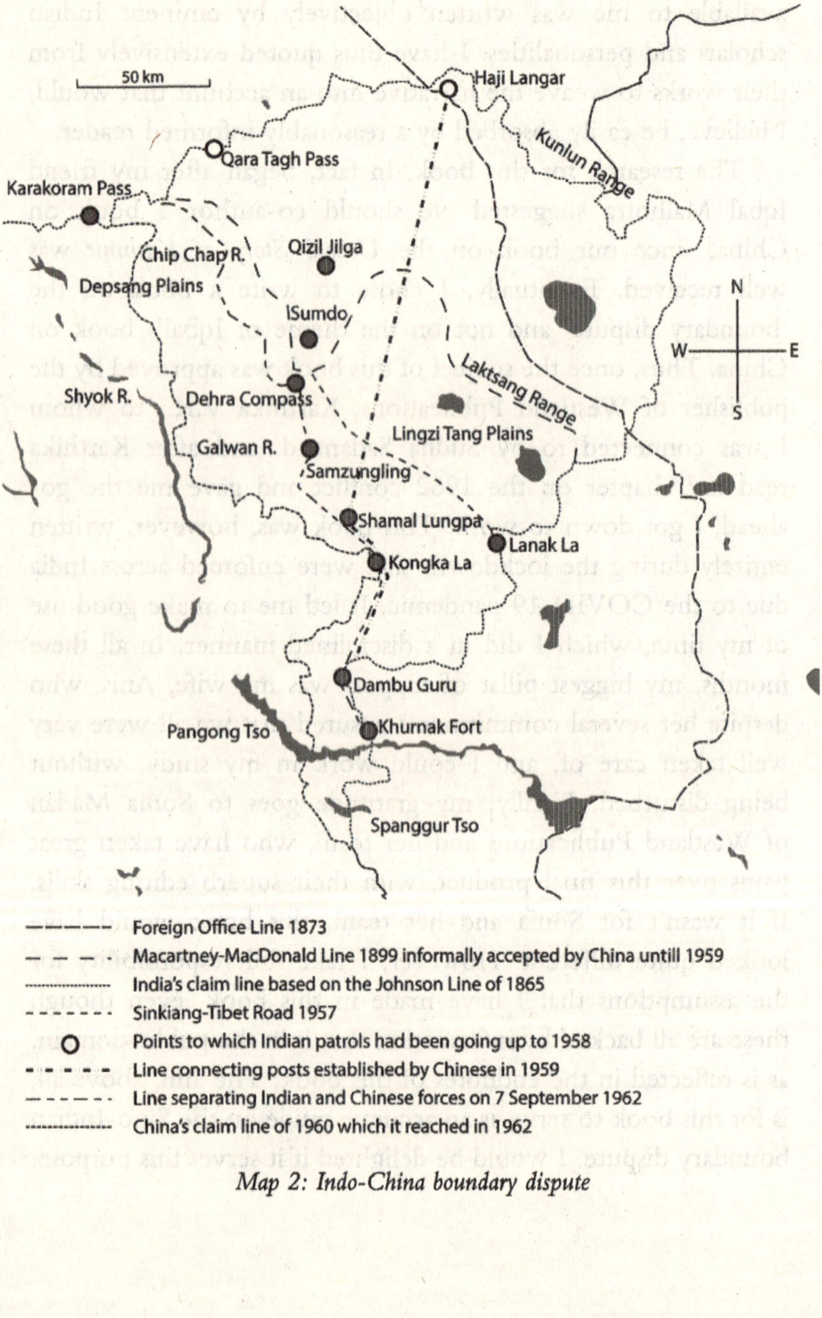

Map 2: Indo-China boundary dispute

1

DEFINING THE BOUNDARIES

In the summer of 2020, China surprised India with its sudden and massive troop build-up along what has come to be known as the Line of Actual Control (LAC), which lies to the east of Ladakh[1] in north India. India's military deployments in response, through the length of the disputed Sino-Indian boundary along the Himalayas, raised questions about the very basis of the territorial claims being made by either side. There was also a sense of déjà vu among the older generation of Indians who had lived through the 1960s, when India almost sleepwalked into a humiliating military defeat at the hands of Mao Ze Dong's[2] post-revolution Red Army. But 2020 wasn't 1962—and India's armed forces wouldn't be overrun despite barely veiled threats by the Chinese state-run media that India mustn't forget the lessons of the past. India didn't. In reality, with the exception of the 1962 Sino-Indian conflict, the record of accomplishment of China's military has been rather dismal. Moreover, the 1962 conflict wasn't even a full-blown war involving all of India's armed forces or the nation's resources—the Indian Air Force (IAF) wasn't used at all, nor was much of the Indian Army.[3]

There were several viewpoints about what led to the military stand-off between India and China in 1962, and what lay behind Beijing's decision to be assertive. There was, however, little disagreement amongst historians and observers that an unsettled Sino-Indian boundary—which earlier was Tibet's border with India—has given China room for its repeated attempts at territorial incursions beyond what is the 'perceived' boundary between India and China.

The History of the Sino-Indian Border Dispute

In the decades that followed the 1962 Sino-Indian conflict, there have been multiple bilateral agreements between the two nations to respect the boundaries that run from the north of India and the Karakoram ranges, along the high Himalayas up to India's border with Myanmar in the east. But India and China have yet to achieve a binding boundary settlement.

A major reason for the contest over the boundaries that, some say, could eventually become a border has been the separate interpretations of history and the legacy of the postcolonial era that China, under Chairman Mao, was adamant on settling on its terms. Notwithstanding the tepid responses of independent India's first prime minister Jawaharlal Nehru to Chinese assertions, China denounced all these treaties over the contested boundaries as colonial constructs that were heaped on China when its power was at its nadir.[4] India, on the other hand, has based almost all its post-Independence boundary claims with respect to China not only on its historical links with the kingdom of Tibet that was absorbed by China in 1951 without any objections by Nehru, but more specifically on the treaties signed by the British Government of India, which India inherited after Independence. In this context, the Treaty of Chushul of 1842 and the Simla Agreement of 1914 are particularly relevant.

India's boundary claims in Ladakh are based on the Treaty of Chushul of 1842, which, in turn, was based on the Treaty of Tinmosgang of 1684 that was signed between Ladakh and

Tibet when both were feudal states and Ladakh was the hub of trade routes into Turkestan and Tibet. Under the Treaty of Tinmosgang, Ladakh had secured an exclusive right to receive pashmina wool produced in Tibet in exchange of tea.

In the early 1840s, to control the trade route to Ladakh, Raja Gulab Singh of Jammu, then a part of the Sikh Empire, sent his troops to battle and defeat Tibet, under the suzerainty of the Qing dynasty of China. The Sikh Empire, invoking the historical claims of Ladakh to western Tibet up to the Mayum Pass—presumably exercised prior to the Treaty of Tingmosgang—conquered and consolidated its territories right up to Minsar and Mount Kailash. This Sino-Sikh War, also known as the Dogra-Tibetan War, fought between May 1841 and August 1842, culminated in the Treaty of Chushul under which both parties sought to maintain the territorial status quo.

When the kingdom of Jammu & Kashmir came into being as a feudatory state of British India, following the Treaty of Amritsar in 1846, the boundaries of Ladakh were promulgated periodically to the Chinese representatives, even though the Chinese never responded. It was only in the 1950s that China became assertive about its claim lines in areas northeast of Ladakh, known as Aksai Chin, a desolate snowy wasteland at an elevation of 5,000 metres (17,000 feet), which served as an ancient trade route between Ladakh and Tibet.

Between 1952 and 1957, it became known that Beijing (then Peking) had constructed a road through it. Nehru and his defence minister, Krishna Menon, had dismissed it as propaganda by the newly created Central Intelligence Agency (CIA) of the United States, and reports of Indian patrols—the first being led by Captain (later Major General) Rajendra Nath in 1952—confirming this fact remain classified till date. By 1957, China formally announced the completion of this road (now known as Highway G219) that finally led Nehru to admit in 1959 that the road ran through what India regarded as its own territory.[5] China, since then, hasn't relented on its claims over Aksai Chin, despite the assertions of India's leaders through the years about Aksai Chin being Indian territory.

Mapping Territorial Lines

India's claims over Aksai Chin being a part of Ladakh are based on lines drawn on maps by the British from time to time, to indicate the extent of their empire in the Indian subcontinent. Thus, there was the Johnson Line (1865), the Johnson-Ardagh Line (1897) and the Macartney-Macdonald Line (1899). The British Government of India chose to regard the Johnson-Ardagh Line as its official boundary with Tibet, and had thus presented this as the boundary to Qing court in Peking (now Beijing) on 24 March 1899. But the then Chinese government didn't respond. The British interestingly used both the Johnson-Ardagh and the Macartney-MacDonald lines on their maps until 1908. However, by 1912, the foreign secretary of British India demanded that India should use the Johnson-Ardagh Line as its boundary, and when the People's Republic of China (PRC) came into being in 1949, Peking accepted the Macartney-Macdonald Line as the boundary. Post-Independence, the Government of India, too, had used the Johnson-Ardagh Line as its official boundary, until Nehru directed a revision of maps to show definite boundaries. However, the one constant with all these boundary lines was that they put Aksai Chin—which China now occupies—within what was to become independent India, as part of the territory of Ladakh that was controlled or claimed by the Maharaja of Jammu & Kashmir.[6]

In 1846, the British had recognised Maharaja Gulab Singh as the ruler of Jammu & Kashmir, which included Ladakh. But the boundary surveys of Ladakh in 1846 and 1847 were inconclusive, as Chinese officials refused to cooperate. Therefore, another survey to identify Ladakh's boundaries was initiated in 1855. The task to determine Ladakh's boundaries was entrusted to a certain William H. Johnson, an Anglo-Indian surveyor after whom the Johnson Line is named. Johnson held a grudge against the British for treating him as an outsider for his Anglo-Indian ancestry. This was exploited by Maharaja Gulab Singh of the princely state of Jammu & Kashmir, who was keen to show through this surveyor the vast north-eastern reaches of his kingdom well beyond the Karakoram Pass. Johnson had stayed on in Ladakh until 1865, by when he had gone through the Karakoram Pass into Sinakiang, into what was believed to be Chinese territory, though there was no field data to confirm this. Thus the boundary of Ladakh as per Johnson was shown to extend from the Karakoram Pass to the Kunlun Mountains, since the Maharaja's troops were already at the fort at Shahidulla (now Xaidulla), where they were stationed since 1863 with custom and trade officials. The Johnson Line, therefore, showed the boundary to include all these territories between the Karakoram Pass and the Kunlun Mountains. The British were unhappy to learn about the Maharaja's territorial designs, but as the Chinese writ then didn't run as far as these areas, this 'line', as demarcated by Johnson, was apparently never presented to China.[7]

By 1866, however, when the Maharaja's soldiers had vacated these inhospitable areas, the Chinese took control of Shahidulla, and placed their own 'Beg' there. During these years, the Russians, too, were exploring how far they could extend their reach towards the Tibetan plateau. Thus, the British decided on a boundary line—with a few modifications to the Johnson Line—along the crest of the Kunlun Mountains, north of River Yarkand to be definitive enough to limit Russian influence. Consequently, in 1897, Major General Sir John Ardagh, the then director of Military Intelligence in Delhi, marked out what came to be known as the Johnson-Ardagh Line. Since India attained independence, even though the boundary in the Aksai Chin sector was described as 'un-demarcated', New Delhi's boundary claims were based on this line.[8]

There was another line used in British maps of the region that London referred to until 1908 as the Macartney-MacDonald Line. It was proposed by George Macartney, the British counsel general in Kashgarin Sinkiang, now known as Xinjiang,[9] with a border along the Karakoram mountain range that was aimed to limit any Russian advances into Tibet.

Incidentally, even though the *Postal Atlas of China*, published by Peking from 1917 to 1933, showed the boundary of Aksai Chin with Tibet along the Johnson Line, it changed when the PRC, also known as Communist China, came into being in 1949. China then opted for the Macartney-MacDonald Line as its boundary. This boundary along the Karakoram Mountains was promoted by British officials—George Macartney in Kashgar—to create a Chinese-held buffer zone, between the vast Russian Empire and Tibet, if the Russians were to advance into Tibet. And though the Qing Empire was silent about its views on this proposal, the post-1949 Communist regime found it the most acceptable boundary for Ladakh.[10] More recently, following the Sino-Indian stand-off at the LAC, China renewed its claims on Aksai Chin based on the Macartney-MacDonald claim line, as formally proposed first by Mao's premier Zhou Enlai (known earlier as Chou En Lai) in 1959. India rejected China's claim then and continues to do so.[11] (This Chinese claim is explained in detail, later in the book.)

Tibet Is Free

Well before India and China became independent states, the British government in India was wary of the ambitions of the

Chinese and the Russians in Tibet and along the Himalayas; though in the absence of any economic stakes there, the British initially felt Tibet was a 'worthless piece of territory'. Lord Curzon, viceroy of India from 1899 to 1905, changed his opinion about the importance of Tibet after an expedition by Colonel Younghusband in 1903–04. Younghusband was tasked to set up diplomatic relations with Lhasa, the capital of Tibet, in order to resolve the border disputes between Tibet and Sikkim and initiate trade with Tibet.[12]

The Tibetans were averse to the influence of outsiders and, initially, they put up a stiff resistance against Younghusband and his Indian escorts, which led to thousands of Tibetans being killed. Though the Dalai Lama then fled to Mongolia (a sanctuary for other Dalai Lamas too), Younghusband, in the typical mould of tough British officers who expanded the influence of the British Empire, returned only after signing the Treaty of Lhasa with the 'regent' in the absence of the Dalai Lama. Later, in 1907, once again without the presence of the Dalai Lama, the British signed the Anglo-Russian Convention, by which both sides recognised China's suzerainty over Tibet.

To cut a long story short, Tibet's fortunes changed when the Qing dynasty, also called the Manchu dynasty, in China collapsed in 1911. Since 1644, this dynasty had commanded complete control over Tibet, spiritually, politically and militarily, to the point that the Tibetans even had to seek Peking's approval in the selection of the Dalai Lama. However, with its fall, Tibet changed. For the first time since 1720, both Tibet and Mongolia became independent and free of Chinese control in January 1913. Both these nations declared independence and signed a treaty proclaiming mutual recognition of their independence from China.

The Dalai Lama returned to Tibet amidst much fanfare. With practically no 'outsiders' on the roof of the world, the

Dalai Lama began to reconsolidate his spiritual authority with the removal of all elements of Chinese influence, like 'priest-patron ties' in Tibet. He also engaged with the American ambassador to China and the Japanese ambassador and military advisor. Tibet drew the attention of all the big powers of that time.[13]

The Dalai Lama had also befriended the British during his time in Darjeeling and Kalimpong in India's Bengal from 1910 to 1912. With his return to Lhasa, the British found in him an ally and brought him on board to accomplish their strategic agenda for Tibet.[14]

Free, Yet Shackled

Britain had a four-pronged strategy to resolve its many concerns over Tibet. One, it sought to define the boundary and the status of Tibet with India and China after consultations with both parties. Two, it looked to delineate the boundaries between Tibet, India and Burma. Three, it aimed to negate Chinese suzerainty following Peking's losses in 1911–12 over a truly autonomous Tibet. And finally, it wanted to keep the Russians away from Tibet. It was then that the British invented the concept of China's 'suzerainty' over Tibet as against its 'sovereignty'.[15] The British sought to make Tibet a buffer state between India and China, without offending the Chinese Republic, which claimed all territories of the former Manchu Empire. The British had hinted to China that 'Chinese suzerainty over a fully autonomous Tibet' was a lot better than a long-drawn and costly military campaign. The Chinese, however, were apprehensive of what Britain might do, considering how the Russians had supported Mongolia's independence.[16]

Although China initially went along with Britain's idea of Chinese suzerainty over Tibet, decades later it bluntly dismissed it as an outmoded concept and a feudal idea. Once the Chinese Communists took control of Tibet in 1951, it claimed that Tibet was a part of China and it was for China to decide the level of autonomy it would be permitted. Strangely, even though China's influence and control over Tibet was non-existent in the four previous decades—from 1912 when the Chinese garrisons were driven out until 1951 when Chairman Mao sent his troops into Tibet—there was no formal recognition of Tibet as an independent nation. Ideally, such a long period of independent existence as a nation state should have carried with it de jure recognition, but the world community neither recognised Tibet nor questioned China's claims over Tibet. This seemed to be acceptable even to the Americans.[17]

In 1913, however, while Chinese influence over Tibet was at its lowest, the British Empire in India was at its most influential. Thubten Gyatso, the 13th Dalai Lama, sought to use his influence with the British. With Tibetan forces having hounded out every soldier of the Chinese army eastwards beyond the River Mekong, the Dalai Lama suggested to the British that a conference to resolve the boundary issues between China, Tibet and India would be useful. Lord Curzon, by then the former viceroy of India, picked up this suggestion. Having earlier initiated trade ties with Tibet through the Younghusband expedition, he was able to get Lord Hardinge, his successor and the viceroy in India, to support the idea.

The British, wary of the Russians' growing influence in Tibet and the region after the Russo-Mongolian Agreement of 1912, invited the plenipotentiaries of Tibet and China to engage with the British government at a conference in Simla and Delhi in India.[18] The Simla Conference of 1913–14 was to be the most decisive event in defining at least one half of the disputed boundary between India and China today, as China occupies Tibet, known as the McMahon Line.

Interpreting Boundaries

Lt Col. Arthur Henry McMahon was formally nominated to represent the British government at the Simla Conference. With the rank of 'secretary' in the foreign department of the British Government of India, McMahon was 'empowered to sign any Convention, Agreement or Treaty, which may be concluded at the Conference'. As a young captain, he had spent two years demarcating the Durand Line that separates Pakistan from Afghanistan today. He was moulded 'in the furnace of responsibility and the anvil of self-reliance and relished the creation and laying down of boundaries'.[19] His task at the Simla Conference, however, was neither enjoyable nor easy.

Besides Sir McMahon, China, wary of a Britain-Tibet deal, took a while to announce their representative or plenipotentiary for the Simla Conference. Eventually, when they did so, the Chinese first stated that Ivan Chen, an experienced diplomat, and Hu Hanmin would be their representatives. However, China decreed that they would be called pacificators, and would carry 'no territorial powers'. The British objected. It was only after threats and prodding that a Chinese presidential order was signed appointing Ivan Chen as their plenipotentiary and authorising him 'to sign articles that may be agreed upon in order that all difficulties which have existed in the past may be dissolved'. He just about made it in time for the opening convention of the conference. In contrast, the Dalai Lama was decisive and swift in appointing Lochen Shastra Paljor Dorje, his prime minister who later impressed everybody with his quiet dignity, as his choice for the tripartite talks. Shastra was described as 'a man of great ability and patriotism'. Moreover, an official statement from the Grand Lama stated 'the Chief Minister Shastra Paljor Dorje is hereby authorized to decide on all questions which may benefit Tibet and to seal all documents relating thereto'.[20]

Both sides made their positions known in the very first meeting held at Simla on 13 October 1913. With the Chinese defeated and evicted from Tibet, Lhasa made it known that it had an 'independent' status and placed a document to this effect. But the Chinese still insisted that Tibet formed an integral part of the Chinese territory and no attempts shall be made by Tibet or by Great Britain to interrupt the continuity of this territorial integrity. For China, unlike the British Government of India, Tibet's precise boundaries weren't important. The British hosting the conference wanted a defined boundary for Tibet, not just with India, but also with China.[21] This was the primary reason for the Simla Conference to have dragged on for over six months, with contestable results.

The Chinese also made a range of ridiculous claims over Tibet, most notably over its territories from the Kunlun Mountains, southeast and south of the River Tsangpo (Brahmaputra) on to the River N'Maikha in Burma (now Myanmar). Even though McMahon was prepared for some surprises, he didn't expect this cartographic aggression based on inconsistent and vague historical assertions. However, there were factors that restrained McMahon from defining the boundaries. For one, a draft prepared by officials at Britain's India Office had only envisaged a two-party meeting between representatives of Peking and Delhi. With Tibet's entry in the deliberations, McMahon had to put up appearances to hide his limitations. In reality, in the absence of clarity about the southern limits of Tibet, McMahon was awaiting some survey reports from the expeditions along the Himalayas, particularly from India's northeast and the tri-junction between India, Tibet and Bhutan. This region had many unsurveyed 'grey areas' along a frontier of over a 1,000 kilometres and was often covered with mist or clouds with many snow-covered mountains that couldn't be easily accessed from the Indian side. This prevented McMahon from presenting a clear proposal to the conference plenipotentiaries on this part of the boundary.[22]

Thus McMahon opened the 'second meeting' of the conference on 18 November 1913 by sharing his dilemma with colleagues. He placed a skeleton map of what should be 'Tibet', admitting—after both sides had made widely divergent claims—that he was 'at a loss as to what really was Tibet'. Thereafter, he conveyed to both the Chinese and the Tibetans that without an agreement on the 'limits of Tibet', further progress was not possible. China's Chen first said he'd have to refer the matter to Peking and then he took to bed after the meeting, claiming he was ill! Thus, with no hope of an immediate headway and with the winter in Simla bringing life to a virtual standstill, the conference venue was shifted to Delhi. It was over subsequent meetings in Delhi, both formal and informal, that there was some movement forward.[23]

The Tibetans brought to these meetings more than ninety records and documents and backed their boundary claims with historical records in their original form, including fifty-six different registers, with numbers of monasteries and details of families, 'where the writ of the Dalai Lama was unquestioned'. The Chinese, on the other hand, made historically refutable claims based on scanty evidence. Moreover, the Tibetans' statements were extremely critical of the 'scorched earth' policies of the Chinese, especially its military commander Zhao Erfeng, who had destroyed many of their temples and villages and massacred hundreds of lamas and people. Erfeng was known to have made paper shoe soles from the leaves of Buddhist scriptures containing the teachings of Lord Buddha! The Tibetans were thus unwilling to accept Chinese claims based on the ruthless military campaigns by Erfeng, stating that 'Chao Erh-feng had been guilty of such glaring misdeeds and that even if he had a hundred lives he should forfeit every one of them to the law…'.[24]

Thus, the hotly contested territorial claims of the Chinese and Tibetans put McMahon in a spot in his attempts to find common ground, to end their 'state of war' and to move the conference towards its conclusion. However, given his vast experience in map-making, McMahon proposed the division of Tibet into two zones—with the approval of Whitehall in London—by drawing lines on a map to mark: Inner (by a blue line) and Outer (by a red line) Tibet. But the Chinese were unwilling to accept the concept of Inner or Outer Tibet. Even then, McMahon was hopeful of a settlement at the fifth conference in Delhi that was to be held on 11 March 1914.[25] At the fifth conference, McMahon, apprehensive that China–Tibet hostilities would stall his best efforts, warned both parties that any attempts to change the ground realties to attain a favourable deal at the conference would have grave consequences. He demanded instead statesmanship from Ivan Chen and Lochen Shatra.[26]

There was, however, a quiet spoiler lurking on the sidelines. Lu Hsing Chi was a Chinese spy at the conference, who set alarm bells ringing in China about a possible outcome that would put China at a disadvantage vis-à-vis Tibet, and thus, Peking virtually rejected the entire draft that McMahon and his team had painfully put together, demanding a better deal. Sensing that the conference might collapse, McMahon threatened to present proposals that were more stringent. This kept the Chinese team on board until the conference shifted back to Simla in April 1914, when McMahon had a private chat with Chen. McMahon warned that if Chen failed to initial the documents in the final meetings, it would be withdrawn. Deep inside he was also prepared for the conference to end without any results even though McMahon had hoped that this was to be a decisive phase of the conference. Thus, he resorted to theatricals. He first began with a summary of earlier conference proceedings and when he ran into resistance by the Chinese and then by the Tibetans, his patience ran out. As a shocker to those in attendance, he ordered the withdrawal of the convention 'with as much ceremony as possible', as recorded by observers, to drive home his frustration with the negotiations.[27]

This unnerved Ivan Chen, the Chinese plenipotentiary in Simla. However, in one last attempt, the conference was reconvened the next day, to give them a final chance to reconsider their positions. Facing the distinct possibility of China being left out of the border arrangements, Chen made up his mind to initial the draft and the map and, much to the relief of all, proceeded with the formalities. However, Chen announced that he was still 'bound to await definite authority from his government in Peking before the convention was formally signed and sealed'.[28] Even as it appeared that matters had finally come to a successful conclusion, this was not to be. Chen informed McMahon's office that his government had refused to accept—'repudiated'—his signing of the convention! McMahon was disappointed, given his multiple attempts to accept Chinese demands.

It soon became known that the man who influenced Peking to put the brakes was Lu Hsing, their Calcutta-based spy, who was elevated to an official position to negotiate with Lhasa. London was brought into these talks and soon Chinese officials suggested that Chen had been forced to agree to the terms of the convention, whereby its venue should be shifted to Peking or London. There is a view that this process reflects a conflict of interest as Sir McMahon was both the arbitrator and the interested party here.[29]

On the brighter side, however, the conference yielded another outcome. After Beijing and Lhasa had presented enough documentation to back their conflicting territorial claims on the Sino-Tibetan frontiers, which had led to no agreement, the focus of the conference shifted to the Indo-Tibetan boundary. On this, the Chinese delegate opted to stay out, as he claimed he wasn't authorised to discuss it. Thus, McMahon and the Tibetan delegate agreed on an Indo-Tibet boundary on 24–25 March 1914. To that effect, McMahon drew a line on a small-scale map and this line came to be known as the McMahon Line. This boundary was marked in red ink along the crest of the Himalayas—the watershed that gave northeast India a defined boundary with Tibet. This was a major outcome after many months of negotiations, even though this was a secondary objective of the Simla Conference. And though the British team and the Tibetan delegation had come to this agreement, the maps with the red markings were shown to China's Ivan Chen, who initialled them without any objections. By then it was clear that China's interests were essentially on the Sino-Tibet boundaries, and not the Indo-Tibet one, since Tibet was an independent nation. These maps were attached to the draft of the Simla Convention.[30]

Economic Underpinnings

With the alarm raised by Hsing Chi, the Chinese were nervous about British designs over Tibet. For the British, the purpose of this cartographic initiative was to give Tibet autonomy, while not entirely displeasing the Chinese. McMahon, therefore, had come up with the idea of an 'Outer' and 'Inner' Tibet, which implied that large parts of Tibet would remain under Chinese control. Lhasa, though unhappy, reluctantly accepted it. However, despite having agreed to a list of Chinese demands that Tibet would remain under Chinese suzerainty and China would have a say in the appointment of the Dalai Lama, the Chinese continued to negotiate endlessly at Simla to avoid committing themselves to a final arrangement. When the Chinese delegation held firm despite threats from the British, McMahon decided to close the conference with only the signing ceremony between the British government in India and Tibet. Chen had retired to another room after the Chinese government had refused to recognise 'any treaty or similar document that might now or hereafter be signed between Great Britain and Tibet'.[31]

The primary British objective at the Simla Conference, though unstated, was to define a frontier between Tibet and the British Empire up to the Burma front, to secure British interests in the tea gardens of Assam and its oil fields. To that effect, a tribal belt to guard the locals and their customs was identified as a buffer between India and Tibet, a peaceful neighbour.

McMahon's 'red line' that delineated this boundary was largely influenced by the explorations of British military officers like Lt Col. F.M. Bailey (better known as FB), who detailed his adventures in a book titled *No Passport to Tibet* in 1957. Besides, McMahon couldn't have achieved so much without the enthusiastic support of his fellow traveller, Captain H.T. Morshead, better known as HM. Having participated in Younghusband's expedition to Tibet, FB became obsessed with the spirit of explorations and especially with Tibet, becoming fluent with its dialects. He went on to head Tibetan outposts of Gyantse and Shigatse and eventually became a close confidant of the Dalai Lama. HM went on to join the Survey of India in Dehradun and became its foremost map-surveyor of what became North East Frontier Agency (NEFA) and is Arunachal Pradesh today.[32]

While the British government appreciated and endorsed the efforts of McMahon, the viceroy of India, Lord Hardinge, expressed appreciation in a formal statement that complimented Sir McMahon and his two key associates, Charles Bell and Archibald Rose. This despite the fact that many observers of the Simla Convention and its outcome regard it as a failure because

China had refused to accept it and the boundary arrangements it offered. However, the boundary of India's northeast frontier that was firmed up on two large-scale maps of 1 inch:8 miles was indeed a farsighted act that came to be known as the McMahon Line, one that India has steadfastly maintained as its border with China since the 1950s. It runs from the northeast corner of Bhutan to the Tibet–India–Myanmar tri-junction. This was in itself an achievement.[33]

However, a month after the Simla Conference ended, a major conflict was unleashed in many parts of the world. The First World War overshadowed many important issues that concerned the world outside its operational theatres in Europe and the Middle East. This included the fate and the future of Tibet, as events were to show.[34]

2
CHINA ON THE WORLD STAGE

During the period 1911–1951, Tibet could arguably be called an independent state, although with the exception of Mongolia, no other country—not even India—recognised it as such. Perhaps, even Tibet did not acknowledge its own independence. In fact, well after the collapse of the Qing dynasty and much after the warlord factions that ruled over parts of China were overthrown, the Tibetans continued to seek Beijing's approval for the selection of the Dalai Lama from the Kuomintang (KMT)[1] party led by General Chiang Kai-shek that controlled China from Guangzhou. Tibetans had thus adopted a contradictory policy of hiding behind Chinese imperial authority when approached by the British directly and standing up to orders from weak Chinese regimes. This can be best seen in the case of the Simla Convention regarding the McMahon Line, which was wilfully signed by Tibet's representative on 3 July 1914, but wasn't ratified later as Beijing hadn't accepted the McMahon Line[2] and barely a few weeks later, the First World War started, engaging most of the principal nations for more than four years.

Inner Conflict in China

In the years between the two World Wars (1919–1939), mainland China grappled with its own political issues, but with little effect, as it toyed with parliamentary elections and even made a brief attempt at restoring the Qing dynasty—as cliques within the Beiyang Army[3] that controlled the government saw clashes amongst warlords. In 1927–28, General Chiang's northern expedition led to the overthrow of the Beiyang government in North China, when he established the Nationalist government in Nanking on 18 April 1927.[4] In the process, however, massacres of Communist cadres in Nanking forced the Communist Party of China (CPC) into an armed rebellion that triggered the Chinese Civil War.[5]

Nation-building efforts and industrialisation, too, suffered in the 1930s from internal strife. In 1931, in search of raw materials to fuel its growing industries, Japan invaded the Chinese province of Manchuria and began to control large sections of the country followed by a full-scale Japanese invasion in 1937, a military conflict that Japan won essentially because China's government was weak and divided. In this scenario, the Chinese leadership of KMT had little time to be interested in events far off in the west, in Sinkiang, where rulers and warlords vied for influence. This did not go unnoticed by the governments in Moscow and Delhi. Both Britain and Russia had territorial ambitions and sought to expand their domains during the interwar period.

By the start of the Second World War, the Soviet Consul in Tihwa was the de facto ruler of Sinkiang.[6] It kept a close watch on the activities of the local warlords, especially the pro-Soviet Sheng Shicai and his rival Ma Hu-shan, who lived closer to Ladakh but controlled southern Sinkiang.[7] In early 1938, however, 'Sheng Shicai's forces along with the Red Army defeated Warlord Ma Hu-shan, whose defeated forces divided up and fled to India via both the Khunjerab and Karakoram passes, respectively. This led to Sheng Shicai closing down both of these passes, and in turn the drying up of trade between Hari Singh's state and Sinkiang. The use of both of these routes by

Ma Hu-shan's several hundred strong forces to flee into India, became a source of worry for (the British) Army headquarters in Delhi. The British perceived an open border as a threat, as it could give refugees from Khotan in Sinkiang easy access into Leh via Aksai Chin. Distrustful of Russia and fearful that it had plans to invade India, Britain wanted to protect all the approaches into India.'[8] By late 1940, Sheng Shicai was forced—as he later claimed—to enter into an extensive agreement with the Soviets, granting them concessions not only in Sinkiang, especially mining rights, but also in Kashmir and Tibet. In turn, Sheng Shicai received additional military cover from the Soviets that added to his trappings of power and strengthened his local political clout.[9] This is explained later in this chapter.

Rivalry for Resources

Ever eager to spread the reaches of its own empire, the British government in India first tried to persuade Hari Singh, the Maharaja of Jammu & Kashmir, to take the Soviet threat more seriously, especially in Gilgit-Baltistan and on its north.[10] The Maharaja was asked to devote greater financial support for the Corps of Gilgit Scouts, the British-officered paramilitary unit and the primary defence forces in the region. However, as Hari Singh was reluctant to do so, the British government obtained from him a lease for the entire Gilgit wazarat (kingdom) north of the Indus and all its vassal states in favour of the then Government of India for sixty years, for a lump sum amount of 75,000 rupees. On 1 October 1935, the Government of India's political agent in Gilgit, Major G. Kirkbride, took absolute charge of the region.[11]

Moscow's eyes, however, were not on Ladakh, but on Sinkiang. It was using the local warlords to gain an advantage by supporting them militarily in return for exploitation of resources and establishing a trade monopoly in the region. In the early years of the Second World War, Sheng concluded an agreement with the Soviets on 26 November 1940, to grant the Russians additional concessions in the province of Sinkiang for fifty years, including the areas bordering Kashmir and Tibet. Sinkiang thus came under the full political and economic control of the Soviets. It remained a part of China in name only. A host of Soviet advisors, the Red Army units and NKVD (The People's Commissariat for Internal Affairs)[12] law-enforcement agents enabled Sheng to become immune to local political opposition. As Sheng recalled in his memoir, *Red Failure in Sinkiang* (1958), the Soviet supremo Stalin pressured him to sign a secret Agreement of Concessions in 1940. This Agreement of Concessions, prepared by Stalin himself, was seventeen articles long and effectively put Sinkiang in the same state as Poland.[13]

Soon thereafter, in 1940–41, the Soviets started to send large-scale geological exploration expeditions into both the Kashgar and Altai regions of Sinkiang. These expeditions discovered large deposits of uranium, beryllium and other minerals used in making a nuclear bomb. The ores of uranium and beryllium were excavated from the Sinkiang Altai mines and delivered to the Soviet nuclear testing site at Semipalatinsk, about 800 kilometres by road from Kashgar. This continued until 1943.

Clearly, Sinkiang had become very important for Moscow, which already had a firm hold on substantial oil and gold production of the region.[14] But Moscow wanted more. It sought a fifty-year exclusive lease on all mining rights in Sinkiang. Towards this end, in 1941, Moscow threatened Sheng, warlord turned military governor who controlled the military occupation of Sinkiang with Soviet support, with dire consequences unless the Russians were given a fifty-year exclusive lease on all mining rights in Sinkiang, over and above the substantial hold they had on the oil and gold resources. The British too were eyeing this region.

The British government in India was relying on the KMT regime to give them this access. However, the KMT couldn't as its writ didn't run in Sinkiang. Moscow was in charge in Sinkiang, though it officially denied it, more so as Britain was Russia's ally in the Second World War, and Moscow needed to work with London on bigger challenges, like the one presented by Hitler and Nazi Germany.

Yet, the British government in Delhi couldn't ignore the fact that its consular presence in Kashgar and trade between the Gilgit Agency and Sinkiang had come to a virtual standstill, ever since the two passes—the Khunjerab Pass and the Karakoram Pass, the frontier between Sinkiang and the Gilgit Agency—remained closed since 1938. The closure of the two passes had meant that Delhi had no land link with the Chinese wartime capital of Chungking, as the Burma Road was yet to be constructed. The British had all along justified their consular presence in Kashgar, but the end of cross-Karakoram trade put the British in a spot, more so as Sinkiang had come under considerable Soviet influence.[15] The Soviets' influence, however, wasn't permanent. Their reverses at the hands of the German Army in Europe were to play a role in their changing fortunes in Sinkiang.

Race for Nuclear Supremacy

With the Soviets on the back foot in Europe in 1942, the control over Sinkiang shifted to the KMT government, as the wily Sheng switched his allegiance from the Soviets to the KMT and expelled all Soviet technicians and military personnel from Sinkiang. A large force of Chinese in the KMT then began the reintegration of Sinkiang with the rest of China by building key roads linking Qinghai[16] with Sinkiang. To prove his loyalty, Sheng arrested several members of the CPC in that region in

1942–43 and executed a number of them, including Mao Tse-min, the brother of CPC leader Mao Zedong. Thus, Sheng was absorbed into the KMT and appointed head of the Sinkiang branch of the KMT party, which allowed the KMT to take root in Sinkiang. The jockeying for power in Sinkiang, however, was of concern to Delhi. The British thus prepared a memo for carefully patrolling the Gilgit-Kashgar boundary—along a line passing through Chamdo, Nag Chuka, Gartok (also known as Garyarsa) and Leh—as this was, then, the contact point between China and India.[17]

The British government was further unsettled with news about the discovery of uranium deposits by the Soviets in Sinkiang and sought to find out more about what the Soviets were planning. One such initiative was for Delhi to build a network of local couriers to bring back excavated materials from Kashgar and carry them across the border to Gilgit, to be transported to the US for tests. To set this in motion, the British decided to place Gilgit under the command of Col. Roger Bacon, whose job was to run an atomic and uranium spying network for what was happening in Sinkiang with the help of the US consulate in Tihwa.

Both the dominant powers, Britain and the US, saw in Sinkiang a route to the resources required for an atom bomb. The US not only wanted to be the first to acquire the 'bomb'—with Britain hoping to be second—but it was also keen to keep a global monopoly of uranium, which the Soviets were excavating in Sinkiang and Tibet. Thus, the Office of Strategic Services (OSS), a wartime intelligence agency better known as the American spy network, was established northeast of Ladakh with transmitters that would open all of Tibet, 1,200 miles east and west of Lhasa. The radios were operational by November 1943 and Tibet became the theatre of the 'new great game'.[18]

The race for nuclear supremacy and exclusivity led the

leaders of the US and Britain—President Roosevelt and Prime Minister Churchill—to sign the top secret '1944 Hyde Park Agreement', in an attempt to ensure that only the US and Great Britain would possess nuclear weapons. Strangely, however, the US copy of this classified document was lost forever among Roosevelt's papers after his death in 1945. So, when the US Atomic Energy Act, also known as the McMahon Act, to control and manage its nuclear technology was passed by both its houses on 1 August 1946, Britain, just like other countries, was excluded access to America's nuclear information.

After the bombing of Hiroshima and Nagasaki by the US, Britain wanted to be the next to have the atom bomb. It thus became extremely important for Britain to find out how close the Soviets were to acquiring the atom bomb, which they were working on in and around the uranium mines in the Koktogai fields, at the foothills of the Altai Mountains in Sinkiang Valley.[19] Britain also established three seismic monitoring stations in the Gilgit Agency (that remained operational until 1956). These were close to the River Indus and within the Hindu Kush Mountains, as it was closest to Semipalatinsk. This generated a daily output of seismic data that was telegraphically reported to the US, which allowed the US to monitor the progress of the Soviet nuclear programme. This also assisted Britain in its technical dialogue with the US well after the end of the Second World War, and scientific data to Britain to acquire its own 'bomb' in 1952, a few years after the Soviets did. On 29 August 1949, the Soviets successfully tested their first nuclear device at Semipalatinsk, a few months before the PRC was established on 1 October.

A Veiled Threat

Just before Mao led the Chinese Communists to victory in the civil war, the Indian political officer in Sikkim, H.S. Dayal, visited Lhasa for a dialogue. The Tibetans were looking to sign an agreement with India to train Tibetan troops and urgently supply them with arms and ammunition. On 8 November 1949, barely a month after the proclamation of the new PRC in Beijing, the Tibetans asked that the strength of the Tibetan Army be increased from 13,000 troops to 100,000. Although it was too late for India to do enough, New Delhi supplied the Tibetans with consignments of arms, including 38 two-inch mortars, 63 three-inch mortars, 150 Bren guns, 14,000 two-inch mortar bombs, 14,000 three-inch mortar bombs and one million rounds of ammunition for Tibet's armoury of Lee Enfield rifles.[20]

This did not escape Mao's attention, as this wasn't the first consignment. The first lot was supplied exactly two years before the PRC had come into being. On 26 February 1946, Tibetan officials had arrived in Delhi with a request for a similar list of weapons that would cost the Tibetans Rs 3,82,162. After the files had done their full circle around the bureaucracy and more, Lt Col. (later Field Marshall) Sam Manekshaw, then posted in Delhi, finally cleared the supply of 14,84,000 rounds of ammunition for the Tibetan Army on 1 October 1947. However, this information was passed on by Chinese spies in Kalimpong to their KMT superiors in Nanking. 'Towards the end of December 1947, the Chinese Ambassador in New Delhi, Dr. Lo Chia Luen handed over an aide memoire to Prime Minister Nehru in which he ominously and prophetically warned that the supply of arms and ammunition to Tibet was not only a hostile act by India but that it would not portend well for Sino-Indian relations in the future,' observes Malhotra.[21]

These supplies were provided based on a confidential memo prepared by the Government of India, titled, 'Appreciation of the scale of direct military assistance which could be provided in support of Tibet'. The memo stated that 'the Soviets in

Sinkiang and China in Tibet were potential threats to India's security. The memo proposed a line passing through Chamdo, Nagchuka, Garyarsa and Leh, and opined that any invasion by the Soviets or the Chinese south of this line would prove to be highly dangerous for India's security. The area south of this proposed line was to be the buffer zone between India and the two expansionist powers of Soviet Russia and China. The memo emphasized on the crucial role the State of Jammu and Kashmir played in maintaining India's military defence.'[22] Before this memo was written, India's Secretary of External Affairs, Sir Olaf Caroe, had stated that the Gilgit-Kashgar boundary was the only direct contact point between India and China and no other contact points should be added.[23]

China–Russia Form Communist Alliance

Following America's nuclear bombing of Japan, Joseph Stalin, the Soviet leader, was keen to catch up with America and thus wanted his nuclear scientists to quickly detonate the first Soviet nuclear bomb. The British were aware of this possibility, as was the US, since the British monitoring stations were passing on seismic data regularly to the US and to London. In the US, these were regularly seen by senior intelligence officers, including Kim Philby, who was a Soviet double agent and then serving as MI6's intelligence chief in Washington, DC. Philby had earlier also informed the Russian KGB that US Secretary of State Dean Acheson was flying to New Delhi in July 1949 to do the groundwork for Nehru's upcoming visit to the US. So, while the US and Britain were monitoring the Soviet nuclear programme, Moscow knew it was being watched, and was in turn watching what Washington was up to, and thus the 'great game' continued.

When the Soviets successfully detonated their first nuclear

device, China's Mao became extremely eager to enter into a bilateral agreement with the Soviets. Mao knew that in order for China to become influential, he needed Stalin's support and military hardware, and Soviet nuclear knowhow, just as Stalin needed the mineral wealth of Sinkiang to enhance his nuclear stockpiles.[24] Radio Peking, which had earlier announced the formation of the PRC, declared in follow-up broadcasts that the immediate task of the PLA was to liberate all Chinese territories, including Tibet, Xinjiang, Hainan and Taiwan.[25]

This announcement from Radio Peking was made only days before Nehru arrived in Washington, DC in October 1949 for a series of meetings with President Truman. However, despite being at the right place at the right time, Nehru apparently ignored these developments. With the imminent alliance between the Soviets and the newly formed PRC, the US was rather keen to have India on board as an ally against the rise of Communism. In retrospect, however, it can be said that Nehru threw away this golden chance, first by ignoring the announcements by Radio Peking, and secondly by going out on a tangent by proclaiming instead that India would be neutral in the ensuing Cold War between the US and the USSR.

Nehru even overruled his more practical home minister, Sardar Vallabhbhai Patel, whose natural inclination was to join the Western Alliance. Thus, Nehru's critics argue—and perhaps rightly so—that in his desire to become the champion of non-alignment, the Indian prime minister ignored the writing on the wall and the strategic challenges before the newly formed Indian Republic.

In the meantime, Stalin was yet to establish a binding alliance with Mao, although he was apparently wary of Mao joining the US camp. Stalin eventually bought out Mao's loyalty following Mao's first-ever foreign trip to Moscow in December 1949. After two months of intense negotiations, Mao signed the

Sino-Soviet Treaty of Friendship and Mutual Assistance on 14 February 1950 with Stalin, under which China was to receive US$ 300 million worth of military assistance divided equally over five years. Half of this amount was earmarked for the Chinese Navy and this loan was to be repaid by China with export of raw materials. More importantly, through this initiative Stalin ensured that Chinese extractive industries involved in extraction of raw materials from the earth were tied to Soviet processing facilities and markets, and deepened China's dependence on the Soviet Union.

The two nations were deeply aligned economically and militarily even as the treaty became public knowledge. Apparently, this alignment didn't create much concern in India despite the fact that Stalin saw the transfer of power by the British to India on 15 August 1947 as a 'political farce' and even refused to send condolences on the death of Mahatma Gandhi.[26] Furthermore, it was believed that Stalin considered Nehru to be an agent of American imperialism while Soviet foreign minister Vyacheslav Molotov considered Nehru to be a British intelligence agent! It also seems strange in retrospect that Nehru chose to abandon the offer of a US-led anti-Communist alliance and his stance of neutrality in favour of the Soviets and officially recognised the newly born Communist China on 30 December 1949.

Communist Support for Korea

Even with the Cold War and the US-Soviet arms race, a major point for concern for the entire world, Stalin had Mao in his fold. This was only too obvious in Korea, which became the first military theatre of confrontation after the World War. Korea had been a unified political entity under Japan's colonial rule. However, following Japan's surrender in the Second World

War, the Allied forces occupied Korea with an understanding that Soviet troops would occupy parts of Korea north of the 38th parallel[27] while US troops would occupy south of this dividing line. This was meant to be a temporary arrangement until the wartime agreement on Korean trusteeship could be implemented and Korea could become a unified state again. But China's support to Stalin played a key role in the turn of events that have left Korea divided.

After several exchanges through their emissaries, Stalin was assured that Mao would support Korea's Kim Il-Sung whereby Stalin gave his consent and support to North Korea to launch its troops across the 38th parallel. North Korea moved thus on 25 June 1950, leading to an announcement by Truman on 27 June that he too was sending troops to South Korea as well as increasing aid to the French in Vietnam. The USA thus joined the war on the side of South Korea while China came to North Korea's aid. The subsequent Korean War, which lasted from 1950 to 1953, ended with a stalemate and left the two Koreas separated by the Korean Demilitarised Zone (DMZ). Furthermore, the Korean War also marked a reversal of America's existing policy of 'non-intervention' towards Taiwan, meant to keep Taiwan protected against Mao's expansionist agenda in the years to come.

By this same yardstick, it can be argued that if Nehru had accepted Truman's offer to join the collation against Communism, then it is possible that the invasion of Tibet from October 1950 and even the Chinese attack on India in October 1962 would never have taken place.[28]

China Controls Roof of the World

With their geostrategic interests now in sync, it is said that Stalin urged Mao to consolidate Chinese control in north-western

Tibet bordering Sinkiang, by building a road to Gartok and sending troops from Sinkiang to keep a watch on the hostile lamas who he alleged were up for sale to the highest bidder, be it America, Britain or India. However, as Tibet did not have a network of roads, the logistics of supporting an invasion would be a challenge for Mao and limit the size of his invading force. Thus, Mao extracted a Soviet commitment to airdrop supplies for the Chinese invasion force in Tibet. Knowing that the Tibetan Army would give a tough response to the PLA, Mao strategically sent his troops into parts of eastern Tibet, which were easily accessible and which could not offer any resistance, to play a psychological game, and circulated a ten-point document, asking Tibetans to co-operate with China in 'liberating' Tibet from foreign imperialists. It was obvious that the 'imperials' were Indians, as Mao viewed India as an extension of the British Empire. He clearly wanted Indian trade officials and the Indian Army escorts in Gartok, Yatung and Lhasa out of Tibet. Also, in keeping with Stalin's advice to secure Chinese control over Sinkiang, the construction of the Sinkiang-Tibet road became a priority for China.

In retrospect, it is difficult to accept that Nehru and his government didn't know about the Soviet-Chinese plans for Sinkiang and Aksai Chin, given the fact that Nehru's sister, Vijaylakshmi Pandit, was India's ambassador to Moscow and Capt. Ram Sathe was in Kashgar as the Indian consul till the autumn of 1950.[29]

On 7 October 1950, some 40,000 PLA troops attacked Chamdo in Tibet from the south. The much smaller Tibetan force, numbering only about 8,000 troops, however, fought fierce battles with the PLA. By 19 October 1950, after the Tibetans had fought 21 battles and lost over 5,700 men, Chamdo fell to the PLA. Less than half a century after Col. Francis Younghusband had marched into Tibet, the Chinese were now in control of the 'roof of the world'.

The PLA then garrisoned itself at Chamdo as it didn't have the wherewithal to advance further, despite Soviet support, and fanned out on a line from Chamdo via Lho Long on the River Salween south to Menkong and Rima on the Indian border and west as far as Riwochi. The terrain and climate further restricted the PLA.

The Tibetan demand for more support and weapons from India was denied, even though the earlier consignment of arms given by India in March 1950 was exhausted. Despite Lhasa's honest plea that it was in no position to resist an armed attack by the Chinese, India refused to help. Even without moral and material support from Nehru, the Tibetans did not cave in and displayed rare grit in holding off the capture of their land by the Chinese.

The Chinese occupation of Tibet was achieved by a combined means of political and military warfare. Measures were steadily implemented to frighten both Nehru and the Tibetan people by disarming their will to resist and by utilising the political factionalism and rivalry, so common whenever a regent ruled for the Dalai Lama, who was only a teenager when Mao and the PLA set their eyes on Lhasa.[30]

India's leadership, however, was divided in their assessment of China's moves. Sardar Patel, independent India's first home minster, saw this as a clear sign of Chinese expansionism and publicly condemned China's 'unjustified' actions in Tibet. He even cautioned Nehru on 7 November 1950 about his complacent approach, but Nehru wasn't worried. Later, Nehru changed his stance and chose to adopt the earlier British principle of recognising China's suzerainty over Tibet, as long as Beijing did not challenge India's control over its frontier with Tibet. He also spoke about the need to protect India's trading rights in Tibet. This was duly conveyed to China by India's ambassador to China, K.M. Pannikar—who, however, had used the term sovereignty instead of suzerainty to describe China's relationship with Tibet, for which he was criticised later—but even then China's first premier Zhou Enlai[31] wasn't willing to accept India's line. In his reply to Nehru, he made it clear that China would establish control over Tibet either by negotiation or by the use of force. Though strategically an independent Tibet was important to the British government in India and later as Nehru's government chose to adopt many of their policies at Independence, control over Tibet was a non-negotiable issue for Communist China. Governments in Delhi—first the British and then the Indian—were desirous of maintaining Tibet's independence, essentially as a 'buffer state' (like Nepal is today between India and Chinese-controlled Tibet), but the Chinese claimed all the territory that was part of the Manchu Empire. Historians, however, are of the view that had Nehru been more realistic and not so obsessed with his own idealism, and had India recognised Tibet as a nation state, China's occupation of Tibet from 1950 could have been legally challenged with a UN resolution. But neither did India nor the US or Britain recognise Tibet as an independent nation, even though Lhasa had been independent of Chinese control since 1912—for at least 38 years—when Chinese soldiers were driven out by the Tibetans. Normally, in international law, such a long period of effective independent existence as a national state carries with it de jure recognition. But the US too, where the terms sovereignty and suzerainty are used interchangeably, didn't initially show much inclination about the status of Tibet.[32]

And while the history of Tibet's relations with China was well known to the British, the Americans who took charge of the western narrative of Tibet from 1950 had little understanding of the historical linkages between China and Tibet. Historians are now of the view that a reason for Nehru's policies—particularly on non-alignment—were countered by the US, because

Washington wanted India to join its collective front against the communists, but Nehru's socialist leanings prevented him from doing so. Ironically, however, Communist China perceived India, as a democracy, to be in America's camp and dismissed its efforts to befriend Communist China as doublespeak. While Nehru was keen to befriend China, his desire for an autonomous status for Tibet was part naivety and part his insistence on adopting a unilateral foreign policy on China. It eventually ran into opposition at home, when his home minister Sardar Patel publicly condemned China's 'unjustified' actions in Tibet, after Chinese troops marched into Tibet in late 1950.[33]

Map 3: Communist China's expansion

Source: Kunal Verma, *1962: The War that Wasn't*, p. 62

Nehru, however, chose to ignore the signs of Chinese expansionism until it became too late. History remains a mute witness to the future foretold by the oracle. The 13th Dalai Lama had prophesised before his death, in 1933, that the institutions of the Dalai Lama and the Panchen Lama 'will be eliminated without a trace', and 'our political system will be reduced to an empty name'. This began to ring true with the events that were to follow in Tibet from 1951. More importantly, with China establishing its writ over the 'roof of the world', the terms and the context of the relations between China and India and its leaders had changed forever.[34]

3
AN AMBITIOUS ADVERSARY

The leadership of Communist China, in particular Mao Zedong, held many grievances against India for where a weak China stood in 1949, having been amongst the wealthiest and most technologically advanced countries two centuries ago. Mao and his team saw India as the direct inheritor of Britain's mantle and hence Britain's legacy, which the Chinese abhorred.

The Chinese resented the British, for British imperialism in China had humiliated their rulers and destroyed their tea industry, allowing for the rise of India's tea exports. Above all, it had made China a nation addicted to opium, which was traded for silver.

Moreover, their humiliation following the British expeditions into China in 1842 led not only to the loss of Hong Kong, but also reverses in Ladakh, leading to the Treaty of Chushul, which defined the borders of Ladakh. By the 1860s, opium had a devastating impact on its society, its economy was shattered and military defeats had humiliated its emperor, even though the Qing dynasty collapsed much later, in 1911, following the cumulative impact of British aggressions on China over seven decades, from 1839 onwards.[1]

Once the Qing dynasty collapsed and Chinese forces in Tibet, too, were routed, the British government in India saw this as an opportunity to set out the boundaries of Tibet, as it did in the Simla Conference of 1914, to pre-empt Russia's desire to increase its footprint over Tibet. It had also learnt about the 13th Dalai Lama's plans to seek a formal union against a rather weak China. Later, with China divided by internal conflicts, even the KMT lasted for two decades until it was driven out of mainland China, to Taiwan, by Chairman Mao and his communist regime.

Driven by power, Mao's CPC told China's population that it would reverse this tide of history, to undo 'a century of humiliation' and instead give China stability, strength and global respect. The Communist leadership went all out with State-led campaigns of 'patriotism', to promote a single ethnic and national identity. Mao was ambitious and wanted to liberate all Chinese territories, including Tibet, Xinjiang, Hainan and Taiwan. Even today, China's stated goal is to establish complete politico-military control over Taiwan and claims territories running along its border with more than ten countries.

Soviet Support Strengthens Mao

Mao's attention was also on Sinkiang, where the Soviets were working on mineral deposits from the Kashgar and Altai regions for making a nuclear bomb.[2] Mao, therefore, engaged extensively with the Soviets and even visited Moscow in 1949. Following deliberations with Joseph Stalin over his two-month long stay in Moscow, Mao, at Russia's nod, joined the Korean dictator to start the Korean War. China provided military assistance to North Korea against the Americans. When the Americans retaliated, the losses to the Chinese were shockingly high, with 1,00,000 PLA soldiers dead. Mao was apparently not worried, as he knew that his only advantage came with the use of 'human wave tactics'.

The Russians were keen to use the Korean conflict as

an opportunity to test their newly built MiG fighter aircraft. Mao, on the other hand, had his sights firmly fixed on Tibet. Therefore, since the start of the Korean War, while the world's attention was focused on the Korean peninsula, Mao pushed in his troops to simultaneously occupy Tibet, which had been under Chinese occupation, yet remained an unrecognised nation. This, however, was accomplished only by 1953, after initial reverses and a stalemate.

Mao's troops moved steadily to expand Chinese control over Tibet that was vast and surrounded by mountains. The Chinese PLA, however, could not be effective as it lacked a rail network and Chinese soldiers were not used to the human challenges of operating in high altitudes. The Tibetan Army, though disarmed, remained a force that could be revived and revitalised, and Tibet had requested military assistance from India.

Nehru in a Bubble

India could have supported the Tibetans, but Nehru let the opportunity pass. Just like he chose to ignore the strategic agenda of Communist China to take over the territories of Tibet and Taiwan, which was broadcast earlier by Radio Peking. Nehru chose to ignore the writing on the wall, giving Mao ample time to forge Soviet support and put his plans into place.[3]

In contrast, Mao remained concerned that India might act against China's poorly equipped forces in Tibet with the help of the Americans, even though Nehru had openly declined America's offer of an anti-Communist alliance on his visit to the US in 1949.[4]

Nehru was inclined to lean towards the Soviets by his friend and alter ego, Krishna Menon, who he had made India's first high commissioner to London in 1947. Menon, much influenced by communist propaganda, was later made the defence minister of India, with disastrous consequences for India in the 1962 Sino-Indian conflict, as discussed later. Nehru, rather naively, believed that the Soviets were only giving China the support that one communist state should give to another. This leaning of Nehru worked well for Stalin and Mao.

Even though the Indian Intelligence Bureau (IB) had begun to share intelligence with Britain's MI-5, which had helped in its creation, the British were only providing Indians inputs on a 'need to know' basis. It led to Nehru making decisions, based on his assumptions coloured with emotions rather than solid intelligence inputs. Truly, Nehru was denied critical intelligence about the Soviets and the Chinese plans to almost concurrently invade South Korea and Tibet respectively, at an important time in India's history.[5]

Nehru thus chose to justify India's neutral credentials, even as China, despite its military limitations and Mao's fear that India could act in concert with the US to stall the Chinese invasion of Tibet, bluffed its way into compelling the Tibetans to sue for peace. The Tibetan leadership wanted to protect the young Dalai Lama in 1950. The 14th Dalai Lama took up his responsibilities—both spiritual and political—at the age of 15, on 17 November 1950, in an atmosphere of apprehension as the Chinese army arrived in Lhasa. The centuries-old Kashag, the governing council of Tibet and a legacy of the Qing dynasty, decided to shift the Tibetan administration along with the Dalai Lama to Yatung, a day's march from the Sikkim–Tibet border. This would allow an easy escape into India, if the Chinese became more aggressive. Yatung was also a centre for Indo-Tibetan trade and the base for an Indian Army military escort. Nehru, however, was not keen to encourage any further dissent by the Tibetans. He even legitimised Mao's takeover of Tibet (with the Panchsheel Treaty of 1954) even though Mao had himself conceded in 1952 that there was no social basis or popular support for the Communist Party's 'liberation' of Tibet. Nehru's stance was to have serious implications for the Sino-Indian boundary question in China's favour. He must, however, be credited for signing treaties for the defence of Bhutan (8 August 1949), Nepal (31 July 1950) and Sikkim (5 December 1950). These nations would act as buffers against any Chinese expansion.[6]

Takeover of Tawang

In contrast with Nehru's faltering ambiguity in Indo-China relations, a few individuals displayed decisiveness, courage and wisdom when India prepared to take over Tawang, even without direct orders from Nehru. This was a major irritant for China, but today strengthens India's claims on the McMahon Line. In January 1951, Jairamdas Daulatram, the governor of Assam,[7] summoned a well-regarded and decorated Indian Army officer, Major Ralengnao 'Bob' Khathing MC, MBE, from the Second Assam Rifles, to Government House in Shillong. In the presence of his advisor, Tribal Affairs, Nari K. Rustomji, ICS, the governor told Major Khathing that he was being entrusted with a top secret mission: 'To go and integrate Tawang into India.' Major Khathing was transferred on deputation to the Indian Frontier Administrative Service, as an assistant political officer, as secrecy of the operation was to be maintained. He directly reported first to Rustomji and then to Major T.C. Allen, political officer of NEFA.[8]

Major Khathing put together a team of two companies along with Captain Hem Bahadur Limbu and a doctor, Captain Modiero, along with 600 porters. After several days of travel in the tough Himalayan terrain, Major Khathing and his team moved onto Tawang via the Jang and Sela mountain pass. At each stop, he made it clear to the villagers that the writ and orders of the Tibetan government, now under Chinese control, would not apply to these areas. His team even established a checkpost and an adjoining barrack on the Sela tract and then moved on to take control of Tawang. The force reached Tawang on 7 February 1951 and the first two days were spent scouting the area for a permanent site, where both civil and military lines could be laid out with sufficient area for a recreation ground. Later, a site for this purpose was chosen northeast of the Tawang Monastery.

Major Khathing then summoned the somewhat reluctant Tibetan officials for a meeting on 9 February, but they didn't show up. Major Khathing, peeved that his authority had been flouted, wanted to show the recalcitrant Tibetans that he were serious. He, therefore, instructed Captain Limbu to order his troops to fix bayonets and stage a flag march around Tawang. By evening, it had the desired effect and Tibetan officials and the abbot of Tawang Monastery came to meet him. They were then given notice that the tsona dzongpens or magistrates or any representatives of the Tibetan government could no longer exercise any power over the people living south of the Bumla range.[9]

On 11 February, Major Khathing visited the monastery in Tawang, called on its abbot and presented him and the other monks gifts that consisted of self-winding gramophone players, bolts of cloth and tiffin carriers. The next day, all the officials of the 11 Tibetan administrative units were called and a general order was issued directing them not to take any further orders from any of the now dispossessed Tibetan officials or pay tribute to them any longer. Tibetan officials asked for time and permission to exercise their authority in the interim, until they heard from the Tibetan government in Lhasa. However, Major Khathing put his foot down and told them that the area belonged to the Government of India according to the Simla Treaty of 1914, and there was no question of a reply from their government in Lhasa. Moreover, being in possession and the dominant authority, there was no question of any extension in the interim or ever. Thus, Tawang effectively became a part of India from that day on.[10] It was a bold and audacious initiative that was implemented with military precision and success. It was perhaps the last such operation on the Sino-Indian boundary, but its significance was lost on Nehru.

Incident Blackout

Major Khathing's orders were to secure Tawang and hand it over to the political officer, to establish a civil administration in Tawang. Having done that, he headed back to Tezpur, en route to Shillong, in response to a wireless message from Rustomji. From Tezpur, an IAF Dakota flew him via Shillong along with Daulatram for a meeting with a furious Nehru, who was reportedly livid. Nehru took the governor to task for transgressing his authority and ordered a complete blackout of this incident from official records. Yet, its evidence remains.

The quintessential bureaucrat Rustomji had his secretary Haliram Datta send a copy of the top secret report titled, 'Major Khathing's Detailed Report about Towang' to Jt Secy S.N. Haksar, ICS, a Punjab cadre officer in the Ministry of External Affairs. Datta wrote, 'In continuation of Shri N.K. Rustomji's demi-official No.CGA.6/51, dated 3 April 1951, I am directed to enclose here with a copy of a detailed report from Major Khathing for the information of the Government of India.' Major Khathing used to refer to Tawang as 'Towang', which is why his report carries this oddity in its title.

Historians are still divided over what was the motivation of the governor of Assam to launch this mission without consent from Nehru, who it was known took personal interest in matters related to Tibet and China. Perhaps it was because the governor, close to India's home minister, Sardar Patel, could have received these instructions from Patel's deathbed bypassing Nehru. If this is true, then this is Patel's important gift to the nation. In fact, there is evidence that in one of his last notes to Nehru on 7 November 1950, Patel did caution Nehru against a possible Chinese infiltration from India's northeast.[11]

Because of Patel's warnings, in November 1950, Nehru set up a committee under his deputy defence minister, M.S. Himmatsinhji, a retired Major General, to look into the challenges presented by the Chinese in India's northeast and the best possible ways to integrate that neglected region into India. Was Nehru keen to act on Patel's advice or to get a 'reality check' about the apprehensions expressed by Patel? The events that followed a decade later showed how right Patel was.

The committee set up by Gen. Himmatsinhji submitted its report in two parts in April and September 1951. As per its recommendations, the Indian government decided to extend its administrative cover over NEFA and take up economic and welfare initiatives into the remote tribal areas. Road-building was also to be initiated as were the establishment of checkposts. Equally important, the Himmatsinhji Committee suggested that in the sectors where boundary demarcations were unclear, even though the McMahon Line had been defined, India should decide its boundary claim lines and take effective steps to thereafter prevent any unilateral territorial occupation by the Chinese or the Tibetans.

In retrospect, it seems ironical that Major Khathing's expedition had done a similar job, as this committee had recommended, yet the governor of Assam was pulled up by Nehru! It has also been argued that the Himmatsinhji Committee was set up to justify the Indian takeover of Tawang so that

Mao's name-calling of Nehru as a 'running dog of imperialism' could be dismissed. This claim, however, contradicts Nehru's livid outburst at Governor Daulatram for initiating the Tawang takeover and shows that Nehru wasn't keen to confront the Chinese. In fact, it is said that Nehru had wanted this report that was to prove extremely useful, shelved.[12]

China's Military Advantage

Mao did not immediately react to the unusual Indian takeover of Tawang. Perhaps he was too preoccupied with the bitter fighting in the Korean War at that time. Stalin was pleased when the Chinese Army took over Seoul in South Korea. However, the US soon counterattacked with massive firepower and eventually took control of Seoul around the same time as Major Khathing's expedition had reached the fort of Dirang Dzong, which was under Tibetan administration.

Despite the huge loss of lives, Mao cabled Stalin that he was willing to use China's huge manpower reserves to exhaust the Americans. This won Stalin over. Pleased with Mao's zeal, Stalin overcame his earlier reluctance and gave orders on 19 February 1951 for the Soviet Union to build factories in China to repair and service its damaged fighter aircrafts. The wily Mao took advantage of this situation and got his technicians to convert these repair facilities into aircraft-making facilities. Thus, by the end of the Korean War in July 1953, even though Stalin was dead and succeeded by Nikita Khrushchev, China had the third largest airforce in the world and more than a thousand aircraft, including advanced versions of the reverse-engineered Soviet MiG fighters. That was indeed an achievement for a country that was still battling poverty. Also, following the end of the Korean War, Mao's attention shifted completely to Tibet, but he moved cautiously.

He saw that having regained its military advantage in Korea, the US was exploring a joint US–UK–India stand against China and its assault of Tibet. The American ambassador to India, Loy Wesley Henderson, had begun to engage with the Dalai Lama and initiated active involvement in Tibet's affairs. Henderson kept Washington posted about his actions. The Chinese leadership was fearful of a US attempt to stall China's plans to take over Tibet. However, once India's reluctance to become involved in Tibet's affairs became clear, the Chinese moved swiftly and strategically.

Unilateral Treaty with Tibet

China had defeated the Tibetan Army on the outskirts of Tibet with its military power, but instead of continuing with its military assault, China asked Tibet to send its representatives to Beijing to negotiate an agreement. By mid-1951, two delegations from Tibet, having the Dalai Lama's consent, arrived in Beijing through different routes. But they were soon held captive by the Chinese establishment and arm-twisted into agreeing on a 'Seventeen-point Agreement' for the so-called peaceful liberation of Tibet!

The delegates tried to escape the fait accompli that the Chinese were imposing on the people of Tibet, by denying that they had the authority to sign any agreement and by hiding their seals that they'd brought along; but the Chinese would have none of it. China did not allow the representatives to communicate with the Tibetan government in Lhasa and forced them to accept the agreement with forged wooden seals! The agreement affirmed Chinese sovereignty over Tibet. This news shocked the Dalai Lama and his team, who were 'transfixed' by the betrayal. They had hoped to effect changes to some of the articles of the Seventeen-point Agreement or to re-negotiate a brand new agreement. In Tibet's view, the document lacked ratification from the Tibetan Kashag. Beijing, however, had other plans. On 28 May 1951, China ordered many PLA units to advance to Central Tibet from different border regions. Multiple forces arriving from different directions thus completed the takeover of Tibet by 30 August 1951.[13] Mao then turned his strategic aggression to quietly go beyond the western boundary of Tibet.

India's Breached Border

The Indian government's attention was focused on its northeastern frontiers, when intelligence reports all through 1952 indicated that the Chinese had started to make inroads into eastern Ladakh by building a road from Sinkiang through Aksai Chin to enter western Tibet near Lanak La Pass. This intelligence was reportedly authenticated by aerial photographs showing the presence of a road, obtained through reconnaissance sorties conducted by the IAF.

To further ascertain the veracity of these reports, the Indian Army chief, General K.M. Cariappa, sent an army expedition with a young army captain, Rajendra Nath, who was selected from the Military Intelligence Directorate. Captain Nath was tasked to carry out an extensive reconnaissance and ascertain the Chinese role in Aksai Chin. Apart from Captain Nath, the team comprised of an engineer officer, a doctor and 15 men from other ranks, mostly from the infantry. The team left on 5 October 1952 and traversed multiple passes ranging from 17,000 feet to 18,300 feet, like the Chang La and Marsmik La passes and the Chang Chenmo river valley. From there they travelled via the Kongka La Pass to the Lanak La Pass and returned to Chang La by 15 November and then travelled to Delhi, where they submitted their report. That report was, however, classified 'top secret' and remains so till date.

As Nehru took all the final decisions related to China, the order to keep the report 'secret' would have come from him. It is reasoned that if the outcome of the report had indicated no Chinese presence in Aksai Chin, Nehru would have publicised it as it would have reiterated his denial of any Chinese intrusion and thereby scotched opposition. The fact that this report was classified—and remains so—confirms that its contents were damning of Chinese actions.[14]

Further, when Indian officials were to formulate their negotiating terms with China, it was felt that recognition of the traditional boundary between India and Tibet was the only way to resolve outstanding border differences with China and Tibet.[15] However, Nehru did not favour this approach. He did not want the border issue to be raised. His instructions were to separate the border issue from the resolution of the Tibet issue. When asked how, Nehru thought the border should be dealt with later as part of a wider settlement! The example of the village of Minsar, a small enclave near western Tibet, is a case in point. It had become a part of the territory of Jammu & Kashmir after the 1846 Treaty of Amritsar and India's historical claim on it was clear. Yet, Nehru was willing to give it up, as per Claude Arpi, a Sinologist![16] This is exactly what the Chinese wanted, the separation of Tibet from the Sino-Indian border issue, as events were to show.[17]

Emboldened by its military power, China communicated its position on Tibet to the Indian ambassador in Beijing in December 1953. China stated that it would not tolerate any further Indian interest in Tibet and neither should India have any objection to the construction of fortifications in Tibet near the Indian and Nepalese borders by China.

India Outsmarted

Nehru, on the other hand, considered China an 'old time friend' and wanted to build friendly relations with India's aggressive neighbour. In fact, to build trust and promote trade and co-operation between the two countries, India weakly negotiated with China for four months and signed an agreement that came to be known as the Panchsheel Treaty. It enshrined five principles of peaceful coexistence: mutual respect for each other's territorial integrity and sovereignty, non-aggression, non-interference in each other's internal affairs, equality and peaceful coexistence. Nehru and Zhou Enlai signed this treaty entitled 'Treaty on Trade and Intercourse between the Tibet Region of China and India', for a term of eight years on 29 April 1954.

The very title of the treaty itself formally conveyed that Tibet was now accepted by India as a part of China! India thus gave up not only its extraterritorial rights over Tibet, but also legitimised Chinese claims on Tibet, when the entire non-communist world was condemning China's occupation of Tibet. Worse still, India surrendered its three extraterritorial Indian Army outposts in Tibet, stationed there since 1904 under the Treaty of Lhasa, when it agreed to withdraw its troops from Yatung, Gartok and Gyantse in Tibet. India also offered China the India-run post and telegraph facilities in Tibet. China thus established not only physical control but also its legal claim on Tibet.

The communist regime then began to claim more territory on the Indo-Tibet boundary, like the Barahoti grazing grounds, and then along India's UP-Tibet border, by using the 1954 Treaty to buttress its claims.[18]

In return, India had expected China to recognise its claims on the Indo-Tibetan boundary, as well as its arrangements with Bhutan, Sikkim and Nepal. However, these expectations weren't explicitly stated in the agreement, whereas China had outsmarted India by placing its expectations explicitly in this agreement.

Gaining Nuclear Capability

Even as the ink was drying on the Panchsheel Treaty, China was primed to achieve two major strategic milestones out of incidents that initially made it uneasy. With India being committed to a non-aligned stance, the US reached out to Pakistan for an alliance. In a bipolar world dominated by capitalist America and communist Russia, both these powers were vying for allies.

In May 1954, Pakistan and the US signed a Mutual Defence Assistance Agreement by which Pakistan agreed to provide the US access to its airbase at Peshawar to fly reconnaissance flights over Tibet and Sinkiang, in return for military and economic aid. The US could also access British nuclear monitoring stations set up before the creation of Pakistan in Gilgit-Baltistan. This was a strategic move as the US was keen to monitor Russian activity in Sinkiang's Semipalatinsk region, the site of the first Russian atomic test in 1949. China was perturbed as it feared that with this positioning, the US would peek into its own nuclear test efforts in Lop Nor in Tibet. This incident, followed by Pakistan's signing of the South East Asia Collective Defence Treaty (SEATO) on 8 September 1954 in Manila, made the Chinese sit up in concern. The purpose of SEATO was to prevent communism from gaining ground in the region and America was signing military alliances to create a chain link of countries around the Soviet Union and China. Pakistan had become a part of it, but India hadn't.[19]

Until early 1955, Mao and the Chinese leadership were

plagued by a sense of unease. Feeling cornered by the US-Pak alliance, Mao was also deeply unhappy with the shoddy treatment China had received in its personal interactions with Stalin, the arrogant Russian dictator who was unwilling to provide nuclear capability that China needed in order to face America's nuclear threats.

Further, Stalin had died of a heart attack just a day prior to Moscow's announcement that Russia was pulling out of the Korean War on 1 March 1953. What Mao had received from the Soviets until then was the assurance that the Soviets would build up China's military potential in addition to the assistance provided earlier to set up over 90 military factories in 1953. It was now Mao's turn to extract a price for the thousands of soldiers he had pushed on the frontlines to face America's firepower in the Korean peninsula. For doing this, he had wanted Russian assistance to have a nuclear bomb that Stalin wasn't willing to part with.

Mao was feeling somewhat short-changed until the arrival of a high-powered Soviet delegation in October 1954, headed by Nikita Khrushchev, who declared that 'after the Soviet Revolution of 1917, the Chinese Revolution was the most outstanding event in world history'. The groundwork was done for China to acquire the 'ultimate weapon'. On 29 April 1955, the Soviet Union signed an agreement with China to provide it with a reactor, cyclotron, fissionable material and required technical assistance to build its own 'bomb', besides training Chinese scientists and technicians at the Dubna non-military research centre near Moscow. Mao couldn't have asked for more.[20]

Following this major win, Mao then turned to tame Pakistan. At the meeting of the leaders of third world countries at the Bandung Conference, also known as the Asia Africa Conference, held in Indonesia in April 1955, China managed to extract a public commitment from Pakistan that though it was a member of SEATO, it would not work against China's interests. In the presence of Nehru and other leaders, China's Zhou Enlai informed the delegates that Pakistan's prime minister, Mohammed Ali Bogra, had assured him that Pakistan's membership of SEATO was neither inimical to China's security nor had Pakistan become part of the alliance to counter any threats from China. Thereafter, China launched its verbal attacks on the US.[21]

Game of Intelligence

While Pakistan's dilemma was how to run with the hares and hunt with the hounds, Nehru had other ideas for India, as he saw himself as a global leader of anti-colonialists in the form of the Non-Aligned Movement (NAM). This initiative, as also Nehru's complacency towards Chinese expansionism into Tibet, drew the US away from him, even as he faced opposition at home, from the media and his partymen.[22] Notwithstanding Pakistan's double game, the US was committed to further its covert anti-China agenda in Tibet that was being shaped since the early 1950s and initiated the groundwork to derail Nehru's non-aligned policy that was viewed as being immoral and opportunistic. The 14th Dalai Lama's eldest brother, Thubten Norbu, had been living in the US (in San Francisco) since mid-1951. Later that year, the CIA invited the Dalai Lama's elder brother, Gyalo Thondup, along with his Chinese wife also to the US, to eventually get him to open a line of communication with the Dalai Lama. On his return, Gyalo initially went to Tibet and eventually set himself up at Kalimpong, a hill town in India, known to be a hub for spies for decades. Here he was visited by B.N. Mullik, India's IB chief. Mullik allowed Thondup to stay in Kalimpong on the condition that he worked for not only for the CIA but also the IB. Thus, Thondup began to work as a double agent to serve the interests of both India and the US. This was probably not known to Nehru, just as the arming of the Tibetans by the CIA remained under wraps.[23] America's surreptitious agenda was thus falling into place.

America's Surreptitious Agenda

Committed to its Tibetan project, the CIA was keen to arm the Tibetan militia that wanted to resist the Chinese occupation of Tibet. However, like any intelligence agency, the CIA wanted to maintain its distance and deniability for its support to the Tibetans. This desire for anonymity led the CIA—in its search for weapons that could somehow be linked with Chinese users—to huge stockpiles of Nazi weapons imported from Germany by private armies and warlords in China between the two world wars.

In these inter-war years, no single ruler or party had control over China. Thus, the CIA set up the 'Foreign Material Acquisition Programme' for purchase of German arms and ammunition that were smuggled into Tibet via India with the knowledge of India's IB. Based on the assumption of commentators about how these events unfolded, it can be assumed that this supply of weapons began in 1954. Although officially declassified papers point to the fact that the CIA'S covert operations in Tibet started rather cautiously only in 1956, evidence points to weapons supply commencing in 1954 itself.[24]

Nehru was mostly kept in the dark. Being deeply averse to covert operations and the games played by intelligence agencies, there was an effort to disguise the close, symbiotic relationship between IB and CIA in addition to play by the British intelligence agencies too. Each of these agencies needed the other's support. In fact, Mullik's predecessor in the IB,

T. Sanjeevi had reassured the CIA that he frequently had to take independent action without the knowledge of his government, and that regardless of the official attitude of his government, he would welcome the continuance of unofficial contacts. Once he had succeeded Sanjeevi, Mullik too maintained IB's links with British and American intelligence agencies as quietly as possible.'[25]

Mostly unaware of these intelligence links, Nehru chose to become unusually accommodative of China's interests in Tibet. The rationale for his policies was that aggravating or annoying the Chinese 'might well bring greater trouble' for the Tibetans. Nehru did not also object to the title of the Panchsheel Treaty, by which India formally pronounced its acceptance of Tibet being a part of China, despite the fact that until then, even Mao's public position was that the Tibetans were 'a completely different people' whereby the Chinese leader intervened to moderate all the steps taken to dismantle the socio-religious identities of the Tibetans. While Outer Tibet was gently handled by Mao, the harsh communist campaign to control Inner Tibet led to a major uprising in Lhasa by 1959[26] followed by the first tranche of Tibetan immigrants into India and Mao's deepening grievances against its neighbour.

4

PRELUDE TO A CONFLICT

Sino-Indian relations began their downward slide from early 1959, coinciding with the Tibetan uprising in Lhasa. Unlike India's demarcated frontiers with Nepal, Bhutan and Myanmar, neither was the Sino-Indian boundary settled then nor was it resolved after the short and bloody conflict of 1962. In fact, it has not been settled even now. There were a number of reasons, largely centred on the 'Tibetan question', which could be attributed to laying the grounds for the geopolitical rivalry between China and India.

While many Indians still regard the Chinese military invasion of 1962 as a 'betrayal', in view of Nehru's efforts to address the concerns of Mao's regime, the Chinese perhaps viewed three factors as most upsetting. First, India's claims on the boundaries of Tibet, which China insisted was an extended territorial part of its mainland along the Himalayas. The other was the exile offered to the Dalai Lama by India after he fled Tibet, which brought into public domain China's high-handed policies. And finally, the role that the US played with India's help in encouraging the Dalai Lama to flee Tibet and providing American military support to Tibetan rebels.

US Efforts to Contain China

Even though Nehru was keen to abandon the British policy of the 'great game' in the Himalayas, the CIA had begun to engage with the leaders of the Tibetan resistance called Chushi-Gangdruk, to challenge China's occupation of Tibet.[1] By some accounts, it was in February 1959 that perhaps the first and only arms airdrop by the CIA took place in Lokha, which lay between Lhasa and the River Tsangpo, which Indians call Brahmaputra. This included 55mm mortars, sub-machine guns, grenades and other ammunition. It emboldened the Tibetan rebels to attack a Chinese army base in Tsethang, whereby they captured all of Lokha and the adjoining land between Lhasa and River Tsangpo,[2] before extending the guerrilla warfare to other areas of Tibet.

Informed publications[3] now reveal that the US president Dwight Eisenhower, in a bid to contain Communist China, had approved a plan to para-drop Tibetan rebels (later referred to as the Khampa rebels), who had been trained, equipped and armed at American bases in Saipan and Okinawa, under CIA's covert operation known as St. Circus. They were then airdropped south of Lhasa, as part of CIA's operation St. Barnum[4] in October 1957 and supported with arms and ammunition.

In fact, the CIA had steadily extended its operational agenda by placing a number of agents in the Indian border town of Kalimpong, near Sikkim and Bhutan, favoured by the Dalai Lama, his brother Thondup and other Tibetans in exile. Once the US became involved in the Tibetan issue, American officials from the US embassy in New Delhi began to reach out to the Dalai Lama,[5] and then other members of the US embassy in New Delhi too became actively involved.

In fact, in August 1951, the American Secretary of State, Dean Acheson, had approved a message to be transmitted verbally to the Tibetans in general and to the Dalai Lama in particular. It said: 'The US government repeats its belief you can best serve your people and country by evading Communist control at earliest opportunity and by denouncing agreement with China after you have reached safe asylum.' This was followed by an official letter to the Dalai Lama by Loy W. Henderson, the US ambassador to New Delhi on 17 September 1951. It read: 'Your Holiness will understand, of course, that the readiness of the United States to render you the assistance, and support outlined above is conditional upon your departure from Tibet, upon your public disavowal of agreements concluded under duress between the representatives of Tibet and those of the Chinese Communist aggression.'[6] The Dalai Lama was, however, not ready to leave Tibet and exile to India until nearly eight years later when matters came to a head.

The Great Escape

From mid-1957, the CIA had initiated their plans to counter China's politico-military presence in Tibet, both covertly and sometimes overtly, through Tibetan guerrillas, armed and trained by the agency and some even airdropped into southern Tibet, as part of the CIA operation 'St. Circus'. This led to violent confrontations between the Tibetan resistance groups and the Chinese army. By early 1959, tensions rose even further when a Tibetan force of 130 men along with thousands of local volunteers attacked a fortress in Teng Dzong by Chinese soldiers, who luckily survived a complete massacre when the Chinese air force straffed and bombed the Tibetans.[7] And then on 11 March 1959, the PLA surrounded Lhasa with troops and artillery. It had become known that the Chinese wanted at best to capture the Dalai Lama and take him to Peking (Beijing) and at worst eliminate him though a military assault. The Chinese military commander around Lhasa, General Dan, had insisted that the pontiff must attend a function in the PLA headquarters without his bodyguards. And when 30,000 Tibetans surrounded the Dalai Lama's summer palace at Norbulingka and forced the cancellation of his visit, General Dan informed the helpless Dalai Lama—since the Tibetan government neither took steps to defend the palace nor appealed for foreign assistance—that artillery shelling would soon follow. Shelling did follow, but that was three days after the young pontiff had secretly left the Norbulingka palace, on 17 March, dressed as a soldier with an escort of Tibetan loyalists for the Sino-Indian border.[8]

News about the Dalai Lama's flight to freedom was communicated by his secret radio operator in Lhasa through 'Morse code' to the CIA in Washington, which led to the US embassy in Delhi reaching out to Nehru on a Sunday, and then conveying to Washington that India would grant asylum to the Dalai Lama. Faced as Nehru was with such a 'fait accompli', he sent a senior official of the Ministry of External Affairs to formally receive the Dalai Lama on his arrival on the Indian border after his 16-day journey, through rough mountains and mostly in the dark. Meanwhile, the Dalai Lama's entourage was supplied with airdrops by unmarked US aircrafts en route, and the escape coordinated by the CIA's Special Activities Division.[9]

Two weeks later, on 31 March 1959, the Dalai Lama emerged in India.[10] The Dalai Lama's exile was but the beginning of a huge movement of Tibetan refugees into India, giving China more ammunition against its neighbour. The Chinese were visibly angry at his escape and slaughtered many Tibetans in Lhasa and wherever they found Tibetan guerrillas, like the Chushi Gandrung forces. And Nehru's talk about India not recognising Tibetan independence, and then his statement on 20 April 1959 that 'while the Dalai Lama would be free to pursue his religious activities in India, he could not participate in political programmes in India', while an attempt to placate the Chinese, fell on deaf ears in Beijing.[11] The uprisings in Tibet and the Dalai Lama's escape was to dramatically alter Sino-Indian ties. Mao openly accused Nehru of encouraging the Tibetan resistance and believed that India was behind the Lhasa rebellion, but Nehru rubbished those allegations. And when China did complain about the CIA's role in the Dalai Lama's escape, as also about a CIA-led guerrilla base that was being used from inside India for raids into Tibet, Nehru denied the Chinese allegations, stating: 'I cannot conceive this could happen without the Indian government knowing about it.' The Chinese leadership did not accept Nehru's assertions because when the Dalai Lama reached India, he had a substantial amount of Indian currency (Rs 2,00,000, that was given by the CIA) and was received by P.N. Menon, a senior official of the Indian Ministry of External Affairs. Much to China's chagrin, the Dalai Lama was escorted by hundreds of loyalists and continues to reside in India. This 'great game'[12] that had begun to be played out in the Himalayas and reached the plains would eventually alarm and annoy the Chinese and alter Sino-Indian relations dramatically.

First Armed Encounter

The Dalai Lama's escape and arrival coincided with Nehru's letter on 22 March 1959 written to Zhou about Chinese incursions. Sino-Indian disagreements on the alignment of their boundary on the Himalayas had become a matter of public concern in India from October 1958, with the news that China had built a 180-kilometre long highway connecting Sinkiang to Tibet via Aksai Chin, historically a part of Ladakh that India regarded as its own. India recognised the McMahon Line, drawn at the Simla Convention that defined the boundaries of Tibet with India. But Mao's regime refused to recognise any boundaries agreed at the Simla Convention, while Nehru decided that India's boundary with Tibet would be in conformity with the McMahon Line, 'map or no map'. Furthermore, he even asked China if 'it wanted amity or confrontation with India'.[13]

This aggressive assertion of India's claims eventually escalated into the 'Longju incident' of 25 August 1959, which marked the first armed encounter between Indian and Chinese forces. Longju was an Indian border post, directly located along the McMahon Line, when it was attacked by Chinese border troops, forcing Indian troops to withdraw. Yet, Indian troops from Assam Rifles continued to patrol the location until the Sino-Indian war in 1962. Today, it is controlled by China, but claimed by India.

As reports of the Longju incident became public knowledge in India, Nehru was further distressed to receive a letter from Zhao on 8 September 1959 that Indian troops had invaded and occupied a number of places in Chinese territory, India was shielding armed Tibetan rebels and Indian aircraft were violating Chinese air space. Although Nehru reassured China that he regarded Tibet as a part of China, it didn't quite help resolve the tensions. In fact, battle lines were being drawn over conflicting boundary claims even as *Shijie Zhishi*, a popular Chinese publication, asserted on 20 September 1959 that 'the McMahon Line was "illegal" and that the Chinese people will never accept it'.[14] As tensions steadily built up between the two nations, Nehru bent over backwards to support China.

Chasing Concord with China

Inside India, the Dalai Lama, though enjoying freedom to practice his religion, wasn't getting the support that he had hoped for, to politicise the Tibetan cause. This may have compelled him to appeal to the United Nations (UN) for intervention on 9 September 1959. In fact, two days after the Dalai Lama had taken the Tibetan cause to the UN, Nehru told the Indian parliament that he was not in favour of this action. Thus, Nehru reaffirmed his twin policy of both appearing politically correct and not annoying the Chinese. To that effect, Nehru distanced India from the Tibet issue, which had first been raised at the UN in 1950 at a time when the world was more concerned with the Korean War and few countries took notice of the tensions between the Chinese and the Tibetans, as the PLA moved in to reclaim Tibet.

Eventually, El Salvador, not India, moved the motion on Tibet, as most countries at the UN General Assembly looked to the US for direction on the Tibet issue. Washington, however, asked the US delegation to take India's directions on how to proceed against China, but India wasn't keen to lead in this matter. Thus, 'the United Nations voted by a margin of 45-9 to express concern over human rights abuses in Tibet'. The US voted in favour but UK abstained, expressing doubts about her recognition of Tibet as an independent nation. Even India did not support this Tibetan initiative.[15]

The Tibetan government found itself alone and friendless. It did not enjoy the status of a nation state as no country, including India, had recognised it as such. Even Britain, which had a long history of engagement with China and Tibet and had tried to define the boundaries of Tibet and China at the Simla Conference, suggested that sufficient autonomy for Tibet could be obtained with Chinese 'suzerainty' not 'sovereignty'. But the Chinese dismissed this as a feudal concept. Neither Britain nor India had used the term 'suzerainty' in the UN or elsewhere, even though in the US, 'suzerainty' and 'sovereignty' were used interchangeably.[16] For Nehru, these were fine distinctions and depended on the power of a state and how far it could go.

Since the early 1950s, Nehru had ignored the gradual erosion of Tibetan autonomy in an attempt not to annoy the Chinese. This approach set a pattern for the Indian government's responses to the happenings in Tibet.[17] India expected only to keep peace with China in the spirit of the Panchsheel Treaty between the two nations. China, on the other hand, chose to ignore the five principles for peace, once the eight years of the treaty had lapsed, leading to the Chinese invasion of India in October 1962, in spite of Nehru's efforts to accommodate Chinese territorial claims over Tibet. For instance, on 4 May 1959, Nehru had told the Indian parliament that India's 'policy towards China remained unchanged and it would continue to support China's entry into the United Nations'.[18] Then on 1 July 1959, Nehru declared that New Delhi would not recognise the Dalai Lama as the head of a Tibetan government[19] as Tibet was a part of China.

Nehru's critics argue that in his zeal to please China, he undid India's historical relations with Tibet that had been forged over centuries. However, the overwhelming evidence of Nehru's policies to appease China, be it the recognition of Tibet as part of China, the treaties of the 1950s or even refraining to support any motion on Tibet in the UN, did not cut ice with Mao. Differences between China and India continued to grow.

Inner Circle Forces

China perceived India as a threat to its complete control over Tibet and it was concerned about members of Nehru's administration helping the CIA to support the Tibetan resistance from India. Benjamin Zachariah's book, *Nehru*, states that prominent members of Nehru's inner circle, including B.N. Mullik, India's IB chief, were working closely with the CIA.[20] Moreover, with Nehru's personal secretary M.O. Mathai being accused of having disproportionate wealth, allegedly from payments for supplying information from the CIA to Indian businessmen, Nehru's biographer, Sarvepalli Gopal, went even further to state that, 'it can be safely assumed that from 1946 to 1959, the CIA had access to every paper passing through Nehru's secretariat'.[21]

It was. however, B.N. Mullik who went much further to push America's anti-China agenda. He was said to be running a sort of private guerrilla campaign against the Chinese, with his team of anti-communist Indian intelligence agents, by using Tibetan rebel groups. By the late 1950s, following the death of Sardar Patel, Nehru's political rival, Mullik had direct access to Nehru and that gave him the opportunity to fight his own private war with China, through the Khampa rebels inside Tibet. 'Not once did Nehru disagree with Mullik's intelligence assessment, nor did he ever object to the IB's overt and covert actions', wrote Giri Deshingkar, India's veteran China expert. Citing Mullik's biography, *My Years with Nehru*, Deshingkar states that 'Mullick engineered the Kongka Pass incident in Aksai Chin that led to the brutal massacre of an Indian police party in October 1959 on the Chang-Chemno Range, on the LAC in Ladakh.'[22] This, more than anything else in those years, was an act brinkmanship that was intended to alter Nehru's views on China and for him to see the threat that China would increasingly pose. It also added to the rise of anti-China sentiment in India, and thus influenced Nehru's views. It has been argued that Nehru's stand on China after 1959 was directly influenced by Mullik. Even as Mullik's colleagues in India's MEA, as well as the military and intelligence agencies, later blamed him for pushing India into a conflict with China, there was no stopping him in the late 1950s. In fact, Mullik's private war against China continued until the 1962 conflict in the Himalayas, as he later admitted in his biography.[23]

Nehru Miffs Army Brass

Whenever Nehru was asked about China's increasing presence in Tibet and their steady encroachment of territory with their claim lines, which could lead to it stepping beyond the 'line' that

India insisted was settled, Nehru would respond with 'liberate Tibet from whom?' Nehru's passive approach attributed to his 'idealism' later had frustrated, among others, India's military commanders. They knew it would cost India dearly in the long run. Thus, when the Longju incident made media headlines and caused an uproar in India's parliament, Nehru announced that 'we have in fact placed this border area of NEFA directly under the military authorities'. It caught the army brass completely off guard as Nehru had made the announcement without having consulted his army chief, the much respected General K.S. Thimayya.[24]

India's northeastern border was then guarded by Assam Rifles, a paramilitary force then under the foreign ministry.[25] By suddenly announcing its move to the army's command, without any consultations, had security implications that Nehru couldn't have even fathomed. Most importantly, it was to bring the ill-equipped and less resourced Indian Army into eye contact with China's army, which would be seen as an added threat by the Chinese. Thimayya, who had often tried to impress upon Nehru the shortcomings of the Indian Army—less manpower, lack of winter clothing and firepower—immediately went to see the prime minister, with whom he had bonds going back to their Allahabad days. Thimayya told Nehru that his decision was clearly against India's security interests. Caught on the backfoot, Nehru then passed the matter to his trusted associate and defence minister, Krishna Menon. Three days later, Menon threatened Thimayya with 'political repercussions' if he went public with his concerns.[26]

Frustrated and fed up, General Thimayya sent in his resignation on 31 August 1959. When Nehru met Thimayya later that day, he persuaded the army chief to withdraw his resignation in the nation's interest. However, news about this incident was leaked and made media headlines until Nehru assured the Parliament on 2 September that he had persuaded the army chief to withdraw his resignation. Surprisingly then, Nehru went on to reproach the army chief for 'wanting to quit in the middle of the Sino-Indian border crisis', which damaged Thimayya's tall military reputation. Nehru, who was known to fear a military takeover just as General Ayub Khan had done in Pakistan in 1958, saw Thimayya as a direct threat.[27] It is said, that from then on until his retirement, Thimayya was publicly sidelined by the Nehru–Menon duo. Their faith began to rest on Lt Gen. B.M. Kaul, better known as 'Bijji', who went on to become one of the men directly responsible for the military debacle of 1962 with China.

Kaul's military career took off after India's independence, even though he had mostly served in non-combat roles in the army during the Second World War. Being a Kashmiri Pandit like Nehru, at a time when the Kashmir issue had gained significance, he was made the military advisor to the Indian delegation to the UN Security Council in 1948 and then put in command of the J&K militia in the early 1950s. Lt Gen. Thorat, under whom Kaul served in Korea and later in India, stated about Kaul: 'A tireless worker and good speaker though given to unnecessary dramatization, … [he had] unbridled ambition in the pursuit of which he was ruthless.' Though his superiors felt that he had reached the limits of his competence as a brigadier, his star was on the rise with Nehru's interventions. A Chinese delegation that had observed Kaul on a visit to India in the 1950s had a similar opinion of him.[28]

India's Faltering Forward Policy

It wasn't just General Kaul and his ilk that worried the Indian Army's brass hats; it was their marginalisation by Nehru and Menon after the Thimayya episode that was a greater cause for concern. As Nehru's carefully cultivated dovish image of a peace-seeking statesman had begun to turn hawkish after the Longju incident, India's military commanders anticipated a border war. In a last-ditch effort to get Nehru and Menon to understand India's limitations if it came to that, General Thimayya directed the very able Lt Gen. Thorat, commander of the Eastern Command, who was responsible for the defence of the McMahon Line, to conduct a detailed assessment of what India could do in the event of a Chinese attack. This was called 'Exercise Lal Qila'. Thorat's plan was to let the Chinese come into Indian territory up to his 'defensive line' and when the Chinese army was stretched without adequate logistics, Indian troops would hit them in India's chosen killing ground. But by now, nobody was listening to the army.[29]

Lt Gen. Thorat even met the defence minister, but his plans cut no ice with Menon, who told him that in the 'unlikely' event of a Sino-Indian war, he would fight it himself at the diplomatic level! Nehru even refused to increase military spending or otherwise prepare for war.

After this failure to get the political leadership to accept the army's assessment, Thimayya and Thorat, who was widely expected to succeed Thimayya, were seen as 'lame ducks'. Nehru and Menon began to rely increasingly on Lt Gen. Kaul, who went past his superiors in army headquarters and reorganised the general staff who resisted the idea of patrolling in disputed areas.

In the summer of 1961, China started patrolling along the McMahon Line and Chinese soldiers would enter India-administered regions. In response, India launched its 'forward policy' that involved creation of outposts behind the Chinese troops that had entered India-administered regions so as to cut off their supplies and force them to return to China. However, the blame for India's forward policy that led to the Chinese invasion cannot be put only on General Kaul.

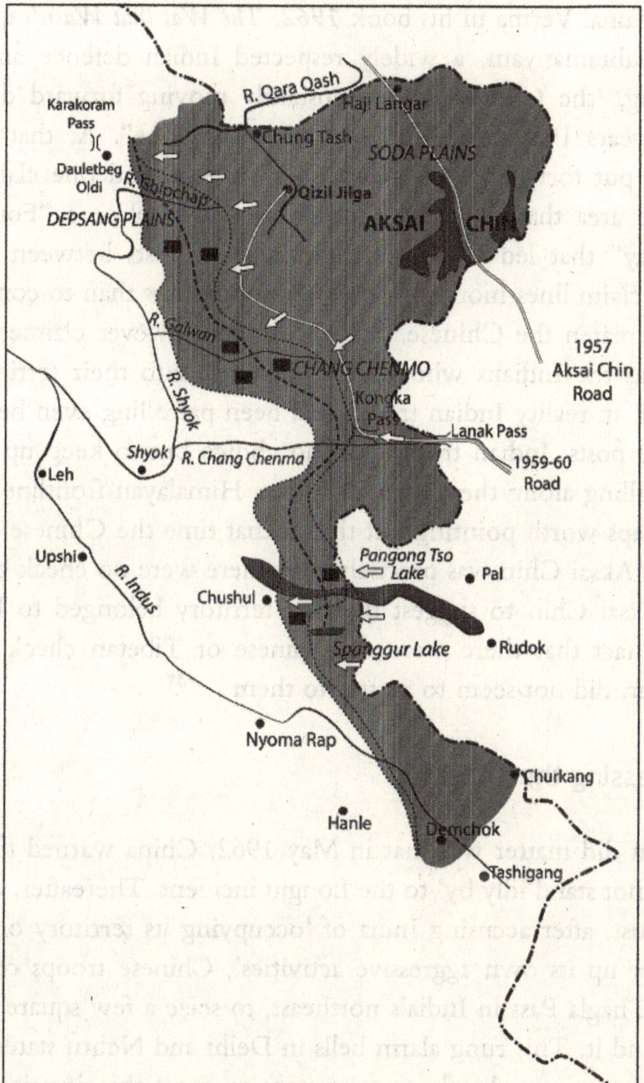

Map 4: China's claim lines of 1960 and 1962, and military offensive in 1962

Source: Arjun Subramanium, *India's Wars: A Military History, 1947–1971*, p. 241

Kunal Verma in his book *1962: The War that Wasn't* quotes K. Subramanyam, a widely respected Indian defence analyst, saying, 'the Chinese were constantly moving forward during the years 1959-1961, up to their "claim line". At that stage they put forward two "claim lines", the second one claiming more area that the first. Thus India put in place a "Forward Policy" that led to the establishment of posts between these two claim lines more for observation purposes than to confront or threaten the Chinese.[30] The Chinese however claimed that it was the Indians who were "nibbling" into their territories, when in reality Indian troops had been patrolling even beyond these posts. Indian troops had no choice but to keep up their patrolling along the vast Sino-Indian Himalayan frontline. It is perhaps worth pointing out that at that time the Chinese claim over Aksai Chin was precisely that–there were no check points at Aksai Chin to suggest that the territory belonged to India. The fact that there were no Chinese or Tibetan check posts either, did not seem to matter to them ...'[31]

Assessing the Threat

What did matter was that in May 1962, China warned that 'it will not stand idly by' to the Longju incident. Thereafter, on 28 August, after accusing India of 'occupying its territory only to cover up its own aggressive activities', Chinese troops crossed the Thagla Pass in India's northeast, to seize a few square miles around it. This rung alarm bells in Delhi and Nehru stated that 'we have immediately to take steps to meet the situation that had arisen'.[32] But the bigger question was how prepared was India to respond to the Chinese?

General Thimayya had retired in May 1961 and was succeeded by General Pran Thapar after the government had side-lined Lt Gen. Thorat, who was expected to succeed

'Timmy'. Soon thereafter, army headquarters came under the full sway of Menon and Lt Gen. Bijji Kaul. The duo had side-lined all those who might have stood up to them and possibly provided a sensible assessment of what to do with the Chinese threat. Further, Mullik, who besides being the IB chief was also Nehru's confidant, was also brought in to put in place India's response to China.

The trio walked India into a conflict that the nation hasn't forgotten yet. But to blame Nehru and this 'gang of three' for the mess that followed is a bit unfair. Thimayya had allowed himself to be marginalised after his resignation saga in August 1959. However, until he retired in May 1961, he could still have found a way of seeking release from service instead of letting the army become a victim of the delusions that prevailed in Delhi.

Thimayya apart, other senior military commanders like Lt Gen. L.P. 'Bogey' Sen, first as CGS and then as commander of the Eastern Command of the Indian Army, must also share the blame. He, along with the likes of Brig. D.K. 'Monty' Palit, the DMO in 1962 and Bijji Kaul's No. 2, Major General Jogi Dhillon and a whole lot of staff officers in Delhi, chose to stay silent or just stood by. They are equally guilty of making India's gallant soldiers 'cannon fodder' for the Chinese in 1962.[33] A few like Lt Gen. Umrao Singh, who stood up to their seniors, were side-lined.

While historians and authors have blamed Mao's decision to 'teach India a lesson' because of the Nehru government's 'forward policy' and for the Dalai Lama's presence in India, it can also be attributed to Nehru's public insistence that the border issue had been settled and that talks weren't possible unless China first withdrew from Aksai Chin. Others might argue that Nehru was repeatedly misled about the ground realities by his close confidants. No wonder he told a group of waiting journalists in Delhi, on his way to Colombo, that he had ordered the Indian Army 'to throw the Chinese out'. This was on 12 October 1962, just eight days before that fateful day when the Chinese attacked India. But what followed was India's Himalayan humiliation that has few parallels in military history.

5
THE CONFRONTATION

After Mao Tse Tung (Ze Dong) had politically bounced back following his disastrous 'Great Leap Forward'[1] (1958–62), he was working on a strategy to teach Nehru a lesson. 'Great Leap Forward', Mao's five-year communist campaign, was undertaken to resolve China's industrial and agricultural problems by accelerating industrialisation and multiplying grain yields through collectivisation. But it was a massive failure and millions died by forced labour, overwork, starvation, exposure and execution. Mao, therefore, had to restore the faith of his people in his leadership and communist goals. Besides, he was already vexed with the increasing American footprint in India to support the Tibetan resistance, and the escape of the Dalai Lama to India was, for him, the proverbial last straw.

In fact, most Chinese scholars still believe that the conflict of 1962—notwithstanding Nehru's efforts to appease China—was to stall India's plans to seize Tibet and to run it as a protectorate, though many neutral observers regard this view as incorrect.[2]

For China though, Tibet was a major source of water and natural resources. Therefore, Mao's decision to go into battle was essentially about Tibet and 'to punish India and end the perceived Indian aggression against Chinese territory along the border'.[3] He proceeded rather methodically towards this goal.

A Clear Plan

To prepare for an attack on India, Mao's specially constituted team studied the Chinese army's operations within Tibet. In path-breaking research into the Tibetan uprising between 1956 and 1959 and the lead-up to the 1962 war, a Chinese scholar Jianglin Li accessed CPC documents and interviewed PLA veterans from the war. His research presented critical new aspects of that period's history. In the three years from March 1959 to March 1962, the PLA fought 12 major battles in Central Tibet, targeting the Tibetan resistance force.[4] Li's research illustrates that Mao carefully watched the operations against the Tibetan resistance by the PLA. It rebuts earlier claims by 1962 war veterans like Yin Fatang, a former CPC boss in Tibet, that the PLA had fought the 1962 war unprepared. Lessons learnt in those earlier battles were to come in use when they attacked India.

Moving into action, early on in the 1950s, the Chinese aggressively claimed large tracts of Ladakh, around 31,000 square kilometres and then another 36,000 square kilometres in NEFA, now Arunachal Pradesh. It built a major road through Aksai Chin, now known as Highway G219, which was completed by 1957. To further test India's response, China published its maps in 1957 showing large chunks of what India called as its own territory. In fact, Chinese maps showed some 120,000 square kilometres of Indian territory as Chinese. When questioned, Zhou responded that there were errors in the maps.[5]

For Nehru, who was keen on maintaining peace with China, these actions were but a 'small matter'. In fact, he dismissed any possibility of a conflict with China, calling it 'preposterous'. In the 1957 winter session of the Parliament's upper house, the Rajya Sabha, Nehru stated, 'I am convinced that there is not the remotest chance, or if I put it more strongly, not the remotest chance of a remote chance of India coming into military conflict with China.'[6] Delhi ignored all threatening signals emanating from China on its own border.

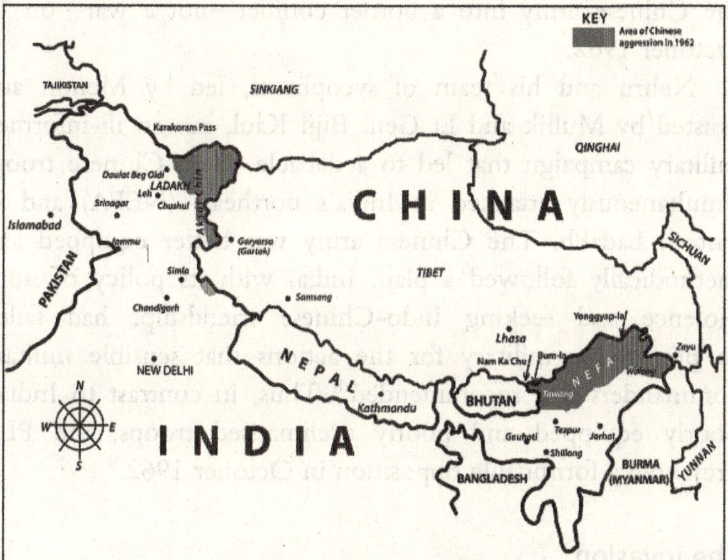

Map 5: Chinese claims in 1962

Source: Kunal Verma, *1962: The War that Wasn't*, p. 60

Strategic Attack

On 1 July 1962, China broke the radio link between Lhasa and Delhi, reducing India's ability to directly listen in to Tibet, even as it continued with its military build-up. On 10 July 1962, 350 Chinese troops encircled an Indian Army post at Chushul and further north of it at Galwan (near the site of the bloody engagement in June 2020), east of Leh.[7]

A few months later, when the world's attention was on the Cuban Missile Crisis during 16–28 October 1962, which many feared could have led to a nuclear war between the US and

Russia, Mao attacked. In October 1962, China moved up three of its well-equipped and battle-hardened divisions onto India's front lines. Sino-Indian tensions about the boundary issue had risen to a point of confrontation when Mao decided to launch the Chinese army into a border conflict—not a war—on 19 October 1962.

Nehru and his team of sycophants, led by Menon and assisted by Mullik and Lt Gen. Bijji Kaul, ran an ill-informed military campaign that led to a debacle when Chinese troops simultaneously attacked in India's northeast (NEFA) and in eastern Ladakh. The Chinese army was better equipped and methodically followed a plan. India, with its policy of non-violence and seeking Indo-Chinese friendship, had failed to prepare its military for the actions that sensible military commanders had recommended.[8] Thus, in contrast to India's poorly equipped and poorly acclimatised troops, the PLA presented a formidable opposition in October 1962.[9]

The Invasion

The border conflict that lasted from 20 October to 19 November 1962 can be said to have started with an event in early September, when a Chinese patrol came down the Thagla Ridge—north of the Namka Chu river in the NEFA region—to an Indian observation post at Dhola and asked it to withdraw. The Indian post commander held his ground and refused. The Chinese then withdrew with no shots fired, which further reinforced the prevailing perception in South Block, New Delhi, that the Chinese wouldn't attack.

However, as the Chinese regarded Dhola in NEFA to be in their territory and viewed India's 'forward policy' (as explained in the earlier chapter) with concern, a stronger patrol of 60-odd well-armed Chinese soldiers again visited the post on 8 September. The post commander—a junior commissioned officer (JCO)—misreported the 60 Chinese soldiers as 600—an inflated figure that he later admitted was aimed to get a quick response. The overstated number caused tempers to flare with outrage. From then on, without checking the numbers, the entire Indian military command chain in India's eastern sector, from the Division and Corps headquarters and eventually to Indian Army headquarters, set in motion a series of actions, which eventually spiralled out of India's control.[10]

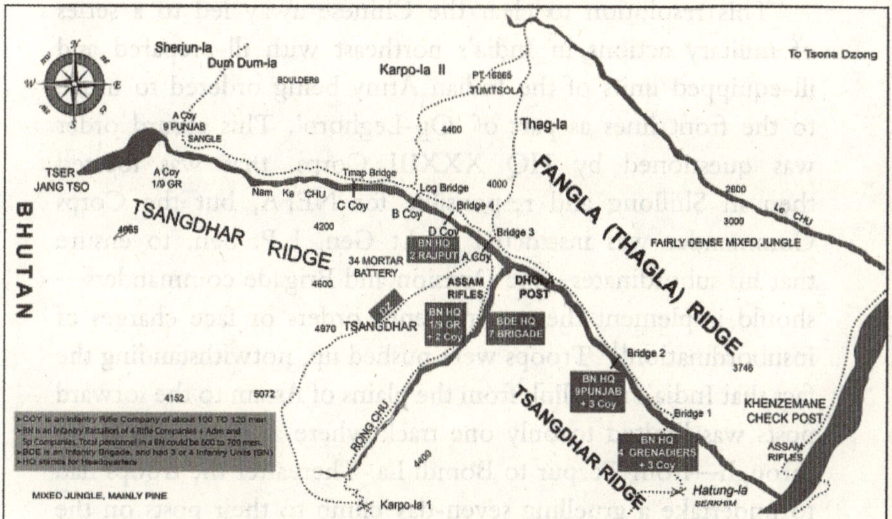

Map 6: Indian Army's deployments in NEFA, 19 October 1962, opposite Thagla Ridge and along the Namka Chu river

Source: Kunal Verma, *1962: The War that Wasn't*, p. 138

Even though Mullik learnt that the initial report by the JCO at Dhola post was exaggerated, he did not inform his superiors. Had he done so, tempers could have calmed down. But he apparently chose to go along with the tide that prevailed in Delhi.

At a hurriedly called meeting in Delhi on 9 September, a decision was taken to evict the Chinese from the areas south of the Thagla Ridge. It was chaired by Menon, and in attendance were B.N. Mullik, the IB chief; General Thapar, the army chief; Lt Gen. Sen, commander of the Eastern Command, S.S. Khera, the cabinet secretary; and H.C. Sarin, joint secretary in the Ministry of Defence, among others. Apparently, there are no records of this meeting, but it is believed that Lt Gen. Sen had given this advice, even though until then he had visited neither Tawang nor any part of NEFA, where the conflict eventually took place.

This resolution to clear the Chinese away led to a series of military actions in India's northeast with ill-prepared and ill-equipped units of the Indian Army being ordered to move to the front lines as part of 'Op-Leghorn'. This absurd order was questioned by HQ XXXIII Corps, that was located then in Shillong and responsible for NEFA, but the Corps Commander was instructed by Lt Gen. L.P. Sen, to ensure that his subordinates—the Division and Brigade commanders—should implement the government's orders or face charges of insubordination![11] Troops were pushed up, notwithstanding the fact that India's road link from the plains of Assam to the forward posts was limited to only one track where a jeep could travel through—from Tezpur to Bomdi La. Thereafter the troops had to undertake a gruelling seven-day climb to their posts on the McMahon Line. Soon the River Namka Chu, south of the ridge, became India's de facto boundary line and orders were issued to 'drive out the Chinese' from Thagla Ridge.

Recipe for Disaster

Orders were given to HQ XXXIII Corps[12] that handled the Indo-Tibetan border, to set up 24 new posts along the McMahon Line. Corps Commander Lt Gen. Umrao Singh protested, as he felt the Indian Army was not in a state of preparedness to take on the Chinese. If Lt Gen. Sen as the commander of the

Eastern Command had accepted the cautionary assessment of his XXXIII Corps commander, the country could have been saved the humiliation that followed. Instead, it was decided to ease him out of operational planning and a new Corps was raised that was headquartered in Tezpur. Nehru's chosen one, Lt Gen. Kaul, who ruled the Indian Army headquarters in Delhi, was appointed the General Officer Commanding (GOC) of the new IV Corps. A new headquarters under Lt Gen. Kaul, a logistics officer without combat experience, was a sure recipe for disaster.[13]

Those giving orders during this critical time for India were either operating out of a vacuum or withholding key information. Like Mullik, who knew later that the Chinese had two regiments deployed at Thagla Ridge with each regiment the size of an Indian brigade with over 2,500 soldiers, and yet apparently chose to withhold this information. Even Mullik's assessment was that if the Chinese would attack, it would be only in Ladakh in the Chip Chap and Galwan valleys, not in NEFA.[14] He was proved dreadfully wrong as the Chinese, in a synchronised move, attacked both these territories simultaneously. In retrospect, it's clear that not only Mullik, but nobody in Delhi too anticipated a serious Chinese response.

After the tense stand-off at the Dhola Ridge in NEFA, Nehru instructed the army on 12 October to 'free our territory'. This was misreported in the press as 'Armed forces ordered to throw out the Chinese aggressor from NEFA'. The message that trickled down was that 'no infringement of our border in NEFA would be tolerated' and these were Nehru's instructions, reiterated the foreign secretary, M.J. Desai. But the orders to throw the Chinese out were in fact given earlier to the army chief, General Thapar on 22 September, when in a last-ditch attempt to buy time, he had asked for orders in writing. The Ministry of Defence order of 22 September 1962, signed by H.C. Sarin, a joint secretary, used precisely these words! It read:

'At a meeting in MMD's (Minister, Ministry of Defence) room, this morning the COAS raised the specific question whether action to evict the Chinese can be taken as soon as the Brigade has concentrated. The decision thought has been, as discussed in previous meetings, that the Army should prepare and throw the Chinese out as soon as possible. The COAS was accordingly directed to take action for the eviction of the Chinese in Kameng Division of NEFA as soon as he was ready.'[15]

With Krishna Menon having left for the UN session in New York on 22 September and Nehru, too, being unavailable, the decision to move the troops forward to confront the Chinese was taken by the junior minister of state for defence, Kotha Raghuramaiah. It is said that when Kaul was asked to move to Tezpur to the new headquarters, he was openly delighted to be given this opportunity as it would allow him to emerge as a hero after 'he threw the Chinese out'! He thus willingly accepted the job of commanding IV Corps—a position actually two steps below what he was holding as chief of general staff (CGS)—to fill a gap in his professional profile. Created just for him, IV Corps had only two brigades as against a minimum of six brigades that a corps should have. Kaul thought this would be just another military exercise that he would stage-manage, as he had done in the past. What he did not know was that the DMO, Brig. Palit, who drove Kaul to see him off at Delhi airport, had withheld a crucial piece of information that 'he would be up against a formidable Chinese force on the Thagla Ridge. This negligence was to cost the Indian army many lives.'[16]

Blunders on the Frontline

When Kaul arrived at Tezpur on 5 October, in an open breach of military protocol he was received at the airport by his superior General Sen. It soon became clear that Kaul was there to fulfil Delhi's mandate and his superiors, General Thapar, the army chief, and General Sen didn't matter anymore. The chain of command now was 'Kaul–Menon–Nehru'. However, with no combat experience, Kaul gave one absurd order after another. The few who objected to the absurdity of the orders were either side-lined or silenced. From then on, things moved at a pace that caught the commanders and their troops on the ground completely off guard.

As Kaul refused to take the Chinese threat seriously, ad-hoc military formations were created with little time for coordination between units to strengthen the defence in the northeast. The example of 7 Infantry Brigade under Brig. John Dalvi that was put out to be slaughtered is one case in point. Its units, 9 Punjab and 4 Grenadiers, were thrown onto the Chinese at Thagla Ridge, only to be butchered. Its two other battalions, 2 Rajput and 1/9 Gorkha Rifles, on their way to peace locations after completing three years on the NEFA frontline, were abruptly ordered to return from the Assam plains, to be re-inducted to face the Chinese without re-acclimatisation or being re-equipped and re-trained. There was little coordination between the senior commanders and army headquarters.[17] From the moment Lt Gen. Kaul landed in Lumpu on 5 October, he issued orders that took formations and units by surprise, such as ordering units to move forward with little logistic support and with only their survival rations! Worse still, Kaul cared little that his frontline troops were ill-prepared to face the Chinese. They were short of ammunition, wore cotton clothing and home-knitted sweaters in freezing temperatures and were unfamiliar with the new locations they were rushed to defend.

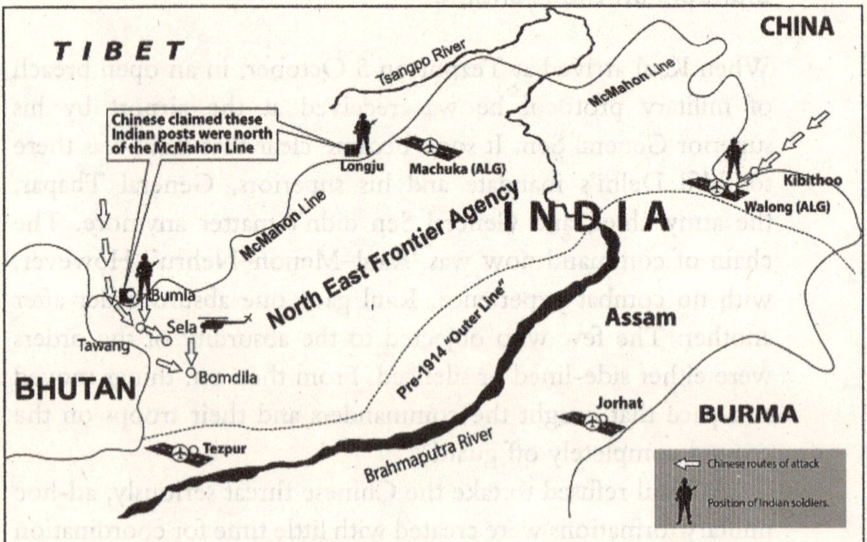

Map 7: Chinese Offensive Lines in NEFA in 1962

Source: Arjun Subramanium, *India's Wars: A Military History, 1947–1971*

Combat Commences

Kaul chose to command troops from the front and not from the location in the rear, like Tezpur where his new corps was headquartered, or the earlier corps headquarters (of XXXIII Corps) in Shillong, which used to oversee the entire Sino-Indian boundary from Sikkim to NEFA and Burma (now Mynamar) border. But the closer he got to the front lines, the more he realised the impossibility of implementing the assurances he had given to his masters in Delhi! As he pompously announced at a conference of officers and JCOs on 9 October, that following the delays in implementing the earlier assurances by the army commander, Lt Gen. Sen, the Chinese would be evicted by 15 September, he had been tasked by the Cabinet to take some action by 10 October. For added effect, he announced that the Cabinet was willing to accept a loss of up to 20,000 lives! His bizarre tactical orders to the units left everyone stunned.[18]

In keeping with Delhi's deadline, Kaul ordered the troops of 7 Brigade—9 Punjab and 2 Rajput—to get across the Namka Chu river valley during the dawn of 10 October. The other two units of this ill-fated brigade, 4 Grenadiers and 1/9 Gorkha Rifles, were placed on the flanks. As they moved up from the valley, the Chinese retaliated with massive firepower that decimated the 7 Brigade. This stunned Kaul, who was present nearby along with the entire senior leadership of his corps. As Kaul's carefully cultivated image took a beating, at the cost of lives of soldiers, he decided to return to Delhi to appraise the prime minister of the seriousness of China's intent, adding as a parting order that 'not a single inch of territory was to be given regardless of the cost'. The departing General also told Commanding Officer (CO) Lt Col. Rikh of 2 Rajput that troops were not to advance across the Namka Chu as 'the situation had changed and the enemy was reacting more violently than he had anticipated'.[19] He never returned to the battlefield, but took to bed in Delhi feigning illness, even as the combat continued.

After completing preparations for their attack, as Indian troops watched with concern, on 20 October 1962, the PLA launched a two-pronged attack against two Indian front lines, 1,000 kilometres apart. At Aksai Chin near Ladakh, China sought to drive out the Indian forces even as it simultaneously moved to capture both banks of the River Namka Chu and Tawang on NEFA. The Namka Chu valley initially became a massive killing field, and then over the next four days the Indian troops deployed in the lower grounds became sitting ducks for wave after wave of Chinese attacks. The other units of 7 Brigade, 4 Grenadiers and 1/9 Gorkha Rifles were later cut off from their adjoining units, and were thus butchered as their platoons and sections were isolated. Normally, infantry units are always deployed to provide defensive fire to their adjoining localities, when either is attacked. A few dozen managed to escape through jungle tracks. This brigade, which had achieved renown in the Second World War in the battles of North Africa, was virtually wiped out. The unrealistic deployment of troops along the River Namka Chu despite protests by Brig. Dalvi would have been repugnant to any officer with basic understanding of military tactics. For Lt Gen. Kaul it seemed acceptable, more so when he directed his command from a 'sick bed' at his official residence in Delhi, even as his superiors and subordinates allowed him to make a mockery of the Indian Army's resistance.[20]

Fearless Fortitude

There is no doubt that the Indian soldier wasn't allowed to fight the battles for which he was trained. Despite the shoddy leadership of India's generals on the NEFA front, the Indian soldier fought with unparalleled courage and resolve, many resorting to fighting with sticks and stones when their ammunition ran out. The example of 2 Rajput, which was virtually wiped out on the first night, is worth citing.

Just after the first night of Chinese assaults on 20 October, many soldiers of 2 Rajput held on to their last round of ammunition in bitter freezing cold. Two hundred and eighty-two soldiers including four officers and seven JCOs were killed, while another 81 were wounded, including three officers and two JCOs. With some soldiers overpowered, only 60 men survived out of the initial 513. The Chinese were to later acknowledge their fighting spirit and confirmed that they suffered the maximum casualties in their entire campaign in NEFA on the first night of their attack.[21]

The adjoining units, particularly 1/9 Gorkha Rifles, also suffered heavily, although 9 Punjab and then 4 Grenadiers—better prepared in their defensive locations—were initially bypassed by Chinese infiltrators. When they were finally attacked, they stood up to the challenge with the same courage and devotion for the motherland that the Indian soldier has displayed time and again. Most of them fought until the end, despite the loss of communication. Telephone lines were crushed in the attacks and as officers were killed by the dozen, the troops did what they had been trained to do—they fought to their last round. A handful who attempted a fighting withdrawal, even though there were no orders for that, died of cold and starvation in that rugged terrain. Worse still, with hardly any officers left alive to immediately tell their tales, many brave deeds weren't even recognised with gallantry awards!

The rout of 20 October was followed by another Chinese offensive at Tawang. A fresh division of about 7,000 Chinese troops advanced on the Bum La between Tibet and Tawang on 23 October. Three Chinese regiments—equal to an Indian brigade of 2,500 soldiers—attacked from the front and the flanks. Even though the brave soldiers of 1 Sikh exhibited exceptional gallantry to hold off the Chinese at Bum La, the Indian garrison at Tawang was abandoned without a fight. Tawang had been prepared for a defensive battle, but the GOC, Major General Niranjan Prasad, was advised by his superiors to instead defend Se La, another mountain pass southeast of Tawang, that fell into Chinese hands. The complete confusion at the highest levels of the Indian Army—with General(s) Thapar, Bogey Sen and Niranjan Prasad—led to knee-jerk reactions like their orders to abandon Tawang.[22]

Finding Scapegoats

Panic had led to chaos and thus on 23 October, during a sudden lull in the Chinese offensive, the Indian Army chief, General Thapar decided to sack Major General Niranjan Prasad, who had repeatedly shown a lack of nerve to act as he indeed should have. Prasad though shouldn't be the only one held guilty of the mess on the NEFA front. All his superiors from Lt Gen. Kaul to Bogey L.P. Sen and the army chief, General Thapar had failed the men they were entrusted to command. But Niranjan Prasad was made a scapegoat. What he failed to do was to stand up to the unimplementable orders that kept coming in from his superiors, and for exercising control over his division, after the Chinese attacks caused panic among the retreating troops.[23]

Although the earlier Chinese attacks on 20 October and the havoc they created in the absence of clear orders to withdraw to suitable defensive locations in the rear, south of River Namka Chu, had led to the rout in NEFA, Prasad was probably a scapegoat for General Sen and Lt Gen. Kaul and General Thapar, as he was following their directives. None had shown any understanding of the ground realities in NEFA.[24]

Prasad was replaced by Major General A.S. Pathania, who had an impressive combat record from previous wars. Kaul was replaced by Lt Gen. Harbaksh Singh (who later distinguished himself as the army commander in the western theatre in the 1965 Indo-Pak war). There was also a lot of talk about the possibility of sacking General Sen and General Thapar to bring back Thimayya and Thorat. Menon had apparently alluded to it in a conversation with Brig. Palit on 28 October.[25]

In Ladakh, Indian Troops were Better Prepared

The consequences of the Chinese attack in Ladakh on 20 October were not as disastrous, as military deployments of units there had been made more professionally. While the severe winter in Ladakh had led to the thinning out of troops in the forward zones as it was difficult to maintain troops on the front lines, the Indian Army faced another problem in the northeast,

Map 8: Indian Army's deployments opposite Aksai Chin

Source: Kunal Verma, *1962: The War that Wasn't*, p. 348

in NEFA. At least a third of the air supplies from air drops along the McMahon Line in the eastern sector—well before and after the Chinese attacks—would often fall into the deep ravines in the absence of maps and suitable 'drop-zones'. A big challenge in the mountains is to ensure that the supplies of food and ammunition are adequate, even though a defender always has an advantage in the mountains if he is sensibly deployed. The lack of troops on the vast Ladakh front line had however led to one division there (of about 7,500 soldiers) being stretched over a few hundred kilometres. Aksai Chin wasn't lost to the Chinese in the 1962 conflict, but the Chinese did make some gains westwards beyond what was their 1960 claim line. As they had been in occupation of the vast Aksai Chin area from the 1950s, the Chinese troops on the Ladakh front were well-supplied.

Indian troops were relatively better prepared in Ladakh for other reasons too. For one, the politico-military establishment in Delhi, especially B.N. Mullik, had all along insisted that if the Chinese did attack, they would first do so across Ladakh. Early into the decade, as the Chinese incursions in Aksai Chin, which India regarded as its own, became public knowledge, Nehru had changed his stance from an accommodative one in 1959 to an aggressive one. He had ordered the establishment of posts in 1960 'to prevent the Chinese from advancing any further'. With the public stand adopted by the Nehru government that 'no talks were possible unless China withdrew from Aksai Chin', the possibility of a conflict was real as both sides began to steadily test each other's resolve to hold on to their claim lines.[26]

Unlike Lt Gen. Bijji Kaul, the military commanders there in 1962—Lt Gen. Daulet Singh as the army commander and Lt Gen. Bikram Singh as the corps commander—were rooted in reality.

Two months before the Chinese offensive in Aksai Chin, Indian Army's Western Command had written to army headquarters that in view of the Chinese military superiority on the border, war must be avoided at all costs, as there were concerns about the availability of troops in the western (Ladakh) sector. However, with Kaul as CGS in Delhi and Nehru's go-to man for military advice, army headquarters had replied less than one month before the attack that the 'forward policy' was a success as the Chinese had exercised restraint. 'We must show our flag' was the order.

The example of the brave men of 14 J&K Militia standing up to Chinese attacks near Ladakh in the northern and middle parts of the Daulat Beg Oldi (DBO) sector and fighting both the inclement weather and the attacking Chinese forces is awe-inspiring. How the soldiers survived against blizzards and freezing cold—when half their yaks and ponies had died in the cold—defies imagination. The high and remote Galwan Valley, in particular, was so difficult to move into that even the Chinese avoided getting into it. The determined Indian soldiers, initially those of 14 J&K Militia and then those of 5 Jat, along with the Gorkhas of 1/8 Gorkha Rifles, stuck it out against several death-defying odds, despite the heavy volumes of Chinese firing from the surrounding high mountains since 19 October. Some of the troops of 1/8 Gorkha Rifles and 5 Jat were then heli-lifted for the defence of Chushul where Brig. T.N. Raina had deployed his brigade tactically, and its units had chosen to stick out when the Chinese attacks came in large hordes just before the conflict ended, between 18 November and 21 November 1962. Their famous battles of Rezang La, a mountain pass adjoining the Chushul Valley, by C Company of 13 Kumaon and Gurung Hill by two companies of 1/8 Gorkha Rifles is now the stuff of legend.[27] The bravery of these soldiers would have received a shot in the arm had India backed up their strength and valour with the use of the IAF.

Air Power Error

Not using the IAF was a grave error. When the option of the use of air power to interdict Chinese troops was brought up in a meeting chaired by Menon on 18 September 1962, Mullik, to everyone's surprise, warned that the PLA Air Force (PLAAF) would bomb towns and cities in India's east, including Calcutta, and may even hit Madras, if India were to use its air power. The IB's assessment was that Pakistan had plans to strike Kashmir if a Sino-Indian conflict did take place.[28]

India's decision not to use the IAF was thus essentially based on Mullik's assessment that the Chinese air force was capable of flying night missions across the Himalayas all the way up to Madras, when in reality it was the IAF that had night flying capabilities with its Vampires that could intercept the Chinese, which had no MiG-21 aircraft despite its claims to the contrary. Moreover, China's air power capabilities in Tibet that could be used against India were virtually non-existent!

The IAF had carried out several air reconnaissance missions in that area from 1960 onwards. Even two years later, the detailed air photography of that region—from Gilgit via the Karakoram range and eastwards into Tibet—had been conducted not once, but several times by Wing Commander 'Jaggi' Jag Mohan Nath, MVC. Since 1960, Jaggi Nath had filmed and reported the presence of Chinese soldiers in Aksai Chin, stating that 'I could not count them, but they were there in good number and I took photographs.' Later, he was taken to see the defence minister. Despite carrying all the evidence—as a junior officer doesn't go to the defence minister's office ill-prepared—all that Menon asked of him was: 'Did you see the Chinese soldiers?'

He answered, 'Yes Sir, I saw them.'

Menon responded, 'That's alright, you can go.'

Later, in an interview given to the historian Claude Arpi, Jaggi Nath stated, 'Even after I told him there were Chinese soldiers there, that was it. It was amazing. They did not know how to handle the situation.'[29]

In hindsight, it seems that no one really took the Chinese threat seriously. Even Air Marshal Aspi Engineer, India's Chief of Air Staff (CAS) then, seemed to be indifferent to all the inputs that came in from IAF's own air reconnaissance missions. Jaggi Nath recalled that after 20 October 1962, he used to go with Air Marshal Elric Pinto, the Air Officer Commanding-in-Chief (AOC-in-C), Western Air Command, several times to meet Aspi Engineer. He mentioned, 'I can tell you, that if Elric Pinto had been the Chief, things would have been so very different. Aspi Engineer was too low key. In 1962, we had all the information about the Chinese deployment as I mentioned to Elric Pinto. If we had sent a few airplanes [into Tibet] we could have wiped them all out. China had NO Air Force worth the name on the Tibetan plateau in 1962. And everything could have been different in [the] 1962 [War].'[30]

Engineer, however, had chosen to accept the IB's assessment and dismissed the vast amount of air photography that his own air force had carried out! But it wasn't just him, even others like Air Commodore H.C. Dewan had apparently echoed the IB chief's line, advising the Indian prime minister 'that the Chinese would bomb Indian cities, including Calcutta'. Even the willingness of Air Vice Marshall (AVM) Jaswant Singh, the AOC-in-C, Eastern Air Command, to send his fighters to defend NEFA was overruled.[31] This was clearly a major strategic error.

With almost all Indian air bases virtually at sea level, the IAF could send its fighters with full bomb loads. The Chinese air bases in Tibet, however, only allowed their aircrafts to take off with limited bomb loads due to the altitude. Though the

Chinese air force was on paper a bigger force, their discord with Taiwan was keeping its aircrafts mostly engaged in China's east. Also, with the Soviets having pulled out of China in 1960, the Chinese air force was nearly grounded, being desperately short of spares for operational aircrafts and facing a serious shortage of aircraft fuel.

India, on the other hand, had enough aircrafts like Canberra bombers and ground attack Hawker Hunters and Gnats available to bomb China's air bases and roads that supported their frontline troops, notwithstanding the Chinese request to the Russians to delay the supply of MiG-21s to India. Most importantly, virtually all Chinese air bases in Tibet that could have been used against India were in the flying range of the IAF, whereas China's PLAAF could only have reached limited Indian air bases and cities. However, credit goes to the IAF for providing our troops on the front lines, much needed supplies by repeated airdrops. Sadly, though, they were denied essential items like pressure cookers, without which one cannot cook a meal in the freezing cold, as the bureaucracy feared that sanctioning these would set a precedent![32]

Weapons Blunder

In addition to supplies, the need for modern and effective weapons to replace the vintage .303 rifles, that were bolt-actioned with a handful of rounds, was more important to hold off large hordes of Chinese attackers. These antiquated .303 rifles were to be replaced with semi-automatic 7.62mm rifles and the 81mm mortars, which remained in use until the 1990s. At the time of the conflict, however, these weapons had arrived, but their ammunition didn't! So, when the Chinese army paused at Tawang for a fortnight to build a road from Bum La, to push up its supporting elements, hasty reinforcements from

India's plains were sent in to beef up the defences in NEFA. It was still not enough as our troops were not acclimatised to the altitude and the cold; they were ill-clad with bare essentials and without training in high-altitude warfare. Yet, as they moved into their positions, the Indian troops put up a fierce fight against the Chinese.[33] Until one day it ended just as abruptly as it had started.

Ceasefire!

With China advancing on its borders, India had declared a state of national emergency on 26 October 1962. In the aftermath of India's failures in the ongoing war was the forced resignation by a chagrined Menon, who was forced to take responsibility for India's military debacle and defeat. Menon resigned and Nehru accepted his resignation in the midst of war, on 1 November 1962.

With Krishna Menon having resigned, Nehru took charge as the defence minister. General Thapar, too, chose to resign than be sacked; but just before he did so, Thapar went on to brief Nehru about the military's shocking reverses in NEFA. However, General Thapar did so without checking his facts. He informed Nehru that Assam would soon fall to the invading Chinese army, when in reality, even at this late stage India's military build-up was taking place and could have held off and pushed back the Chinese army. But on the basis of his advice, Nehru wrote a letter on 19 November 1962 to then US President John F. Kennedy to urgently provide India the necessary air support to stop the Chinese army from taking over Assam, and blowing up its oil wells and its cities. India had effective air power but its leaders chose not to use it. In fact, Nehru's letter to Kennedy went in to minute details about the aircrafts and equipment that India required from the US.[34]

On the same day, China unilaterally decided to end the conflict just as abruptly as it had initiated it. Was it a coincidence or something more was at play? Zhou as the Chinese premier personally called the Indian chargé d'affaires in Beijing on the night of 19 November and briefed him about China's decision to withdraw. However, the Indian government learnt of this crucial decision 36 hours later, on 21 November!

The day after Zhou conveyed China's unilateral decision to conclude the conflict, America's naval blockade of Cuba also ended. China's abrupt decision to withdraw its troops after the many bloody battles the PLA fought, without retaining control on the spoils of war and the swathes of territory it had captured, raised many questions that historians are still trying to answer.

The Chinese withdrawal apparently wasn't due to any fear of the harsh Tibetan winter that usually sets in by December that would have severely restricted their movement and supply lines. While the reasons for initiating the conflict are still obscure, it is clear that it was a measured battle that was fought and ended on China's terms, at a time chosen by China when the world was too busy trying to avert a nuclear conflict between the US and the Soviets, to bother about a strategic border conflict between China and India. Following the ceasefire, it was time to assess the damage, count the dead and figure out what went wrong.

The Blame Game

Taking into account the size of the Indian Army in 1962, only a fraction of it was engaged in trying to counter the Chinese attacks. Yet, the number of Indian casualties was far more after the ceasefire than during the conflict, as the Chinese 'ruthlessly indulged in the slaughter of Indians'. Indian troops too inflicted heavy casualties on the Chinese wherever they fought.[35] Although the total Chinese casualty figures vary, the official Indian count is 2,616, including all the Chinese killed and seriously wounded. This number is mirrored by the officially reported figures of Chinese casualties in this conflict, stated to be 2,400.

Although both Western and Indian historians have contested these figures, they are of one mind in squarely putting the blame for India's defeat on its senior military officers, particularly in NEFA, where senior officers 'left the scene without even making sure that all the units had been informed [of the ceasefire] and that the withdrawal was according to plan. The panic gradually spread to the units who tried to keep together but were so dispersed into smaller and smaller groups till all semblance of control was lost.' This was particularly so after the battle of Namka Chu and the fall of Tawang, where Major General Pathania, who succeeded General Prasad as GoC, 4 Division, chose to abandon the scene when his superiors gave no clear orders to do so.[36]

It is generally customary to blame the Nehru–Menon duo for all that went wrong on the front lines—especially as Nehru had brushed aside the serious warnings about China given by the Army chief General Cariappa in the early 1950s, going as far as to say: 'It is not the business of the C-in-C to tell the PM who is going to attack us where.... You mind only Kashmir and Pakistan.' However, as matters began to slip out of Nehru's control from 1962, General Thapar should have warned him about being misled by his inner circle, including Mullik and General Kaul, which would cost the nation its reputation and many brave men from the army. Yet, a bigger question that still haunts India's military historians is whether we should blame Bijji Kaul or the politico-military leadership in Delhi for imposing him on the NEFA front? If he wasn't there, would the narrative have been any different?

Apart from Mullik and Kaul, many others in the military

hierarchy too cannot be absolved of responsibility for India's military rout. Included on this secondary list of men are General(s) Thapar and Bogey Sen besides Prasad, who was responsible for the fall of Namka Chu, Tawang and Sela. At best, they all acted as messengers or simply as bystanders. Another big strategic error by the military brass was to not use the air force in an offensive against the Chinese, despite all the advantages it entailed. In fact, Air Marshal Aspy Engineer is known to have prepared a detailed plan for the IAF's attack on both the Chinese PLAAF bases in Tibet as well as the Chinese army's garrisons there. His plans, however, were ignored by General Thapar who outranked him. General Thapar could not change the prevailing wisdom in Delhi's South Block that the use of the IAF would only escalate the conflict.

Apart from Menon, even Mullik and the US Ambassador John Galbraith went to great lengths to pressurise Nehru to desist from using combat aircraft against the Chinese. It was also the influence of Professor P.M.S. Blackett, British advisor to Nehru on defence, that kept the IAF grounded barring its reconnaissance and logistical roles. They all believed or at least claimed that the Chinese air force would cripple India's military efforts. In reality, however, the Chinese PLAAF had virtually no air assets in Sinkiang or Aksai Chin, as the many low-flying air reconnaissance and photography flights by Wg Cdr Jaggi Nath of the IAF's 106 Squadron had shown. He was never intercepted nor was his aircraft damaged by anti-aircraft fire. All that the Chinese did was to complain of more than 180 Indian air violations between March and June 1962.[37]

Curious Conflict Timing

While historians have probed China's reasons for the attack and accused its pent-up resentment against India and its own internal strife for which it blamed India, they have wondered about the timing of the conflict. What led China to first declare war and then, just as abruptly, end it?

While historians argue that Mao was waiting for the right time to strike India, and the Cuban Missile Crisis from 16 October to the end of the Soviet blockade on 20 November 1962 provided him the window of opportunity, a deeper examination of certain issues could point us towards a new narrative.

Was it the Chinese worry that the IAF's air photography flights across the Himalayas into Tibet could let the Indians onto China's plans to acquire nuclear weapons? Mao had initiated the highly secretive nuclear Project 596 in the Lop Nor area in June 1959 and he feared that photographs with the IAF that had been passing over that area included images of this plant that may be passed to the US through Mullik. There is also some conjecture that an advanced US satellite programme (CARONA) had provided some coverage of China's nuclear plant by December 1961. Or was this fact finally authenticated by the IAF's flights, as Lop Nor was beyond the flying range of the U-2 flights of the US based in Taiwan?[38] Whatever effective air power China could bring to bear against India in the initial stages of its invasion was focused on Taiwan, as Beijing feared a US intervention with the help of Chinese nationalists in Taiwan. It was only after Washington assured the Chinese leadership that it wouldn't militarily support the Taiwanese in the event of a Taiwanese attack on mainland China, that Peking (Beijing) chose to attack India, and that too with large numbers of troops on the ground using human wave tactics. Much of the aircrafts that it had deployed in Tibet were either unoperational or would've been ineffective against India.[39]

While too many questions remain, the bigger question that begs an answer is: what led Mao to choose the one-month window to attack India, from 20 October until its unilateral decision to stop the conflict on 19 November 1962?

It is believed that the final nudge to Mao to attack India—whether to hide any further US-led probes on his secretive nuclear sites or simply to destroy Nehru's standing—apparently came from a message that the Russian dictator Krushchev gave to the outgoing Chinese ambassador at a grand banquet in Moscow, that he would stand by the PRC, if it went for a border conflict with India. He had also revealed that he had secretly installed nuclear missiles in Cuba. Thus, on the day the Cuban Missile Crisis became public, China attacked India.[40]

Also, it was only when Kennedy stood strong against Russia and Khruschev was compelled to step down, that the US naval blockade of Cuba ended, the day after the Chinese had conveyed to India its unilateral decision to end the conflict.

India's reverses in that 30-day conflict in the high Himalayas dramatically altered India's view of China. Nehru died in 1964, a broken man, the Chinese successfully tested their nuclear bomb at Lop Nor in 1964 and Khruschev abandoned the Chinese and moved closer to India. Historians still question whether Nehru's acceptance of America's offer of an alliance in the 1950s against the Soviet Union could have changed the narrative and whether the story of the 1962 conflict would have been different then, notwithstanding the blunders of all those guilty men.[41] Perhaps we shall never know, or we may learn about the secrets long hiding in India's closets once official reports are made public.

6
THE POST-WAR REPORT

The Chinese invasion of 1962 resulted in a painful defeat for India that tore the country's reputation and Nehru's ambitions into tatters. While China's triumph had a negative impact on India, there was an unexpected positive outcome too. In that moment of national humiliation, the country became so united that Nehru's government even suspended the committee for national integration, the National Integration Council! Some even went so far as to argue that: 'If Dunkirk[1] has gone down in history as the best example of British courage and determination in the face of the greatest odds, the planned withdrawal of several thousand Indian jawans (soldiers) and officers from the besieged 14,000 ft Se La region in NEFA will surely be regarded by future historians as a great page in military history.'[2] Of course, to put it mildly, that was certainly an exaggeration.

In the depths of India's ignominy, Y.B. Chavan succeeded Menon as defence minister and General J.N. 'Mucchu' Chaudhuri took the reins from General Thapar as army chief. Nehru's desire to make the blundering Lt Gen. Kaul the army chief was overruled by President Dr S. Radhakrishnan. Apparently, Nehru had then even considered recalling Lt Gen. Thorat from retirement to replace Thapar.

Thorat was flown to Delhi in an IAF plane to meet Nehru on 20 November 1962. But his brief meeting ended abruptly when he informed Nehru that the army had warned early on what the Chinese could do in India's eastern theatre, an assessment that was sent to General Thimayya, who in turn had passed it on to Menon. But these files had apparently not been shown to Nehru. Once again, when Nehru found the finger of blame pointing at Menon, he exploded in anger and the meeting ended abruptly![3] It is said that Nehru had to protect Krishna Menon to protect himself. Nehru's arrogance and Menon's disdain cost India dearly. Yet, even after the conflict, Nehru was unwilling to take the responsibility for the disaster and its impact on India's defence forces.

Tethered Enquiry

The Indian Army's morale was shattered after the border war. It is for this reason that General Chaudhuri as the new army chief, under the orders of the Nehru government, initiated an enquiry into the drubbing endured by the Indian Army in the border war with China. The Nehru government had asked the army headquarters to prepare a report only of the events that led to the fiasco.

In March 1963, four months after the war had ended, Chaudhuri commissioned a team of two unimpeachable officers of the Indian Army to conduct this enquiry, Lt Gen. T.B. Henderson Brooks and Brig. Prem Bhagat. Both Lt Gen. Brooks, an Anglo-Indian officer who was the GoC of XI Corps, and Brig. Bhagat, VC, Commandant, IMA, Dehradun, were sound professionals, and they were not perceived as 'Kaul's boys'. Brooks, a second-generation army officer, was from the Maratha Light Infantry regiment and Brig. (later Lt Gen.) Bhagat, VC, was a widely respected Victoria Cross winner.

It is said that General Chaudhuri was keen to initiate a full-fledged study of the 'debacle of 1962'. He, however, was advised to avoid any investigation on the higher direction of that conflict that would require the Brooks–Bhagat team to access files pertaining to governmental decisions, which would be unacceptable. Officially, even the functioning of army headquarters, not just the politico-bureaucratic establishment in Delhi, was outside the purview of the commission. As Chavan later stated in Parliament, the enquiry was in no way meant 'to undertake a witch-hunt into the culpabilities of those who were involved in or took part in these operations' and the government 'did not wish to institute an enquiry into high level policies and decisions'.[4]

Naturally, Brooks and Bhagat were denied access to crucial exchanges between the leadership—civil and military—in Delhi. The commission only had access to directives issued to the lower levels of the army command. Their terms of reference for this enquiry were to look only at what went wrong militarily, including issues like training, equipment, physical fitness of troops and the role of military commanders. The purpose of the exercise seemed to fix the blame only on the 'failure of military commanders and to the tactical mishandling of troops on the ground', as Chavan later declared in a low-key statement to Parliament. Thus, Nehru ensured that he and his government survived despite the 'series of reverses', as Chavan was to put it.[5]

'Top Secret' Document

The Brooks–Bhagat Committee submitted its two-volume report to the Ministry of Defence in May 1963. Naturally, being commissioned by the Nehru government and without access to critical files, the report did not contain any names of the political leadership of the day, namely Nehru, Menon, etc. Although Chavan read out selected extracts from the report in Parliament, the gist of the report seemed to be missing. The report was never made public and, even 57 years after the border war, remains a classified document.

In fact, the leadership in New Delhi did everything to cover the debacle, but there is now sufficient amount of literature—even without making public the findings of the Brooks–Bhagat report—which shows that the responsibility for the disaster of 1962 lies with both the political leadership and the military commanders of 1962. Very few people had access to the very few copies of the report, although there have been speculations for long that General Chaudhuri, who commissioned the Brooks–Bhagat report—for which he is most remembered—apparently leaked volume I of the report to the British journalist Neville Maxwell.

Maxwell became one of the few people outside the Indian establishment who were allowed to read the report and to make his notes without exposing its findings in detail. Maxwell used the report's findings in his book, *India's China War*. In 2014, a substantial part of the report was released on the internet, apparently by Maxwell, on his blog, and it allowed a free download too, allowing people to keep copies![6] Needless to state, the Indian government never validated this 'published' version of the report, but it is generally taken to be authentic. The Brooks–Bhagat report remains a strongly guarded document in the vaults of India's Ministry of Defence in South Block. What led to classifying the Brooks–Bhagat report?

Unforgiving Analysis

R.D. Pradhan, who was Chavan's private secretary between 1962 and 1965, provides some insights in his memoirs, *Beyond Expectations*. He states: 'During the conduct of the enquiry, Chavan was apprehensive that the committee may cast aspersions on the role of the prime minister or the defence minister....

His (*Chavan*) main worry was to find ways to defend the government and at the same time to ensure that the morale of the armed forces was not further adversely affected.' So, Y.B. Chavan's secretary concluded that Chavan 'earned the gratitude of the prime minister'.[7] This confirms why the government of the day clearly did not wish this inquiry to look into high-level policies and plans.

The investigation, even if it had been permitted, would have had no access to records of meetings in the Ministry of Defence because Menon had categorically disallowed any notes or minutes to be kept of his conferences, stating that these were top secret in nature. So, the Brooks–Bhagat team was unable to get crucial information to lay the blame on Menon and his core team, where it belonged. It thus absolved them of responsibility for their blunders in the ultimate analysis. Although Lt Gen. Brooks was clearly directed not to fix responsibility onto specific individuals, Maxwell had no such restriction. Maxwell wrote: 'Henderson Brooks and Bhagat place the immediate cause of the collapse of the resistance in NEFA in the panicky, fumbling and contradictory orders issued from corps HQ in Tezpur to a "triumvirate" of officers they judge to be grossly culpable: Lt Gen. "Bogey" Sen, Lt Gen. "Bijji" Kaul and Brig. Monty Palit.'[8]

The focus of the Brooks–Bhagat enquiry was only meant to be on the operations of IV Corps, that was responsible for the debacle in India's northeast in 1962, not even the Ladakh sector, where tensions had first started![9] However, what these two officers are said to have eventually produced was an unforgiving analysis about the problems along the entire Sino-Indian border, discovering along the way a great deal that Lt Gen. Kaul—regarded by many as a lackey of Nehru and Menon—and the government of the day wanted to be kept hidden. If that was the purpose of classifying the Brooks–Bhagat report, why then does it still remain such a closely guarded secret?

Opposing Disclosure

In 2005, veteran Indian journalist and former MP, Kuldip Nayar requested the Ministry of Defence under the Right to Information 'to make me available a copy of the report'. The defence ministry's stand was articulated during a hearing of the commission in March 2009. It was said, 'Disclosure of this information will amount to disclosure of the army's operational strategy in the northeast and the discussion on deployments has a direct bearing on the question of the demarcation of the Line of Actual Control between India and China, a live issue under examination between the two countries at present.'[10]

In 2008, answering a question on the report, defence minister A.K. Antony from the Congress-led UPA government in India told Parliament that the Brooks–Bhagat report could not be made public because an internal study by the army had established that its contents 'are not only extremely sensitive, but are of current operational value'.

Again, in 2014, Arun Jaitley, then the minister of defence, in the NDA government, gave a written reply to the Indian Parliament (Rajya Sabha) that 'The Henderson Brooks report is a top-secret document that has not been declassified so far. Release of this report, fully or partially, or disclosure of any information related to this report, would not be in national interest.'[11] That incidentally, was a clear U-turn by Jaitley, who had earlier as part of the political opposition asked 'why the Henderson-Brooks report was not made public'.[12]

A handful of people have apparently had a look at the Brooks–Bhagat report. This includes those at the defence ministry's historical division tasked to research and write the official history of the 1962 conflict with China, and those like the late Jaswant Singh, an ex-army officer and a rare soldier-scholar in Indian politics. Having read it, when he was foreign and briefly defence minister in the A.B. Vajpayee government, Singh too preferred 'to let sleeping dogs lie'. Some have cited examples of how the report lays the blame on army headquarters for its direct interference, bypassing the established chains of command or even deployment of troops on the frontline against the Chinese. One example is of the General Staff in Delhi giving direct orders to HQ 7 Brigade, bypassing the headquarters of Eastern Command, IV Corps, and 4 Mountain Division to (a) capture a Chinese post 1,000 yards northeast of the Dhola Post, and (b) contain Chinese concentration south of Thagla, a ridge on the NEFA frontline. This order could be seen to be as incredible as the order for 'the charge of light brigade'.[13]

Such observations would lead us to believe that as against common belief, the Brooks–Bhagat report does not expose the blunders of the political leadership as it was meant to only look at what went wrong militarily and that too on the NEFA front. Other accounts, however, indicate that the report alludes to political interference as well.

Decoding 'National Interest'

An authoritative voice and a champion of the need to go public with the Brooks–Bhagat report is the veteran Sinologist Claude Arpi. In an article, Arpi quotes from a 'decision notice' of India's Central Information Commission, dated 19 March 2010, which states that the 'report's findings would bring into question the lay of the India-China border and thus could impact the ongoing negotiation between the two countries on this matter.'[14] So, what were these findings? Does it influence the Indian position on the lay of the McMahon Line?

Arpi's article quotes largely from the memoirs of those Indian Army officers who fought in the 1962 conflict and then in later years penned their instructive, but bitter, accounts of what led to the conflict and why there was such confusion about the boundary lines.

For instance, Major General Prasad, in his book *The Fall of Towang* (Tawang), describes the setting of the operations: 'The McMahon Line from just north of Khinzemane, as drawn by Sir Henry McMahon in 1914 with a thick blue *(in fact, red)* pencil on an unsurveyed map, was not an accurate projection of the Himalayan watershed line... In this process, the position of Thagla Ridge was, to say the least, left ambiguous. The story goes that the officer surveying the area had completed an admirable task of delineating the watershed up to this point when a pretty Mompa girl claimed his attention and the work was left uncompleted.'

The survey was completed in 1913 by Captain(s) Bailey and Morshead, but it is true that it was rather sketchy (1 inch: 8 miles). If one follows the watershed principle as well as the ownership of customary pastures' rights, the Thagla Ridge was the border, but the fact remains that the old map that was the reference for India's position on the 'genuine' location of the McMahon Line showed the Thagla Ridge and the Namka Chu, north of the red line. Further surveys were unfortunately not conducted after India's Independence'.[15] Prasad also cites Brig. John Dalvi's *Himalayan Blunder*, an honest, heart-wrenching account of his brigade that became the first to face the Chinese onslaught on 20 October 1962.

Dalvi questioned how the Dhola Post on the Namka Chu near the Thagla Ridge came into existence: 'We seemed to have ventured most casually into a potentially explosive commitment. Instead of working in water-tight compartments, we should have alerted the whole Army and prepared for a clash. Even Mullik, Nehru's trusted man in the IB, who was involved with the operations before the fighting started and one who implemented the infamous "forward policy", had probably no clue about the exact position of the border and the Chinese preparations.'[16]

Ambiguous Boundary Line

That was one of the major shortcomings of India's boundary policy towards China in the 1960s. The men responsible for delicate matters, some of which directly led to the border conflict, had immense authority but no accountability for the mess they created. The subject of the 'Forward Policy' as mooted by the Nehru government apparently figures in the Brooks–Bhagat report, especially how it led to a Chinese attack. Arpi argues that the 'Forward Policy' was Menon's initiative and he had Nehru's full support, although the prime minister did state that posts should not be established in 'disputed areas'. The sighting and exact locations of these posts, however, were decided mainly by the IB and not the Indian Army.

This matter caused great unhappiness with the military commanders on the front lines. Brig. Dalvi recalled that many generals, including General Umrao Singh, from the IV Corps Commander, had opposed the indiscriminate opening up of more posts. Arpi too writes, 'The setting up of posts in disputed territory is a different matter. It is an act of rashness, whoever decreed it and with whatever authority, unless we had the means to settle the resultant dispute on the battlefield.' Arpi then states that 'as the local GOC of the 4 Infantry Division, Major General Prasad noted, the local commanders had no choice. Though they could certainly have resigned, in an almost war situation, it was not an easy decision to take.'[17]

In his memoirs about the war, Gen. Prasad writes, 'I told the DMO that the establishment of Dhola Post could lead to very serious consequences if in fact it lay north of our claim line.' He claims he had informed Brig. Palit, then the DMO, when he visited the corps headquarters in Tezpur on 14 August 1962. This led Palit to take up this matter of the posts on the Sino-Indian boundary with the Director of Military Survey, which was confirmed by Brig. Palit in his account of the 1962 conflict, *War in the High Himalayas*.

Palit wrote, 'On my return to Delhi I referred the Thagla dilemma to the Director of Military Survey. The latter commented that as the existing maps of the area were "sketchy and inaccurate, having been compiled from unreliable sources", the map co-ordinates of the new post quoted by the patrol leader were of doubtful accuracy. He confirmed that the recognised border was the watershed, but qualified this statement by adding "the exact alignment of [this] will depend on an accurate survey, which would take two to three years to complete".' But it was going to be a matter of a few weeks only, as Brig. Palit would soon know.[18]

Clearly, there was ambiguity about the McMahon Line, and thus Brig. Palit decided to seek the opinion of the MEA and more particularly, the historical section that's part of the MEA. To clarify the exact position of the line, Palit met Dr S. Gopal, then the director of the historical section, a historian of repute and President Radhakrishnan's son. Dr Gopal confirmed to Palit that since the boundary talks with the Chinese in 1954, the Government of India had been aware of certain ambiguities on the boundary such as in the area of the tri-junction based on the terrain that led to a different understanding than what was depicted on the quarter-inch scale Simla Conference maps.[19]

Palit quotes Dr Gopal to say: 'The Chinese had been told *during the talks of 1960* that the alignment *of the McMahon Line* followed Thagla Ridge, which is also the ridge shown by Army Headquarters in the sketch.' He then adds, 'What Gopal had not told me—and I found out only later—was that the Chinese had not accepted our arguments and had counter-claimed Thagla Ridge as Chinese territory.' Palit then sent Dr Gopal's remarks to HQ of the Eastern Command in Lucknow for onward transmission to 4 Infantry Division: 'By then it was mid-September and events in that remote region on the border of Bhutan and Tibet had already reached a critical stage.'[20]

The Brooks–Bhagat report is said to bring out the fact that despite nobody knowing the exact lay of the boundary, there were solid presumptions in India (though not accepted by China) that the Thagla Ridge on the northern edge of NEFA was the 'actual border'. This led to the positioning of Indian troops as far ahead as possible along the McMahon Line, on the Sino-Indian boundary, even though these detachments were in the form of lookout posts, and not a forward defended locality with adequate ammunition and food supplies. Soliders were thus ill-clad and ill-equipped to hold onto their locations in the event of a probing attack. It is believed that these orders had come from the IB in Delhi and not from army headquarters.[21] It also led to Chinese intelligence reports to Beijing that India was planning an attack on the Thagla Ridge on 10 October 1962. However, when Indian troops were pushed up with orders to 'throw out the Chinese' or 'take the Thagla Ridge', it became evident that such orders came from Delhi because no one in South Block had envisaged a confrontation.

After the fiasco, all efforts were made to shift the blame onto the commanders on the ground. Brig. Dalvi, the commander of the ill-fated 7 Brigade, was to ask, 'Who forced me to open Dhola?' He was referring to the Dhola post that was the scene of one of the initial confrontations. Historians say, Nehru's orders to throw out the Chinese was just bravado based on little understanding of ground realties. 'It is probably what the Henderson–Brooks report discovered, which is why it will continue to remain classified,' writes Arpi.[22]

Political Failure

The Brooks–Bhagat report shows that eventually India's confrontation with the Chinese led Chairman Mao to conclude that: 'It seems like armed coexistence won't work. It is just as we expected. Nehru really wants to use force. This isn't strange. He has always wanted to seize Aksai Chin and Thagla Ridge. He thinks he can get everything he desires.'

In retrospect however (as this book has argued), Mao was waiting for an opportunity 'to teach India a lesson' and the Indian government offered him that opportunity. The Chinese attacks occurred simultaneously in all sectors (NEFA and Ladakh) from which it is clear that the operations had been prepared well in advance by Mao and the PLA, which was working to a plan and Mao didn't really need a pretext.

The findings of the Brooks–Bhagat report make it evident that the real failure for the 1962 debacle was not only military, but also political, a view echoed by Ram Madhav, an eminent member of the Bharatiya Janata Party (BJP), who wrote in 2014: 'As the news of the leak of Henderson Brooks report tumbled out in the media, the Congress Party's reaction was that there was no mention of Jawaharlal Nehru's name in that and hence he shouldn't be blamed for whatever had happened then. This is a weird argument. As the prime minister of India not just during the period of war but at least a dozen years prior to that, Nehru cannot be absolved of his failures that led to defeat in the war, loss of territory and loss of face.'[23]

Madhav then identified four reasons for the fiasco of 1962. First was Nehru's decision not to confront the Chinese after they began the occupation of Tibet, despite repeated requests from the Tibetan government. Further, when El Salvador raised the Tibet issue at the UN, Nehru had instructed India's representative B.N. Rao to make sure that the UN doesn't include it in the agenda.

Second, the encouragement that China received with the Panchsheel Treaty in April 1954 proved fatal for the Tibetan cause. With the buffer of Tibet gone, China was positioning itself to confront India, This agreement had officially and fatally undone all that good work done over decades to uphold the independence of Tibet.[24]

Britain's understanding of the importance of guarding Tibet's independence had led to the creation of the Indo-Tibet border and the McMahon Line. Thus, the Panchsheel Treaty was naturally a windfall for China. Interestingly, while Nehru claimed credit for Panchsheel, Zhou told US President Richard Nixon in 1973, 'Actually, the five principles (Panchsheel) were put forward by us and Nehru agreed. But later on he didn't implement them,' wrote Ram Madhav, who says 'Panchsheel brought nothing but ignominy to us. Friends felt betrayed; China never believed in the spirit of the agreement and violated it just within three months after signing. Originally conceived for eight years, the agreement died a natural death exactly in the same period with the Chinese attacking India in 1962.'[25]

Thirdly, since 1952, Nehru's government turned a blind eye to China's encroachments into Aksai Chin area. Mullik's assessment in 1952 was that the Chinese were only converting a mule track into a jeep track in the Aksai Chin area. By 1953, however, Nehru was informed that the jeep track was being fast updated into a highway. This information was kept under wraps, despite a Chinese media announcement in 1957 that China was building a highway linking Sinkiang with Tibet through Aksai Chin. Yet, Nehru chose to keep the country in the dark until 1959, when he was faced with no option but to finally concede this information.

Aksai Chin was on China's radar since the Communist regime took power. All that India did was to issue a letter to China insinuating that the Chinese workers working in Aksai

Chin region 'had not secured valid visas', as if that was the real problem! Thereafter, Nehru and Menon were both unwilling to take up the issue at the UN. Menon dismissed media questions on the matter that 'the UNO has not defined aggression'![26]

Finally, Madhav goes on to argue that 'Chen Yi, the foreign minister of China had assured Menon in New York in mid-1962 that there would be no reaction to the Indian Army trying to evacuate the Chinese. Zhou told Nehru in 1960 that there would be no war between the countries. Nehru himself had the belief that China would never attack India because 'Is it imaginable that a war between India and China will remain confined to those countries? It will be a world war.' Hence there was no preparation; no planning. 'Defence against whom?' was the duo's (in)famous response. So, when the Chinese attacked, Menon was in New York while Nehru was first in UK, then in Africa and later in Sri Lanka.

Further, as the 'Brooks-Bhagat Report also pointed out there was no road link between Srinagar and Leh until November 1961; there were only four air bases; and just one brigade to man the entire 2,000 km border. The army wanted one additional brigade and they were given just one battalion. Shortage of ammunition plagued the army throughout.'[27] The writing was there on the wall, but no one in Delhi was willing to read it.

Who Was the Aggressor?

The Brooks-Bhagat report underlines the deep disconnect between Delhi and the military commanders on the ground. Those in the establishment who are aware about its contents are, therefore, still divided over who was the aggressor and whether or not the report should be made public. It is feared that the publication of its 200 pages would only undo the myth that the 1962 conflict was a Chinese aggression. A series of studies have, over the years, clearly shown that the Indian Army was in fact ordered to challenge the Chinese for a military confrontation, which they could only lose. The culprits were in South Block in New Delhi, who repeatedly pushed troops forward into positions that would bring them into eyeball-to-eyeball contact with the Chinese; place them into indefensible positions and with no scope for a fighting withdrawal, an operation of war. The commanders on the ground from corps HQ to brigade HQ, with a few exceptions, chose to follow meekly their absurd orders.

Apparently, there are three groups opposed to the declassification of the Brooks–Bhagat report. First is India's political leadership, whether it is the Nehru loyalists or those who operate on hearsay. Very few have actually read the report even when they had access to it. As the 1962 conflict was a political disaster, Nehru's family and followers in the Congress party, a major political entity in India, would rather forget and pretend it never happened. Even the Indian bureaucracy that controls the Ministry of Defence, the intelligence services and the historical bodies, among many others, prefers to keep the issue buried. It would inconveniently open up a new debate on who ordered the army into a confrontation and raise questions about the role of the bureaucracy in the Ministry of Defence. Finally, the armed forces too oppose the declassification as they would rather prefer to hide the critical details and their own shortcomings. The 1962 conflict had in fact exposed the underbelly of India's civil and military establishments and everyone must share the blame.

Birth of Conspiracy Theories

A few years ago, Maxwell, then an old man living in Australia, published part of the report—or what was purported to be part of the report—on his website.

Maxwell's release of the Brooks–Bhagat report took place as the election season was heating up in India. Predictably, it added to campaign rhetoric. Since the 1962 war is seen as Nehru's biggest failure, the leak was highlighted by the BJP to embarrass the Congress. Among the strongest voices in the BJP was that of Arun Jaitley, who demanded the report be declassified.

This is what made Jaitley's about-turn once in government more embarrassing. In effect, he echoed the words of his predecessor, A.K. Antony, who declined to release the Brooks–Bhagat report in 2010, arguing it was 'sensitive' and of 'current operational value', even though the war had been over for half a century.

Opacity is the mother of conspiracy theories. The chief conspiracy theory surrounding the Brooks–Bhagat findings has been that by keeping them under cover, the Congress is protecting Nehru. This may or may not be true. Nehru's failure on the China front, his dependence on a reckless defence minister and the circumstances of the 1962 war, including the decision to push Indian soldiers into aggressive positions in disputed territory without providing for the hapless soldiers weapons or logistical support, have all come out. Many of the participants in the tragedy of 1962 have written their own accounts.

That apart, Henderson Brooks was a professional solider. He was asked to scrutinise where the army erred. He is unlikely to have commented on the politicisation of the army brass or that individual generals were currying favour with certain politicians and ministers and feeding them a mythology they wanted to hear. This was an important element of 1962, but could not possibly have been part of Henderson Brooks' mandate.

So, from where does the opposition to the release of the report emanate? There are four sources. First, 1962 was a national tragedy that sections of the Indian establishment would rather forget and pretend never happened. Second, 1962 was a political disaster that the Congress establishment would rather forget and pretend never happened. Third, the bureaucratic inertia in the defence ministry would prefer to keep the report sealed. It would rather use this secrecy as a carrot or stick depending upon the situation in the perennial battle between defence ministry civil servants and army generals. Fourth, the army would not want critical details revealed—presuming Antony was right in 2010 and the report does have operational minutiae that are still of use—or want it to be known that the army headquarters and tin-pot, Bonapartist generals flagrantly and unconscionably let down the gallant jawan.

This coalition has been so persuasive and stubborn that it thwarted even George Fernandes. As the defence minister in the Vajpayee years, Fernandes, like Jaitley, came from an entirely non-Congress political tradition. On taking office, he spoke with clarity on the Chinese strategic challenge. In 1998, he was instrumental in pushing the publisher Penguin to reissue D.R. Mankekar's *The Guilty Men of 1962*. Yet, Fernandes too failed the Brooks–Bhagat test.

What is there in the report that causes a politician like Fernandes or Jaitley, who forcefully asked for its declassification in favour of transparency, to take what would seem to be an indefensible position? What mysteries are contained in the report that a confident nation and a confident army can't address before its release or can't face up to?

The defence minister cannot declassify the report on his own. There is a cabinet decision that will have to be revoked. It is also feasible that the report is only made public with a few paragraphs or sentences blacked out in the interest of 'national security'. While not ideal, this situation with redactions can be lived with. A blanket refusal to release the report cannot be lived with.

India's democracy and its people deserve better. The memory of Major Shaitan Singh, Subedar Joginder Singh and all those valiant men who died for India in those icy heights in 1962 deserve better.

Especially when the border issue is not resolved and Chinese incursions have not stopped yet.

7

A FORGOTTEN VICTORY

The saga of the conflict of 1962 had put an end to the 'Hindi-Chini bhai bhai' slogan of projected brotherhood and injected a deep distrust and antagonism between the two sides, as tensions continued to run high along the Himalayan border. After the traumatic humiliation of the 1962 conflict, India's political leadership was rattled and demoralised. The experience of the politico-military debacle was also sharply etched in the memory of India's Army, that issued clear orders that Indian troops must move up to the McMahon Line cautiously and avoid provocations. This strategy became uniform throughout our northern borders.[1]

The border conflict also shaped the foreign policies of these two nations. While Pakistan was compelled by America, in the spirit of being a member of the Southeast Asia Treaty Organization (SEATO), to not take advantage of India's war with China, Ayub Khan used this opportunity to build its equation with China. Three years later, Pakistan attacked India.

In fact, as part of its plans to wrest Kashmir from India in 1965, Pakistan had asked China to engage in military activity that would divert India's attention towards the Himalayan borders. Although China did not violate the operational boundaries along the Himalayas, it increased the frequency of its movements along the watershed line. It led to minor skirmishes and a few instances of firing by troops.

Rising Political Tensions

As India and Pakistan went to war on India's western front, the Chinese also initiated action in the eastern Himalayas. Around this time, a series of conflicts broke out on India's Himalayan borders as China made its first attempt to occupy the strategic Nathu La mountain pass in Sikkim during Indo-Pak hostilities in 1965. However, from August 1965, Indian troops had a no-nonsense commander, Major General Sagat Singh of 17 Mountain Division, responsible for the Sikkim front, headquartered in Gangtok. He successfully rebuffed this attempt by the Chinese, who would then make another bid for the strategically located Nathu La in September 1967, only to be thwarted once again by Sagat.

Towards the end of the India-Pakistan conflict on 19 September 1965, tensions between India and China escalated as Chinese troops crossed the LAC into Ladakh, which divides Indian and China-held territories along eastern Ladakh, beyond which lines Aksai Chin. The term LAC, however, came to be formally used after 2003, and is different from the Indo-Pak front lines in J&K and north west Ladakh, known as the Line of Control (LoC), that replaced the ceasefire line in 1972. They kidnapped and killed three Indian armed personnel near Tasaskur on the LAC.[2] Relations grew more strained in the following months, as the Chinese side made effective use of radio broadcasts to propagate anti-Indian sentiment among its listeners.

The tense equation between these neighbouring nations is reflected in the records with the Indian embassy. From 1966, a flurry of official dispatches, each following the other in quick succession from the Indian embassy in Beijing, suggest that Indians residing in China were being 'ill-treated', even though a paltry 24 Indian passport holders lived in China at the time. A secret annual consular report that was sent from Beijing revealed that a Gurudwara in Tianjin (then Tientsin) had been desecrated and a Parsi temple in Shanghai was occupied by the Red Army.[3]

A secret CIA assessment (declassified in 2011) had identified this unattended build-up of political tension between the two nations as the real source of the eventual border clash.[4] For their part, the standard Chinese response to any diplomatic protests remained that India was the 'aggressor' in all instances of conflict. The Chinese establishment had even accused India of adopting 'shabby tricks' and suggested in 1966 that New Delhi compensate Beijing for losses and damage incurred during the initial skirmishes on the China-Sikkim border. China stated that these were entirely initiated by India.[5] Tensions at the border and the anti-Indian sentiment resulted in action against an unlikely person—an Indian diplomat in Beijing.

A Spy Story

A career diplomat, K. Raghunath became India's foreign secretary and architect of the 'Gujral doctrine' that guided India's foreign policy in the 1990s. In 1965, however, Raghunath was posted to the Chinese capital to head the Information Services of India (ISI), the government's public information unit. Two years into his stint serving as a young second secretary at the Indian embassy in Beijing, Raghunath became embroiled in a bizarre spying scandal.

By all official accounts, the ISI's toughest job was coping with Chinese restrictions. Every conceivable interaction ran into some kind of ban or the other, frustrating the unit's intentions. The best Raghunath could manage was putting up posters conveying the Indian government's messages on the walls of the embassy. Then, in early June 1967, Raghunath and another Indian diplomat, P. Vijai, were caught taking photographs on what appeared to be their tourist jaunt to a temple of the Sleeping Buddha near Beijing.

The Ministry of Foreign Affairs in Beijing alleged that the photographs were taken to create a topographical map of a 'prohibited area'. Raghunath was accused of collecting 'political and military' information, sneaking into Chinese government institutions and impersonating embassy members of 'friendly countries like Pakistan and Nepal'. He was put on public trial as all of China went into an uproar. A film, *Severely Punish the Indian Spy Raghunath*, was made and screened for the Chinese public to showcase his alleged crimes and further indict him.[6]

India responded with indignation. New Delhi strongly refuted all accusations and denied all Chinese charges of espionage. Protesting Raghunath's mistreatment by the Chinese, his return to India was expedited. On his arrival in India, he was given a hero's welcome at a packed airport lounge in the Indian capital. It brought back memories of the distrust that had led to the 1962 conflict and thereafter.

Defending the 'Watershed'

By the time Raghunath was accused as a spy, the already strained relations between India and China had well and truly soured as was evident in the frequent border scuffles that occurred on the Indo-Sino border.

On India's eastern boundary, on China's border with Sikkim, then an independent state with an Indian military presence, lay Nathu La. This mountain pass overlooked the Chumbi Valley at a tri-junction between territories held by the Chinese army in South Tibet and Bhutan. (This was the area where Indian and Chinese troops were engaged in a long military stand-off in 2017.) Another mountain pass, Cho La, lay about 30 kilometres northwest of Nathu La in Sikkim. Sagat Singh, the commander of 17 Mountain Division was responsible for the Sikkim front and the forward positions in Nathu La and Cho La.

About 15 kilometres southeast of Nathu La was Jelep La, near the tri-junction of India, Bhutan and Tibet, which came under 27 Mountain Division[7] headquartered in Kalimpong on the east. Both these mountain divisions—17 and 27—were under the Siliguri based HQ XXXIII Corps, which in turn came under India's Eastern Command.

While observation posts were located on the mountain passes, the main defences of both the 17 and 27 Mountain Division were at Chhangu and Lungthu respectively. These frontline formations were, however, under clear orders that in case of hostilities, they were to vacate the posts on the watershed and fall back to the depth positions at Chhangu and Lungthu respectively, leaving behind only observation posts at the passes.

Even Sagat's predecessor, the earlier GoC of 17 Mountain Division, in the winter of 1964, had chosen to use the 'watershed areas' only to delay the Chinese up to the main defences in the rear, located on the Changgu and Lungthu ridge lines in Sikkim. This was the operational thinking on the Indian side that was followed by the adjoining Indian force of 27 Mountain Division, headquartered on the east in Kalimpong. For instance, in a particularly tense stand-off against Chinese soldiers that resulted in an exchange of intense fire, 27 Mountain Division, responsible for Jelep La and the tri-junction area, having fought a defensive battle in 1964, eventually gave up its advantageous position. It withdrew its troops to their rear positions, vacating the dominating heights, which were promptly occupied by the Chinese. Captain (later Major General) Randhir Sinh, who as ADC to Sagat Singh had witnessed these events, confirms the pull back by 27 Division: 'It vacated Jelep La Pass and the "watershed" and occupied its defences on the Lungthu Ridge.'[8] Jelep La fell into Chinese hands and continues to remain so.

Yet, as Delhi continued to insist on a non-confrontational approach, the Chinese encouraged by their gains once again took up threatening postures across the 'watershed line'. A tense situation continued to prevail for two years. Patrols would walk shoulder to shoulder along the 'watershed' jostling each other. There were at least four provocations, which involved small arms and mortar fire. Additionally, in Nathu La, the Chinese had initially installed 21 powerful loudspeakers and subsequently eight more, which would blast out non-stop anti-India propaganda. The Indian government's response to what the Chinese were doing was cautious. The Chinese thus felt confident enough to try their luck again at Nathu La in 1967, but here they overlooked the presence of a determined commander like Sagat.

Drawing the Line

Sagat realised that the defence of Nathu La was crucial to stall any ingress by China towards the 20 kilometre narrow Siliguri corridor, where the borders of India, Nepal and then East Pakistan, presently Bangladesh, met. Nathu La was critical to the defence of Gangtok, which lay only a few thousand feet lower and not too far from the pass. Otherwise the Chinese would have a free run all the way downhill to the plains of north Bengal and the Siliguri corridor that connects Assam to the rest of the country. He, therefore, decided that if Sikkim was to be defended and any Chinese attempt to roll down into the area was to be stalled, then a re-deployment of his forces and the defence of the 'watershed' line was important. Such a formation brought Indian and Chinese troops into eye-to-eye contact.[9]

By August-September 1967, there was a lot of pushing and jostling (the likes of which was shown on Indian television in

2017), but Sagat refused to allow his troops to fall back as he considered the watershed at the passes and adjoining heights to be the natural boundary between India and China. Also, fed up with these Chinese pin pricks, he decided to demarcate the LAC, without a change of its status from what was available on the maps with India since the Simla Conference of 1914, more so, as the Chinese had already carried out an intrusion across the LAC and constructed a structure at the hilltop called North Shoulder (north of Nathu La) on 17 August. This had led to a tense confrontation as Indian troops wanted to demolish this structure.

He went about having the border clearly demarcated by laying a wire fence at the pass, along the natural boundary. Sagat understood that in the mountains, anyone who controlled the heights had an unassailable advantage. So he went about strengthening his positions. Furthermore, he placed his observation post sites at strategic locations from where they could look deep into the Chumbi Valley and bring down effective artillery fire right up to Yatung.[10] Thus, mere months after the expulsion of India's young diplomat from China, when Indian forces in the eastern Himalayas started to erect a fence along the border at Nathu La, they once again found themselves in the midst of a military clash.

A Confrontation

From 18 August, the Chinese objected vociferously to the laying of the fence on the LAC. Five days later, they were still trying to stall the efforts of Indian soldiers. Yet, Indian troops stood their ground despite Chinese provocations like bayonets being poked through the clothing of those on patrol to stop their tactical activities.

On 23 August, about 75 Chinese soldiers carrying rifles with bayonets advanced towards Nathu La in a line and stopped at the border where they shouted out slogans from a red book. The Indian troops watched and waited as these soldiers left after an hour and returned to continue with their protests.[11]

It was becoming clear that further escalation may occur. Notwithstanding Delhi's tepid responses, Sagat ordered his troops to stand fast in their positions. Sagat had briefed his superior commanders, the Corps Commander, Lt Gen. Jagjit Singh Aurora, and the commander of the Eastern Command, Lt Gen. Sam Manekshaw, MC, about his plans.[12] They agreed that a physical barrier might help stop daily arguments between soldiers over who should stand where and how on that part of the border. The Chinese, evidently, disagreed as several attempts were made to stop Indian troops from erecting the fence and tensions around Nathu La were high in the first week of September 1967.

On 10 September, Sagat briefed the units and ordered Lt Col. Rai Singh, CO, 2 Grenadiers, to strengthen the existing fence with a military-style cat-wire fence, for which he was given two platoons[13] of 18 Rajput and a Platoon of Pioneers, besides a Company[14] of Engineers. The brigade commander, Brig. M.M.S. Bakshi, an MVC winner from the 1965 Indo-Pak war, had moved forward to Nathu La, to monitor developments closely since a confrontation was expected, while Sagat himself moved to Sherathang nearby. And as trouble was anticipated, Indian medium artillery guns (that had a range of 15–20 kilometres then) were moved forward. No one, however, expected the severity of the Chinese reaction on 11 September 1967.[15]

The day dawned bright and sunny at Nathu La, unlike the normal foggy days. Early in the morning on 11 September 1967, the engineers and jawans started erecting long iron pickets from Nathu La to Sebu La along the perceived border while officers of the 2 Grenadiers and Artillery Observation post at Sebu La and Camel's Back were on alert. As they worked on the fence, Chinese loudspeakers blared out the 'Hindi-Chini bhai bhai' slogan and Bollywood songs. Shortly thereafter, a Chinese commissar led a section of the infantry from the Chinese outpost to stop Indian troops. An argument ensued, a tussle broke out and incredibly, for the second time in a week, the same commissar was roughed up and his glasses were crushed during a heated exchange.[16]

'The Commissar was the only representative of the People's Liberation Army who could converse in English and he seemed perpetually to be goading his troops,' recalls Major General Sheru Thapliyal, then a young artillery lieutenant, posted barely a kilometre from Nathu La.

Long after that eventful September, this incident with the unnamed Chinese commissar remained fresh in Thapliyal's memory. As Thapliyal wrote later, 'The commissar's role in the Chinese system was important and his stature was high. Having his spectacles crushed in undignified jostling with the Indians may well have dealt a blow to his self-esteem.'

Defending Nathu La

Thapliyal also chronicled the day of the clash. 'The Chinese Political Commissar, came with a section of Infantry to the centre of the Pass where Lt. Col. Rai Singh, was standing with his commando platoon.'[17] The commissar asked Rai Singh to stop laying the wire.

Sagat's orders to the Indian Army were clear. They were not to blink. An argument started, which soon built up into a scuffle in which the commissar was roughed up. Thereafter the Chinese returned to their bunkers and Indian engineers resumed laying the wire. But within a few minutes, a whistle was heard on the Chinese side followed by murderous medium machine gun fire from the north shoulder. As the Nathu La Pass is completely devoid of cover, the jawans of 70 Field Company and 18 Rajput were caught in the open and suffered heavy casualties, which included Col. Rai Singh who was wounded.

That morning was marked by some exceptional displays of bravery from the Indian forces. There were close to 70 casualties in that first strike itself, when the Indians troops found themselves exposed and unprepared as they stood out in the open'. Thapliyal writes that they 'rallied a few troops' to assault the Chinese gun, but they too died heroically in the attempt. Though 2 Grenadiers opened small-arms fire on the north shoulder of the pass, the volleys accomplished little.

The Chinese then even opened artillery fire on Indian soldiers. General Sagat could only fire his artillery on clearance from army HQ. He waited for five hours, but when clearance was not forthcoming, he ordered the guns to open fire. The officer at the Artillery Observation post located on the heights around Nathu La opened devastating fire into the Chumbi Valley and the road axis, which caused heavy Chinese casualties. 'On Sagat's orders, an attack was planned on 12 September, postponed to 13 September and ultimately cancelled on orders of higher HQ. It took nearly four days for the situation to stabilise,' writes Randhir Sinh.[18]

Meanwhile, official exchanges between India and China, already bad-tempered, filled up with references to the skirmish in the mountains. A note from Beijing on 10 September, the day before the Chinese opened fire, had given an account of 60 Indian soldiers allegedly intruding into Chinese territory, installing barbed wire and wounding two Chinese guards with bayonets.

On 12 September, the day after open hostilities, detailed notes were exchanged again. China again blamed India's 'aggressor troops' that opened fire and killed or wounded 25 Chinese guards and destroyed Chinese temples and houses. The note complained that 'Indian reactionaries' were at the 'height of their frenzy', and issued a warning in no uncertain terms: 'Do not misjudge the situation and repeat your mistake of 1962.'

Indeed, India did not repeat its mistakes. Over the next five days, the Indian Army hit back with superior artillery and fought a few hand-to-hand battles at Nathu La. The duel continued for four days after which the Nathu La fight effectively came to an end without any ingress by the Chinese. This conclusion for India may not have been possible without Sagat and his troops. Having gained an upper hand since he took command in 1965, Sagat was not the man to give it up, come what may. Keeping national interest in mind, Sagat was prepared to take on the Chinese with all the resources at his command, even at the risk of incurring the disapproval of his superior commanders and putting his future career prospects on the line.[19] It is said that Sagat made himself unavailable on radio and telephone during the course of the fighting as he continued to conduct the battles according to his own plan and until all Chinese positions at the pass had been neutralised. Thereafter, a ceasefire was declared and bodies of the dead exchanged.

The Cho La Conflict

The situation remained volatile for some time, resulting in several clashes after the Nathu La 'incident' as it came to be known. The most serious one, however, was the firefight that broke out at Cho La, north of Nathu La on 1 October 1967. Chinese troops surrounded an Indian sentry post that was located at point 15,450, which was claimed by the Chinese. A heated argument took place between the Indian post commander, Nb. Sub. Gyan Bahadur Limbu of 7/11 Gorkha Rifles and the local Chinese company commander.

A Chinese soldier bayoneted the Indian JCO in the arm, which led to a close quarter battle. While the Gorkhas beheaded a number of Chinese, the officiating company commander, Lt R.S. Rathore was killed, along with 21 Indian soldiers. The Chinese were able to occupy the post, but only temporarily.

According to Major General V.K. Singh's accounts, 'this Gorkha unit launched a brutal khukri assault to evict the Chinese who had intruded. They gave the Chinese side a "bloody nose", compelling them to vacate the post so that once again, they could occupy the higher position'.[20] In fact, on that day, Indian soldiers of 7/11 Gorkha Rifles fought and pushed back the Chinese by a couple of kilometres.[21]

It took some time for the situation to revert to status quo, but an aura of menace hung over the sector. The Chinese, however, did not push matters much. Over a period, India's forward policy resulted in the 'watershed' being occupied in strength. It is said that Sagat Singh's actions had annoyed people in Delhi. He was posted out in December 1967, although he had commanded this division for the required two years. (Sagat later earned fame for his daring blitzkrieg to Dhaka in the 1971 Indo-Pak war.)

The Inside Stories

When the skirmish broke out in 1967, Sagat was at the forefront giving ground instructions to his troops to hold on. However, when some troops fled from the battle scene, he directly intervened. The two platoons earmarked to support the troops did not react. Some of them even ran away. Major General Sagat then snatched a sten gun and stood on the road coming down from Nathu La, along with the Subedar Major of 2 Grenadiers, to stem the rout. He threatened to shoot anyone he found moving to the rear. So, they collected whatever men were available and sent them forward.[22]

Another account of Nathu La is drawn from the personal diary of Col. N.C. Gupta, who was a young second lieutenant posted to Nathu La at the time and recorded the events in his diary. His version reveals a detail missing from official records.

Sent to restore communication at the south shoulder post at the height of fire, Gupta found that faulty communication was not the reason why the post was not responding. It was in fact because the post was deserted. Designed for an entire platoon, Gupta found it completely empty. He then 'resorted to intermittent firing' to give the impression that the post was occupied. He held the post alone for four hours before reinforcements reached him. He also had to leave the post briefly to find a platoon headed by Attar Singh, and then guide them back to the post and re-group. Gupta recorded that over 90 soldiers of the 2 Grenadiers had abandoned the post. More than 36 were later court-martialled. Gupta received a Sena Medal, and was acknowledged for his bravery during 1967 within the army.[23]

Aftermath of Battle

Many acts of unprecedented valour were performed and Sagat Singh ensured that they received due recognition. The injured Col. Rai Singh was awarded the Mahavir Chakra for his actions under fire. Of the officers who were killed at Nathu La, Major Harbhajan Singh of 18th Rajput was awarded a Mahavir Chakra and Capt. Dagar of 2 Grenadiers was awarded the Vir Chakra posthumously.

There were also a few cases of desertion of duty which Sagat enquired into and the guilty were brought before military courts. Those found guilty were severely punished.[24] Each of these incidents, coming as they did just five years after the 1962 war, was a short and bloody affair. The skirmish at Nathu

La lasted just four days from 11 September to 15 September while the Cho La incident was for just one day, on 1 October. Officially, India claimed to have lost 88 soldiers (with 62 at Nathu La, 21 later at Chola, about five from the adjoining post of 10 JAK Rifles)[25] and inflicted up to 340 casualties on the Chinese. Beijing admitted to losing 65 soldiers at Nathu La and an unknown number in the Cho La incident. Though no civilian lives were lost, there was massive loss to property due to Chinese bombardment of civilian areas in Sikkim.

Forgotten Victory

The 1967 battles of Nathu La and Cho La changed the Sino-Indian political dynamics dramatically. Yet, why has this resounding victory, which was achieved after India's humiliating military rout in 1962, been forgotten? Indian Army veteran Probal Das Gupta says, 'When you look at 1971, China didn't interfere in the India-Pakistan war. Not many have asked why. There are many reasons why 1967 is an important yet underrated reason why China did not go down the Siliguri corridor and cut India out. At various subsequent stand-offs, whether it is Daulat Beg Oldi or Doklam in 2017, India has always used that template and obtained a dominating position in confrontations against China. Hence, there was a parity that was obtained in 1967, which got back India's pride and was also responsible in conveying to China that they may be militarily a bigger power, but they could not overrun India anymore. I believe peace is obtained when you achieve parity.'[26]

In retrospect, had General Sagat Singh not stood his ground, Chinese troops stationed at Nathu La would have captured the pass. Could the Chinese have moved up into the Doklam plateau in those snow-filled winter months and threaten the Siliguri corridor, which had considerable importance for India's operations in East Pakistan? This is still a matter of debate in Indian military circles.

The clash didn't cause much international concern. The Indian deputy prime minister, Morarji Desai, was on a visit to the US when the clashes started. In Washington, DC, the Nathu La skirmish ranked second only to an update from Vietnam—where the US had entered the second decade of its war as per US president Lyndon B. Johnson's secret daily briefing from the CIA. Yet, despite the severity of the incident, it appears that Washington never believed it could grow into a larger conflict.

They were right, for the skirmish did not escalate into a full-fledged war. This was perhaps due to another player in the game. A CIA assessment from the time notes a sudden increase in Soviet military build-up on the Chinese border from 15 divisions to 21 ground divisions. It is difficult to establish its cause and effect, but the pressure on Indian borders may have eased because Chinese attention was diverted to its Manchurian border, where Russia, a former ally, now branded 'Revisionist Traitors' by the CPC, had sent in tank divisions in a dispute that culminated in 1969's Sino-Soviet border conflict.

Nonetheless, the diplomatic chill continued. A note from China to India dated 8 October 1967 expresses displeasure over an Indian secret agent following and interrogating non-Chinese embassy personnel in New Delhi. In December 1967, China made another strong protest against the harassment of a Tibetan who left the Chinese embassy in Delhi with Chairman Mao badges, Chinese tea and cigarettes.

In spite of these hostile exchanges, all visible Chinese aggression or Indian assertiveness on the border that led to further violence had ended. The two countries returned to the relatively safe cover of covert operations in each other's ambit as in India's northeast, where the Chinese continued to lend secret assistance to insurgents.

India's attitude towards China remained defensive despite some successes against Pakistan in the 1965 war. Thus, despite a fierce fight by the soldiers of the Grenadiers and Gorkha units, which suffered hundreds of casualties, these actions was reported little in the media.[27]

Today, China is building up its infrastructure on the Tibetan Plateau at an alarming pace and training troops for high altitude warfare. Its build-up for any offensive action hereafter would be at a faster rate than hitherto fore. It also remains aware that operations across the watershed will be on much difficult terrain and against an army, which will not be a pushover as it was in NEFA in 1962. The ill-feeling was exacerbated, on India's side, by growing evidence of Sino-Pak collaboration. A series of notes passed back and forth between the MEA, New Delhi, the Indian embassy in China and the Chinese foreign ministry reveal a palpable nervousness over the emergence of a dangerous new strategic reality.

8
CHINA'S STRATEGIC INTRUSIONS

China appeared to be willing to resolve the Sino-Indian border dispute until the early 1980s. Thereafter, it changed tack. On a visit to India in April 1960, Zhou had offered to settle China's boundary dispute with India by swapping territories based on the respective claims of both countries, which meant that the Chinese would give up their claim beyond the McMahon Line in the territory of NEFA in return for China being allowed to keep Aksai Chin. New Delhi, however, rejected this offer.

The Indian government believed that the Thagla Ridge was a clear delineation of a watershed line that marked the McMahon Line, which was stated to be India's boundary claim line in India's northeast since the time of Nehru. Even after the bitter border conflict in 1962, there was no exchange of territories on the NEFA front even though Chinese troops had entered way beyond the McMahon Line up to Tawang. To India's surprise and Nehru's relief, the PLA had unilaterally withdrawn to their original positions in NEFA, unlike in eastern Ladakh. Unlike Tawang, China had chosen to hold on to its territorial gains along Aksai Chin in 1962 and still controls this region. Until the Nathu La and Cho La incidents in 1967 (as explained earlier in this book), the Chinese did not make any major intrusions on the Sino-Indian boundary.

Two decades later, apparently keen to settle the border

dispute with its neighbour, Chinese leader Deng Xiaoping offered India a package boundary deal. In 1979, in his meeting with Atal Bihari Vajpayee, then the external affairs minister, Deng offered Vajpayee a comprehensive settlement based on the exchange of claimed territories in the two sectors, which would settle matters for good, subject to certain adjustments 'here and there' as necessary.[1] Further, if the package deal as a solution to the boundary dispute 'was not possible at an early date, Deng recommended cooperation in other domains'.[2] Talks on the boundary issue thus commenced in 1980, but went on without any swift resolution.

Differences of opinion began to re-emerge between India and China from 1984 on the exact alignment of the McMahon Line, which divides the Indian territories from Chinese-held parts of southern Tibet. This was more so essentially in the areas north of Tawang and around this monastery town. The Chinese, too, lay claim on this territory.

Tawang is the birthplace of the sixth Dalai Lama, habituated largely by an ethnic group called the Monpas, who are not Tibetans, but follow Tibetan style Buddhism. These Monpas have had an allegiance to Lhasa's religious-cum-temporal governments. Apart from traditional donations, taxes were collected by both the monasteries and administrative officials with allegiance to Lhasa. Based on this administrative history, China claimed that the Tawang tract or region belonged to China—which now controlled Tibet—and not because of any ethnic links. The Monpas of Tawang have, however, repeatedly stated that they have no wish to be a part of China, both individually and through their elected political leaders.[3] But since early 1951, India had established control over this region, following the expedition of Major Bob Khathing.[4] Thus, neither China nor India was in any mood to give up Tawang. Moreover, India, having learnt its lessons from the 1962 military debacle, had built up its capabilities to defend the entire region south of the McMahon Line.

It soon became apparent to the Chinese that India wasn't keen to settle all the outstanding boundary issues and wanted to leave it hanging indefinitely, as 'giving away' of any territory claimed by independent India, for a 'give and take' settlement would have a serious negative fallout across India. Thus, China changed its position. It decided on a 'grab what you can' approach across the unsettled boundaries. The military intrusions in the Sumdorong Chu Valley near Tawang, south of Thagla Ridge, where the 1962 conflict had begun, is a case in point. These intrusions commenced in 1986–87 in Arunachal Pradesh and took several years to diffuse.

A Military Stand-off

The area north of Tawang up to the Thagla Ridge was considered neutral until 1980. Indian troops began patrolling those areas from 1981 onwards. By the summer of 1984, the Sashastra Seema Bal, India's boundary paramilitary force, established a post in the area that was vacated in the harsh winter. Even the Indian Army commenced patrols in this area south of the Thagla Ridge in 1984. The Indian detachments would vacate the area in the winter months and return in summer next year. However, when Indian troops returned in 1986, a patrol of 12 Assam, an Indian Army infantry unit, detected Chinese troop intrusions on 16 June 1986.

The actual region of the incursion near the Thagla Ridge has been described as the Thandrong pasture on the banks of the Sumdurong Chu and the Wangdung region, which falls in the Zimithang circle of Tawang district. This region has been located to the north of the McMahon Line as per Indian accounts. Sumdorong Chu—referred to as Sangduoluo by the

Chinese media—is a rivulet flowing north–south in the Thag La triangle, bounded by Bhutan in the west and the Thag La Ridge to the north. This region falls along a traditional route from Lhasa to Tawang, and from there to the Brahmaputra Valley, which had witnessed serious clashes in the 1962 conflict. However, since then (1962/63) it was considered neutral zone, and wasn't monitored by India between 1977 and 1980. However, with the improvement of communication lines and the ability to better maintain its troops in the forward localities, the Indian Army sought to reinforce its defences in Arunachal Pradesh in the early 1980s. Patrols resumed in 1981 and by the summer of 1984, India had established an observation post on the bank of Sumdorong Chu which allowed Indian troops to view Chinese positions on the other side of Thag La Ridge. This observation (look out) post was manned by personnel of the Special Security Bureau through the summer and vacated in the winter.[5]

Prior to 1986, IB teams also made visits to Sumdurong Chu, on the far side of the Nyamjang Chu, the river that originates in the eastern Himalayas and flows through Tibet into India. Both the Sumdorong Chu and Namka Chu rivers flowed into this north–south flowing river, the former from the east and the latter from the west. The IB teams did not report anything unusual. But when Indian troops returned in 1986, a patrol of 12 Assam detected Chinese troop intrusions on 16 June 1986. This was confirmed by Col. A.K. Jayachandran: 'There was no Listening Post of the Intelligence Bureau (IB) there. For most part it was an unoccupied area from both sides. The IB was located way behind at T Gompa and Sungetsar. They gathered their Intelligence by talking to grazier and local shepherds. The Chinese presence in Sumdorung was noticed first by local graziers who reported it to the IB, sometime around early 1986, who further reported it up their chain. The Army was told to verify this and a patrol of 12 Assam under Capt. S.M. Tabib was despatched post haste on 16 Jun 1986. The patrol went up to Lungrola and beyond, covering approximately 4 days at an altitude of about 14000 ft. Capt Tabib's patrol confirmed the presence of Chinese at Wangdung.'[6]

However, in June of 1986, once the patrol from the 12 Assam had reported that a sizable number of Chinese troops were already present and engaged in constructing permanent structures, the Government of India, on 26 June 1986, lodged a formal protest with Beijing against intrusions in this region by Chinese troops. Beijing denied any such intrusions and maintained that its troops were in a location north of the McMahon Line, while the official Indian stance was that the Chinese troops had intruded south of the McMahon Line.[7]

India protested against this intrusion through diplomatic channels on 26 June 1986 and the matter was 'intensely' discussed during the seventh round of border talks, held between 21 July and 23 July 1986. It is said that the Indian government made an offer that if the Chinese agreed to withdraw from the areas around Sumdurong Chu, the Indian troops wouldn't occupy the areas vacated by the Chinese the following summer. The Chinese denied any intrusions and insisted that their troops were north of the 'so-called' McMahon Line. Thus, as the stand-off continued, the Chinese 'dug in' and prepared to stay for the winter.[8]

Initial reports had indicated that around 40 Chinese soldiers had led the intrusion, but soon their numbers increased to 200. The Indian army patrols found that the Chinese had even constructed a helipad at Wangdung for visitors, troops and air-supplies of rations and essentials by August 1986.[9]

This issue became a matter of public debate in the Indian parliament. By October 1986, Deng issued a warning to New Delhi, that if India continued to nibble away at Chinese territory, China would have to 'teach India a lesson'. This threat was sent through the US Defence Secretary, when he arrived in New Delhi from Beijing.[10] The threat had echoes of 1962, but even as the Rajiv Gandhi-led government fumbled with its responses, the Indian Army chief decided to step in.

General Sundarji

General Krishnaswamy Sundarji, Chief of Indian Army, is perhaps the most cerebral chief that the Indian Army has had. An infantry officer of the Mahar regiment, his forte was the planning of large-scale mechanised operations. In late 1986, Sundarji had directed the mobilisation of the Indian Armed Forces along the Indo-Pak border in Rajasthan as part of Exercise Brass Tacks, which he had planned and war-gamed at various levels. He knew his options against Pakistan rather well, having also commanded India's then most potent Pakistan-centric military force, the army's Western Command.

Early in his career as an infantry officer, Sundarji was the first to be given command of India's first armoured division and was compared in hushed whispers with Germany's General Erwin Rommel. He also knew the Chinese front on the McMahon Line well, having commanded the Siliguri based XXXIII Corps, the same corps under which Major General Sagat Singh had given the Chinese a bloody nose at Nathu La.

Sundarji's higher command course report at the Command and General Staff College in the US had apparently stated that 'he was fit to command the NATO army'. This was not possible as Sundarji was in the Indian Army and India was not a part of NATO. However, Sundarji went on to do something bigger than what NATO forces did with their annual military training exercise, Autumn Forge. Hence, Exercise Brass Tacks[11] against Pakistan and then the stand-off with the Chinese following the Sumdurong Chu incident afforded General Sundarji just the opportunity he was waiting for!

Exercise Chequerboard

General Sundarji decided that the situation on the Indo-China border merited a military response. He ordered the airlift of troops between 18 October and 20 October 1986. This initial heli-lift operation involved a brigade of over 2,000 infantrymen from 5 Mountain Division. They were well acclimatised and knew the terrain well. It was commanded by Brig. 'Bantu' Batra, a dynamic armoured corps officer, who was towards the end of his tenure and was later relieved by Brig. (later Lt Gen.) B.S. 'Bhupi' Malik, of the Gorkha Regiment, after the unit in location was suitably deployed.[12]

Code-named 'Op-Falcon', the Indian Army had deployed additional troops on the Hathung La Ridge overlooking Sumdorong Chu along with three other key mountain features, to breathe down the Chinese in that valley by 20 October. Ironically, it was the same day 24 years ago that China had attacked India at these very locations! In 1962, the Chinese were on the high ground; this time, it was the Indians.[13] It didn't stop there. As China had to save face, it ordered a general mobilisation along the entire Sino-Indian front. But this was also in keeping with General Sundarji's prediction and prepared plan of action.

He initiated a major operational deployment code-named 'Exercise Chequerboard'. For this, Sundarji used the maximum possible heli-lift capability of the Indian Air Force. He ordered almost all the reserve formations of the Indian Army to move up towards the McMahon Line.

It involved 10 divisions of the Indian Army—with about 7,500 men in each division—and several squadrons of the Indian Air Force and saw the redeployment of troops at several places in the North-East. For instance, the Indian Army had reportedly moved three divisions to operational positions around

Wangdung, where they were supplied and maintained solely by air. These troop reinforcements were over and above the 50,000 troops, which in itself were at least five times more than what had existed in 1962, when China had attacked. These troops were positioned as per their traditional deployments across Arunachal Pradesh.[14]

This impressive demonstration of military power had China quite literally stumped and the Chinese leader Deng Xiaoping himself issued a threat. As stated earlier, in October 1986, he warned New Delhi that if it continued nibbling across the border, China would have to 'teach India a lesson'. This threat was identical to that made to Vietnam in 1979.

Political Action

Rajiv Gandhi learnt of the seriousness of the situation on 4 December 1986 at the Navy Day reception in Delhi, where it is customary for political, bureaucratic and civilian leaders to be present. Suitably alarmed, Rajiv summoned Sundarji and all civil and military officials connected with such matters of national security to the Operations Room in South Block.

During this meeting, General Sundarji held his ground while the civilian leadership weren't clear about India's policy on dealing with the Chinese on the boundary and what should be done.[15]

Indian journalist and author Manoj Joshi sums up the situation: 'Sundarji told him (Rajiv) that they [the Indian Army's actions] were a result of a Cabinet Committee on Security decision in 1983 ordering the Army to take up positions that would enable the defence of Tawang. While the Army had gone about the process methodically over the past years, the politicians and "babus" had simply not paid attention. There was a heated argument at this point, with some officials wondering whether the Army had exceeded its brief and whether it was really necessary to occupy Hathung La and the surrounding features. Sundarji riposted that in the Army's professional judgment, it was. And, offering them the pointer he was using [to show places on the map], he said that if they wanted other advice, they were welcome to seek it. It didn't take much to remind the officials that civilian interference in operational matters was what had led to the disaster of 1962—they backed off.'[16]

Later, to further strengthen its ownership over the region, the Indian parliament voted for statehood for NEFA and the new state of Arunachal Pradesh was created in December 1986. The Indian government elevated the status of Arunachal Pradesh into a full-fledged state of the Indian Union. This sent a clear message to China that this territory was non-negotiable. Beijing and its various media arms protested, but India's response was that this was India's internal matter. Yet, China was unwilling to relent on its claims. By 1987, the Chinese army on the frontlines appeared determined to stay, having deployed its troops around Sumdurong Chu in the winter before Indian troops could return in the spring of 1987.

High-level Talks

China already had a sizeable military presence on the Tibetan plateau, but by early 1987 it is said that Beijing had further augmented its forces with another 20,000 troops from the 53rd Army Corps in Chengdu and the 13th Army in Lanzhou, along with heavy artillery and helicopters. By early April, it had moved eight divisions into eastern Tibet as a prelude to possible belligerent action. On India's part, troop movements that had begun with Operation Falcon in late 1986 continued through early 1987 under the massive air-land operation exercise 'Chequerboard'.

As the border became tense, Prime Minister Rajiv Gandhi acknowledged the situation in his speech to Parliament on

3 March 1987. He stated: 'There has been tension on our border with China. We want a peaceful settlement of the border issue. It will need wisdom and statesmanship. It will need vision and firmness. Firmness is included in wisdom.... It is this perspective that should guide our countries in seeking a solution to the problem.' The stand-off, however, continued until May 1987, despite the warnings issued by China and with troops in eyeball-to-eyeball contact in Hathung La. The rapid and powerful response by the Indian Army in 1986–87 had made it clear to China that the equation had changed and the Indian Army was no more a pushover.

This strained situation was resolved after the Indian foreign minister, N.D. Tiwari, made a deliberate stopover in Beijing on his way to Pyongyang in May 1987. During this visit, both sides affirmed a desire for dialogue on the boundary issue. Thus, in August 1987, Indian and Chinese troops moved back to their original positions that placed them reasonably far apart, following a meeting of their field commanders. In the eighth round of border talks in November 1987, it was agreed that the level of engagement must be upgraded from the bureaucratic level to a political level.[17]

India's firm response to China's threats paved the way for Rajiv Gandhi's visit to China in 1988, when China extended the 'olive branch' and where he was treated with new-found respect. Both countries agreed to the setting up of a Joint Working Group (JWG) that would discuss ways for alignments of the LAC, with confidence-building measures (CBMs). Eventually, this led to an agreement to maintain peace and tranquillity on the border in 1993.[18] This led to a relatively peaceful Sino-Indian front, at least after the Sumdurong stand-off until the Doklam stand-off in 2017, with the exception of Chinese firing on an Indian patrol, where four Indian soldiers were killed in October 1975.

Incident Analysis

For India, the Sumdurong Chu incident was certainly a wake-up call. General Sundarji used the new awareness in South Block about the China threat, to push the authorities in New Delhi to undertake many road construction schemes, building of air strips and advance landing grounds for the IAF that had been withheld until then, on the presumption that good roads in the border areas on the Sino-Indian front would allow Chinese troops to easily roll into the plains, as they were poised to do after the rout of the Indian frontlines in 1962!

It also led to China inviting General Sundarji for a visit, as the Chinese were apparently keen to meet and gauge the man who had put them in a spot! His reputation preceded him as the Chinese believed he had put the fear of a possible Indian invasion amongst the Pakistani generals, with Exercise Brass Tacks.

However, a visit by an Indian Army chief to China didn't happen until 1994, when General B.C. Joshi went to China.[19] Sundarji, by the autumn of 1987, had fallen out of favour with Rajiv Gandhi and the Indian civilian establishment for what was seen as brinkmanship following the intervention by Indian Peace Keeping Force (IPKF) in Sri Lanka becoming a mess. Nevertheless, Sundarji was regarded by some as the only Indian general after the 1971 Indo-Pak war 'to have had a marked influence, by the sheer force of his personality'.[20]

Finally, there are differing opinions about why border tensions had escalated in 1986–87. The Australian author Neville Maxwell is said to hold India solely responsible for the escalation just as he has largely done in his book on the 1962 conflict. He didn't blame General Sundarji though. He blamed Gandhi for using the military stand-off as an opportunity to rouse nationalistic sentiments, so that he could impose an internal emergency and unite the nation.

He was clearly off the mark, as the course of events explained earlier have been confirmed by several keen observers. The other view is that India wanted to test the extent of Sino-Soviet ties and how that could have an impact on Indo-Soviet relations. This too has little basis, as India's diplomats and the political establishment only realised the gravity of the situation on 4 January 1987 (as explained earlier), well after General Sundarji had initiated Op-Falcon and the subsequent deployments.[21]

In India, it became evident that following the Sumdurong Chu face-off, Beijing wasn't able to micro-manage developments on the Sino-Indian front, as it had done in earlier years, more so as India had reacted in the past in a predictable manner, by steering clear of upsetting the Chinese with any aggressive counter actions. But Op-Falcon and Chequerboard sent out a strong message to Beijing. After this incident, China was keen to reach a settlement over the boundary issue.

The Line of Actual Control

China agreed to sign the Border Peace and Tranquillity Agreement (BPTA) during the visit of India's prime minister P.V. Narasimha Rao to Beijing in 1993, though its officials had emphasised that arrangements for maintenance of peace and tranquillity on the LAC 'should not automatically imply agreement between India and China as to the alignment of the LAC'.[22]

Neither was India comfortable in accepting the ceasefire line nor the proposed 1959 or 1960 claim lines by China as the boundary in Aksai Chin in east Ladakh. Hence, India went a step further to state that the LAC of 1993 reflected the ground realities then, not the territorial claims, thus implying that representatives of the two nations were expected to clarify the overlapping claims between the two neighbours in their meetings and talks. Therefore, a group of experts, including both diplomats and military men was assembled under the JWG with the primary responsibility of ironing out all the differing views about the LAC. Although the JWG held some 15 meetings between 1989 and 2005, the differences about the LAC remained.[23]

Historically, China has been interpreting the boundary line as per its own convenience. The former Indian National Security Advisor (NSA), Ambassador Shivshanker Menon stated that 'China has been using the term "Line of Actual Control" to shape the border discourse in their own favour.' He further stated: 'In their occupation of Aksai Chin in the western sector for instance and in the east, China declared that the LAC largely followed the "illegal McMahon Line", which was delineated on a map and generally followed the Himalayan watershed. Similar conditions were absent in the west. Neither India nor China exercised any settled jurisdiction or regular administration in the Aksai Chin area.' In fact, there was a vacuum that China had filled because it had used the old trading track that passed from Xinjiang through Aksai Chin to occupy Tibet. Thereafter it had built a case to justify its occupation.

For instance, on 23 January 1959, Premier Zhou Enlai had for the first time informed Nehru that 'the Sino-Indian boundary has never been formally delineated'. Later, Zhou wrote, 'There are certain differences' over the border. He proposed that the two sides maintain the status quo with 'each side for the time being keeping to the border areas at present under its jurisdiction and not go beyond them'. In another letter in November 1959, Zhou had proposed that both sides withdraw 20 kilometres from 'the so called McMahon Line' in the east and 'from the line up to which each side exercises actual control in the west'. At the end of the same year, on 17 December, Zhou told Nehru that 'the line up to which each side exercises actual control in this sector is very clear, just as it is in the other sectors of the Sino-Indian border'. He said this conformed to a map that had been published in China in 1956.[24] It took nearly four decades, but discussions by the JWG managed to change the narrative.

A Slew of Pacts

By 1996, there was one major breakthrough. When China and India signed a significant CBM in November 1996, they sought to not just maintain status quo along the LAC, but to actually attempt a purposeful thinning of military forces and deployments through negotiations contingent upon working out a mutually acceptable LAC! This was to be followed by arrangements that had long titles, but actually meant the same thing. For instance, there was the 'Agreement on Political Parameters and Guiding Principles for the Settlement of the India China Boundary Question' signed on 11 April 2005, with its key element—Article IX—reiterating that the JWG experts must continue to work towards the 'clarification of the line of actual control'. On the same day, the two sides also signed a protocol to deepen the CBM regime on the border. These 'Modalities for the Implementation of Confidence Building Measures in the Military Field along the Sino-Indian Border' set up the Standard Operating Procedures (SOPs) for the military in the event that a Chinese patrol met an Indian one in a contested area, or vice versa. They would display a banner on which would be emblazoned, 'This is Indian/Chinese territory.' They would then unfurl a second banner with the words, 'Turn around and go back to your side.' Such incidents where these banners were shown came to be known as 'face-offs'.[25] Then came the global economic crisis and a revolt by the Tibetans that threatened to upset the apple cart.

SOPs to the Rescue

The year 2008 was significant for a number of reasons, for both China and India. China was drawing praise for how its economy had weathered the global economic crisis of 2007–08. However, China's coming-out party—the clinical efficiency with which it had organised the Beijing Olympics in 2008—was spoilt following a major revolt by the Tibetans. It took the CPC leadership by surprise, as Beijing was under the impression that the situation in Tibet was well under control. No sooner had the revolt begun in Lhasa, the unrest rapidly spread to Tibetan-inhabited areas in China, outside of Tibet. Beijing blamed the unrest on the Dalai Lama and the Tibetans residing in India.[26]

Adding to China's concerns was the signing of the Indo-US nuclear agreement and New Delhi's decision to upgrade the infrastructure on the Sino-Indian boundary areas, in accordance with recommendations from the China Study Group (CSG), a multi-agency that was established in 1975 by the government of Mrs Indira Gandhi. It is mandated to advise the Indian government on the policies to adopt on China.[27] This required the completion of 73 China–India border roads and tunnels to connect the highways as well as a trans-Arunachal highway besides enhancement of Indian military capabilities across the board along the LAC. Thus, the Manmohan Singh led 'UPA government sanctioned the creation of two new mountain divisions for the Indian Army and the deployment of additional armoured, mechanised units along the LAC. Four advanced landing grounds were activated by the IAF in Chushul, Fukche, Demchok and Daulat Beg Oldi with top-of-the-line fighter aircrafts like the SU 30MKI stationed in Tezpur, Chabua and Bareilly. Importantly, these decisions were backed by a steadily growing Indian economy.'[28] However, with the increase in capabilities and enhancement of troops deployed, there were more reports on boundary incursions by patrols on both sides.[29]

For a decade, between 1993 and 2013, China and India had followed a predictable routine: their troops patrolled to the extent of what they saw as the LAC and both sides followed the SOPs that had been worked out in 2005. In 2013, however, when the PLA established an isolated camp of five tents 19 kilometres inside what India considers the LAC in the Depsang plains, alarm bells started ringing in South Block, leading the Indian government to re-examine the boundary dispute and its role in the bilateral relationship. The three-week stand-off, however, ended as suddenly as it had begun, perhaps because New Delhi threatened to call off the visit of Chinese premier Li Keqiang, scheduled for 18 May 2013. Eventually, this led to the signing of a new Border Defence Cooperation Agreement (BDCA) in October 2013, which called for a freeze on the military situation on the boundary. It had an interesting aspect: it brought the Chinese military directly into border management, as the Chinese signatory to this 'agreement' was Admiral Sun Jianguo, the Deputy Chief of Staff of the PLA.[30] On India's part, the signatory was the defence secretary, who is responsible for the 'defence of India', not the service chiefs as is commonly believed.

However, China's continued pattern of encroachments and incursions was not uncommon in the undemarcated areas along the LAC. Thus, after Depsang in 2013, it was Chumar in 2014 and Pangong Tso in 2019. In each case, the Chinese went on to physically occupy some parts of the LAC and then prevented the movement of Indian patrols, particularly in places where the claims of the two countries overlapped. The permanent occupation of any territories, however, was avoided (until the Chinese incursions in Ladakh in 2020) and tense situations were averted after both sides took recourse to the accepted SOPs. What was the purpose of these Chinese incursions?

Battle over Boundaries

There seems to be a general consensus in India that the Chinese motivation for pushing troops forward on the Himalayan boundary was part of its strategy to convey that the boundary issue was far from settled, more so after India had shown little interest in its earlier proposal of settling matters by swapping Aksai Chin for Arunachal Pradesh.

Former Indian NSA and a former foreign secretary, Shivshankar Menon summed it up in an interview in 2015 when he said: 'We have got it to the point where it (a settlement) can be done by an act of political will on both sides. Multiple rounds of talks by special representatives of both governments have done the required technical work and it is now the matter of a political decision.'[31] However, Shyam Saran, also a former Indian foreign secretary and a media commentator, asserted that 'for any settlement to be politically acceptable in India, it must be "LAC plus"'. This implies that India retains what it has in the east and China concedes some territory to India in the west! For India, this is the additional territory that China occupied in the west, beyond its own 1959 claim. Until then, 'the current situation will continue fairly indefinitely', predicts Joshi.[32]

On the other hand, Saran points out that given China's repeated insistence in demanding Tawang, the border settlement has a wider context. Since the mid-1980s, the Chinese have strategically adopted an approach of linking the western (Ladakh) boundary issue with that of the eastern (Arunachal) boundary, in contrast to the Indian stand that the boundary issues in these two sectors should be considered separately. Thus, it was only in the middle sector, where the claim lines ran along the Indian states of Himachal Pradesh and Uttar Pradesh, that the Chinese were willing to even exchange maps and discuss India's claims on the disputed Himalayan frontiers. Any future disputes that arise—as witnessed in 2020 following the fighting and the military stand-off on the LAC—can only be resolved if the Chinese would be willing to at least exchange maps. The Chinese have been extremely reluctant to do so.[33] Further, it wasn't just the battle over boundaries between China and India that was the issue. In June 2017, Indian troops became engaged in what perhaps became, until 2020, their longest ever stand-off on an issue that actually was a matter between Bhutan and China, but had serious security implications for India.

Doklam Stand-off

Even as the leaders of India and China—Prime Minister Narendra Modi and President Xi Jinping—were meeting on the sidelines of the Shanghai Cooperation Organisation's summit at Astana, in Kazakhstan, there were reports of a new Sino-Indian stand-off on the boundary tri-junction between China, Bhutan and India. This is a region in north Sikkim and a part of India which lies between Nepal and Bhutan.

This stand-off took place around the Doklam plateau,[34] presently referred to as the Dolam Plateau, which is Bhutanese territory, but China lay claim to it based on its interpretation of the Anglo-Chinese Convention of 1890 to which Bhutan was not a signatory. This convention has in any case been overtaken by later-day agreements with Bhutan in 1988, 1998 and 2012, which clearly advocate the maintenance of status quo in the disputed areas until the issues are resolved through dialogue.

To prove their claim over this region, the Chinese also incorrectly cite a letter written by Nehru on 22 March 1959. Nehru had stated in this letter that the Convention of 1890 also defined the boundary between Sikkim and Tibet, which was later, in 1895, demarcated. There is thus no dispute regarding the boundary of Sikkim with Tibet region. The letter clearly refers to the boundary in northern Sikkim and not to the tri-junction region, which needed to be discussed with Bhutan and Sikkim, which is today being disputed due to differences in map interpretation. Also, let us not forget that the 1890 treaty was an unequal treaty as Tibet, Sikkim and Bhutan were not involved.[35]

It is in this contentious tri-junction region that the so-called Chinese intrusion took place. The Bhutanese call this tri-junction region Doka La. The Chinese, however, believe the tri-junction is located at a place called Gamochen, about 15 kilometres south of Doka La. The Chinese are building a road in this direction and the Bhutanese are objecting to it, saying Beijing is intruding into its territory. India states the tri-junction is located at Batang La, about 6.5 kilometres north of Gamochen.[36]

In fact, while several terms were used to describe the area of tensions—from Dokla to Dolam to Doka La—Doklam, is referred to as the 'Dolam Plateau' by the Indian Ministry of External Affairs and the Embassy of Bhutan in New Delhi.[37] Although the military stand-off came to be known as the Doklam stand-off, the Doklam Plateau is about 30 kilometres away from the stand-off point at Dolam, near Doka La! As this study has shown, claims and counter-claims have dominated the century of discord on the Himalayas.

More than two dozen meetings had taken place between Bhutan and China on this issue without any headway. In fact, two decades prior to the stand-off, in 1996, China had offered Bhutan a deal, 'to exchange Pasamlung and Jakarlung valleys (495 square kilometres) with the pastureland of Doklam, Sinchulung, Dramana and Shakhatoe (269 square kilometres). Sensitive to the threat Doklam may pose once handed over to China, Bhutan has evaded Chinese pressure. Till date, there have been 24 rounds of border talks between Bhutan and China and

Beijing seems to have been frustrated after the Bhutanese failed to yield to their demands,' says Col. Anil Bhat.[38] Therefore, the Chinese resorted to grab what they could. 'China's attempt to build a road through the Dolam plateau is an attempt to change the status quo and is in violation of the agreements between Bhutan and China,' writes the scholar Apoorva Goel, in an essay detailing the cause underlying the stand-off near Doklam.

India's Security Concerns

With the Chinese following their infamous strategy of salami slicing into parts of unoccupied territories, India was rightly concerned with this Chinese attempt to once again try and unilaterally alter the status quo, even as the agreement between the special representatives of India and China in 2012 provides that 'the two sides have to maintain the status quo until their competing claims are resolved in consultation with the third party'. Bhutan is the third party here as the territory claimed by China is that of Bhutan, but which the Bhutanese weren't equipped to defend.[39]

It was this Chinese attempt to alter the status quo, which could have major security implications for India, which led to the 72-day long military stand-off in 2017.

Chinese encroachments in this area towards the Jampheri Ridge would allow the Chinese to come closer to the southern tip of the Chumbi Valley, from which the district of Jalpaiguri—a major road and rail communication centre—could be threatened by any future Chinese attack and could even cut-off the entire northeast region of India from the rest of the country.

The Chinese had already constructed a major class 60 road that can carry heavy vehicles from Lhasa to Gyantse, which extends deeper inside the Chumbi Valley. Beyond that, it had built a smaller 20 kilometres long, class 5 track for light vehicles that came close to the Indian Army post at Doka La, which was the de facto border outpost frequented by Chinese military patrols. However, when China tried to encroach further, Indian troops stood up to Chinese intrusions. China had upped the ante by closing the pilgrims' route to Mansarovar via Nathu La Pass in Sikkim and issued veiled threats—as it often does—through its state-controlled publication *Global Times*, that it could review its policy on Sikkim and Bhutan.[40]

Despite Chinese intimidation, the Modi government chose to stand firm as India's ties with Bhutan were at stake. Also, the stand-off was being closely watched not only by the smaller countries of South Asia, but also Southeast Asia to see if India would blink first. There was hope that the Modi-Xi meeting at SCO in Astana would offer a way out. The joint statement that followed the meeting of these two leaders stated: 'There was an understanding that where we have differences, it is important that differences should not become disputes.'[41]

Triggers for Doklam

What had India done in this region that led to the Doklam stand-off as a consequence?[42] It was true that China was alarmed with India's infrastructural developments south of the McMahon Line in Arunachal Pradesh, Assam and Sikkim. China was also concerned with India's desire to raise a mountain strike corps with two army divisions and the construction of new bunkers. Thus, China initiated the construction of roads in that area and when the Royal Bhutan Army (RBA), which is trained and mentored by the Indian Military Training Team (IMTRAT) in Bhutan, had attempted to stall the Chinese, it was pushed back. In retrospect, the occurrence of a series of events could have triggered the crisis at Doklam.

For one, the Chinese army had been reorganised into theatre

commands with its Western Theatre Command (WTC) being the largest military command, after a merger between China's Chengdu and Lanzhou military regions. Soon it became clear that the WTC was being prepared for high-altitude permafrost zones like that in Xinjiang and Tibet as well as India's Ladakh and Arunachal regions. In May 2016, the *Global Times* also ran an editorial highlighting the importance of the WTC, especially in its role against India.[43]

In April 2017, the Dalai Lama, normally confined to the remote township of Dharamshala in India, was allowed to visit Arunachal Pradesh. This expectedly attracted Chinese criticism, and the Chinese foreign ministry was quick to threaten India, stating that 'India in disregard of China's concerns had obstinately arranged the Dalai Lama's visit to the disputed part of the eastern region of China-India border, causing serious damage to China's interests and China-India relations.'[44]

In May 2017, India refused to hail Xi's biggest project—the One Belt One Road (OBOR) that is now the Belt and Road Initiative—and declined to participate in its launch functions. Instead, on 26 May, barely three weeks before the stand-off, Modi inaugurated the Dhola-Sadiyabridge on Assam's River Lohit. The operation of this bridge would not only improve connectivity with Arunachal Pradesh, but also allow the Indian Army's 60-tonne Arjun and T-72 main battle tanks to be deployed in that region. On 16 June, 100 PLA soldiers shifted earth-moving units and four to five bulldozers to Doklam and began building a road towards Doka La.[45] For over two months thereafter, China remained adamant that it wouldn't back off.

Beijing's mouthpiece, *Global Times* asserted: 'India should abandon the fantasy of a long-term stand-off at Doklam. China will by no means agree to the withdrawal of troops from both sides in order for talks to be held. Doklam is Chinese territory. The withdrawal of Indian troops must be a precondition for talks and China will not compromise on this stance.... China cannot afford to lose an inch of territory. If New Delhi remains stubborn, India should be prepared for all possibilities from a potentially grave escalation of tension in the future.'[46] Reading between the lines, there was at play here a larger strategic Chinese game. Did China need a crisis?

Power Games

Doklam had a strategic implication for Xi's position in the Communist leadership. 'The episode was a tactfully timed move taking place just before the 19th Communist Party Congress was about to take place, where Xi was expected to further strengthen his position. Chinese muscle-flexing during the run up to the Doklam crisis played a major role in this affair. Hence, Doklam was meant to be a master move by Xi to win over the military and demonstrate his power to the Chinese people. It was for this reason Beijing continued to stir up the crisis even after both the sides had respectfully disengaged,' writes Col (retd) Anil Bhat.[47]

For India, the stand-off between Indian and Chinese troops near Sikkim was a clear departure from the Sino-Indian disagreements about their long-standing boundary disputes in the past. For the first time, the dispute was about a third country's territory. The Doklam Plateau belonged to Bhutan that already had an agreement with the Chinese recognising the same. India, however, had got embroiled in this Sino-Bhutanese issue for its own strategic reasons, even though Indian officials were citing the Indo-Bhutanese treaty of friendship as a reason for India to offer military support to Bhutan, if it were attacked or threatened.

India's reasons for taking on the Chinese, however, were primarily driven by the Indian Army's assessment that any further encroachment by the Chinese through road-building and other military activities on the Doklam Plateau would allow the Chinese to come closer to the Siliguri corridor which connects mainland India to India's north-eastern states. Therefore, India's military commanders, over the years, have watched the Chinese very carefully, especially as China continues to build a vast layout of roads and rail networks on the Sino-Indian frontline across the Himalayas. China's modus operandi is also well known as it has a notoriously long history of walking into others' lands, claiming the territory by changing the ground position and then citing ancient historical claims. China's approach to maps is also different from everyone else's because they are all about Beijing's intentions. Therefore, during the Doklam stand-off, Chinese diplomacy was about pressure and coercion, threats and intimidation, even though India was at a military advantage in the stand-off along the Sikkim frontline with the Chinese.

Doklam Impact

The Chinese had long been exploring an opportunity to enhance and strengthen their military positions in the Doklam part of the frontline, despite their agreement of 2012, not to alter the territorial status quo with India. The region is close to where India's military commanders had given Beijing a beating, be it through their proactive actions in Nathu La in 1967 or Sumdorong Chu in 1987.

India's handling of the Doklam stand-off, however, had successfully conveyed to her neighbours that India was unwilling to be browbeaten by China and it was willing to stand up for its friends like Bhutan, if push comes to shove.

Although India had stood up to the Chinese in support of Bhutan, Beijing was not willing to give up on its claim over the Doklam Plateau and the two valleys adjoining it, as it had added considerable strategic value to China's boundary claims with new infrastructure.

A few months after the Sino-Indian disengagement, news began to come in about the construction of a military complex by the Chinese in the disputed region. Chinese foreign ministry spokesman Lu Kang said: 'I have also noted the relevant report. I don't know who offered such kind of photos.... In order to patrol the border and improve the production and lives of border troops and residents, China has constructed infrastructure including roads in the Donglong (Doklam) area.'[48]

As India wasn't keen on pushing its card any further, the Chinese occupied an adjoining disputed site of about 90 square kilometres on the Bhutanese plateau and built another road there that gave them a somewhat similar access, to areas they could use in the event of a conflict.[49]

With China, India cannot ever let its guard down. This stand-off had not only questioned the limits of China's military power, but also sent a message to Pakistan, its closest ally in the region, that China can be challenged and still has some limitations. However, experts warn that India too must be prepared for consequences as China would instigate Pakistan to ramp up its terror game and show itself more aggressively in the unsettled boundaries around Kashmir and Ladakh, and in the Indian Ocean region.

A former Indian Army chief, General V.P. Malik, who had successfully led the Indian Army to evict Pakistani army, led intrusions from the heights around Kargil in 1999, wrote that 'while India had operational advantage at Doklam, it has to be prepared for skirmishes in any part of the Line of Actual Control—from Ladakh to Arunachal Pradesh'.[50]

India's problem, however, wasn't simply China's habit of minor intrusions, but the absence of recognition amongst India's leadership and policymakers that there could be a major intrusion

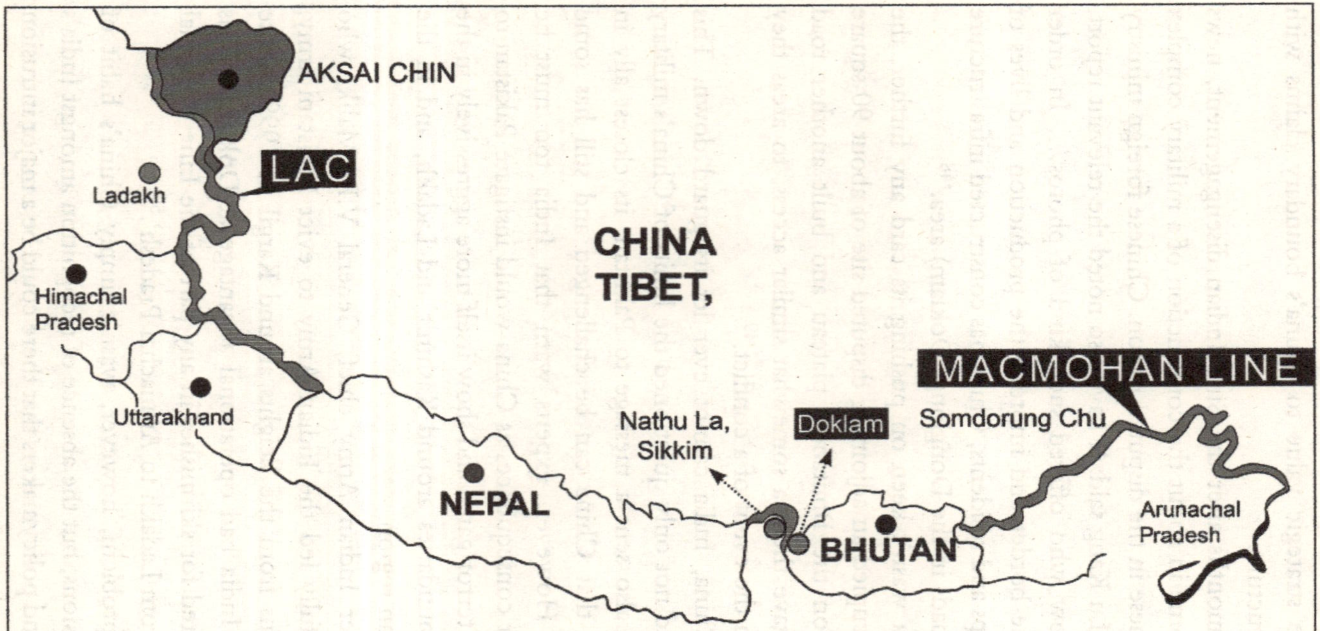

Map 9: LAC, India's boundary with China

Source: Outlook magazine

that could set the stage for a serious confrontation sooner than later. As Malik said, 'The mindset in the government, has never recognised that we can have a serious confrontation with China sometime or the other. Otherwise, why should our infrastructure on the northern border be so weak? We have been talking about infrastructure on the northern border from the time I was the army chief nearly two decades ago. Plans were made, but they remain on paper mostly.'[51]

He was proved right when in April 2020 the Indian establishment was caught unawares when the Chinese swiftly occupied parts of territory along the LAC in east Ladakh. At first there appeared to be a sense of déjà vu with events before the 1962 Sino-Indian conflict. However, the swiftness of Indian response from a well-coordinated Indian Army, Air Force and Navy took the Chinese by surprise.

9

LAC: 2020 WAS NOT 1962

In early May 2020, Indian and Chinese soldiers engaged in fist fights and stone pelting at the beach of Pangong Tso, a lake shared between India and Tibet/China with the LAC passing through it. More brawls followed at 14,000 feet. Later, in mid-June, soldiers fought fiercely with fists, rocks and wooden clubs spiked with nails and wrapped in barbed wire, but as the border code dictates, no shots were fired.

As the snow melted in early 2020, the Chinese army had dramatically increased its presence in Aksai Chin along the LAC, which India mistook as military exercises, even though there were substantially larger elements of tanks and artillery. The PLA had encroached beyond its usual deployments on the LAC at four locations in Ladakh—in the areas of Galwan, Hot Springs, Pangong Tso and Demchok—besides one location in Sikkim. This initially led to a lot of pushing and jostling between the troops patrolling the LAC, until the stand-off turned extremely violent and led to the much reported clash in Galwan Valley on 15 June 2020. This much publicised conflict resulted in the death of at least 20 Indian soldiers and a larger number of Chinese soldiers, including the commanding officers of both the military units, even though the Indians were vastly outnumbered.[1] Thereafter, China made its intentions known.

Beijing was in no mood to pull back its army and as it

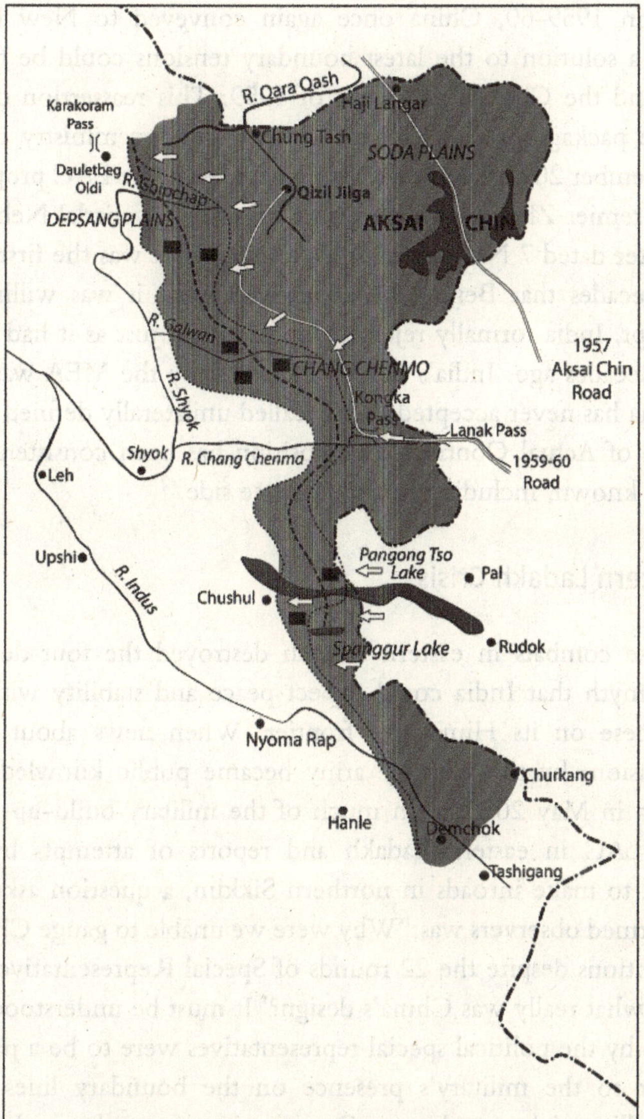

Map 10: China's claim lines of 1960 and 1962, and military offensive in 1962

Source: Arjun Subramanium, *India's Wars: A Military History, 1947–1971*, p. 241

did in 1959-60, China once again conveyed to New Delhi that a solution to the latest boundary tensions could be found around the Chinese proposals of 1959. This reassertion of the same package proposal by the Chinese foreign ministry on 29 September 2020 stated that 'Beijing abides by the LAC proposed by premier Zhou en Lai to prime minister Jawaharlal Nehru in a letter dated 7 November 1959.' Although it was the first time in decades that Beijing had conveyed what it was willing to accept, India formally rejected the proposal, just as it had done six decades ago. India's official statement by the MEA was that 'India has never accepted the so-called unilaterally defined 1959 Line of Actual Control. This position has been consistent and well known, including to the Chinese side.'[2]

Eastern Ladakh Crisis

These combats in eastern Ladakh destroyed the four-decade-old myth that India could expect peace and stability with the Chinese on its Himalayan frontier. When news about these intrusions by the Chinese army became public knowledge in India in May 2020, with much of the military build-up along the LAC in eastern Ladakh and reports of attempts by the PLA to make inroads in northern Sikkim, a question asked by informed observers was: 'Why were we unable to gauge Chinese intentions despite the 22 rounds of Special Representative talks and what really was China's design?' It must be understood that talks by the political special representatives were to be a parallel track to the military's presence on the boundary lines with patrolling pickets and posts. One wasn't meant to be a substitute for the other, though in the aftermath of the 1962 conflict, China 'did not permanently administer or patrol many parts west and south west of Aksai Chin for decades'.[3]

India had also set up the 'China Study Group' (CSG), a

secretary-level grouping which includes the foreign secretary, home secretary and defence secretary besides the vice chiefs of the three services and chiefs of IB and R&AW. The NSA convenes meetings from time to time, which are attended by the service chiefs. The CSG, set up to advise the government on its China policy, has been carefully monitoring and assessing Indian military activity for decades now. For better border management, the CSG also recommends revised patrolling limits, rules of engagement and the pattern of Indian military presence along the Indo-China boundaries. Accordingly, the CSG identifies specific patrolling points on the LAC that act as 'designated spots to be patrolled according to a pre-determined schedule by the security forces'. This means patrols are sent to a numbered point with no prominent geographical feature, that 'serve as a guide to a location on the LAC for soldiers, acting as indicators of the extent of "actual control" exercised on the territory by India'. Therefore, the Indian Army's movements are controlled by the CSG, which has a formal political mandate of 1975, later reviewed in 1975, even though the frequency of patrols is not controlled by the CSG. That is left to the army or the Indo-Tibetan Border Police (ITBP). It is said that 'close observation of the LAC' is done even more stringently than along the LoC with Pakistan in western Jammu & Kashmir.[4]

On the other side of the border, the CPC leadership too exercises overall control over the PLA, but lacks the political drive to find a solution to the boundary dispute. Especially after the 2013 and the 2017 Doklam stand-off, China's desire to position itself at an advantage has become more noticeable, with 'nearly 75 percent of the transgressions' by Chinese troops taking place across the LAC that lies east of Ladakh, while only 20 per cent have occurred in India's eastern front along Sikkim and Arunachal Pradesh. This makes it apparent that for the Chinese, the Aksai Chin area is 'a valued piece of real estate' and the Ladakh crisis could thus be explained as a 'belated reassertion of China's original claims over the area'.[5] Belated because in the past, intrusions or attempts at it had occurred mostly in a few sensitive 'grey areas' on the disputed Sino-Indian boundary, that by many accounts is said to be 3,488 kilometres long, but as per a former Indian Army chief, General J.J. Singh, the entire Sino-Indian boundary is 4,057 kilometres long.[6]

No Solution in Sight

A mutually acceptable settlement is still a far cry despite the multiple 'agreements' in 1993, 1996, 2005 and 2013. These pacts did provide a clear direction, but a sincere desire and the political will needed to settle this long-standing issue was missing. In some ways, this territorial dispute is like the India-Pakistan conflict over Kashmir. Neither side can be seen to be giving in, with so much at stake for their political leadership.

For China, there is the vision of Mao, who saw Tibet as the palm of China's right hand and Ladakh, Nepal, Sikkim, Bhutan and Arunachal Pradesh as its five fingers that China has to 'liberate'.[7] For India, it meant 'horse trading' as Nehru put it, as Zhou's proposal involved accepting all the Chinese territorial claims 'whether Arunachal Pradesh in the east or Aksai Chin in the west, which were Indian'.[8] For many years even after Nehru had passed away, Indian diplomats were loyally hanging on to this legacy. This stand in due course has become an Indian article of faith!

Even meetings by later leaders of these two nations have not resolved the dispute despite Modi and Xi Jinping having visited each other's countries and having engaged in 18 meetings from the time Modi became prime minister until the Galwan clash in June 2020. They first engaged in 2014. Later, following the stand-off over Doklam in 2017, they met over structured summits at Wuhan in 2018 and then at Mahabalipuram, near Chennai, in 2019. Yet, there were major Chinese intrusions across the LAC in 2014 and again in 2020, despite the issuing of 'strategic guidance' to their respective militaries to have better and more frequent communication and strengthen the existing CBM, so that the special representatives could 'seek a fair, reasonable and mutually acceptable settlement to the border question'.[9] It still remained delightfully vague.

So it seems that with talks leading nowhere, China perhaps decided to try and once again 'teach India a lesson'. China's leaders have perhaps chosen to ignore the fact that the myth of invincibility of the PLA was put to rest by its neighbouring country Vietnam in 1979, after Deng Xiaoping had similarly sent the PLA across China's southern borders to 'teach Vietnam a lesson'.[10] Similarly, by hanging on to their experience of the 1962 conflict, China's civil and military leaders do tend to ignore that much has changed since then. That '2020 wasn't 1962'. India's leadership, conscious of the 'lessons' learnt from 1962, is determined to defend India's territorial frontiers with deliberate action that may be perceived as intimidating by China.

Catalyst for China

As China saw it, matters came to a head following several actions initiated by India in recent years. First was India's effort to improve infrastructure—roads, bridges, tunnels and communication arteries—at various points along the Sino-Indian boundary, which had been long neglected for fear that better roads from the Himalayas onto the plains would aid invading Chinese forces to roll down! Then, in July 2013, India took a decision to raise a strike corps for the Indian Army in the eastern sector, with offensive defence capabilities to monitor

China's activities and conduct trans-border strikes. This corps would have acclimatised army units for rapid responses. Finally, another action by India that put China on the edge was the Modi government's decision to abrogate Article 370 of the Indian Constitution that gave J&K special status, the creation of a new union territory of Ladakh and the call thereafter given by the home minister himself 'to liberate 38,000 sq. km of Aksai Chin'. These events had all contributed to China's aggressive behaviour.[11]

The fighting at Galwan Valley was a turning point with China's incursions along the LAC in 2020 and its large military build-up that woke up India's policymakers to the reality of the Chinese military threat. It led one major Indian newspaper to state in its editorial that 'the LAC is the new LOC'. This implied that India must now prepare for a permanent increase in its deployments and constant friction like the military situation on the LoC—the fiercely contested Indo-Pak front along Jammu & Kashmir. Moreover, this time there would be no rollback by China because 'there is now insufficient trust between the militaries for such a move. If India were to accept the status quo, on paper this will seem as if India had conceded a chunk of land behind its version of LAC.'[12] What is the way out? Is China now keen to establish a 'new normal'? Should both sides bring the boundary issue to the fore and seek a settlement?

New Delhi adopted a multi-pronged approach of talks to tell Beijing that its expansionist approach was unacceptable, followed by several highly publicised visits by the leadership, including that of Modi. It was soon clear that India must adopt a new approach with China. To allow China to gain either territorially or psychologically would have been politically disastrous for the Indian prime minister and his government. So, to begin with, India chose to match Chinese deployments on the LAC. In the summer of 2020, India and China had deployed about 1,00,000 troops around the LAC in Ladakh. Clearly, New Delhi wasn't going to repeat the mistakes of the past. Besides, it became apparent to India that the 2020 ingress by PLA troops across the LAC in Ladakh had a greater strategic design, unlike Chinese intrusions in the past, that happened regularly only to be withdrawn after diplomatic talks.

Three Warfare Strategy

The bigger question 'why China chose to adopt a sudden military build-up along the LAC in 2020' has many answers. On the face of it, China saw the time when the world order was in shambles due to COVID-19, as an opportunity to address its ambitions and to tell doubting Thomases at home that Beijing was still strong and working towards Xi's 'Vision-2050' for China to stand tall in the world.

It has been argued that beneath the surface of China's aggressions lies a plan to humiliate India, to damage its economy and its industry.[13] China does it through its 'Three Warfare Strategy…. to subdue nations. This strategy is composed of public opinion warfare, psychological warfare and legal warfare. Additionally, China practises a three-pronged approach at the geo-political level conducted through "debt trap, wolf warrior diplomacy and military coercion" in seeking a bipolar world order,' writes Lt Gen. Bhatia, India's former Director-General of Military Operations.[14]

Debt Trap Diplomacy: With this strategy, China makes investments and provides infrastructure loans to developing nations eventually to leverage the debt to achieve Beijing's strategic objectives. Research and reports[15] indicate that since 2015, Chinese tech investors have put in amounts from $4–8 billion into Indian start-ups and 18 out of 30 of India's unicorns are Chinese funded. Additionally, there were reports of Chinese investment to the tune of about $3.5 billion in multiple enterprises like Alibaba, Xiomi, Flipkart, Paytm and Oppo besides pharma and electronic companies. All this is part of China's slow and creeping entry into the Indian economy, which has led to India's massive annual trade deficit of over US $50 billion.

Even though its investments were welcomed partly because India was happy to attract foreign direct investment (FDI) as an indicator of its economic growth, Indian consumers, like so many others in the world, had become heavily dependent on Chinese pharmaceutical, electronic and telecom products, often cheaper and better made than the local competitors. Thus, New Delhi has to work hard to wean itself away from the huge inroads that Chinese goods have made into India.[16] The stand-off at the LAC changed the status quo and it wasn't business as usual anymore. Alarm bells had finally rung in the Indian finance ministry that this could be the classic Chinese 'debt trap', in which China had already entrapped Sri Lanka and Pakistan.

Wolf Warrior Diplomacy: China has used wolf warrior diplomacy as a tool of state policy to deflect attention away from negative press, attack other nations and defend its national interests. In the short term, this brand of China's diplomacy was evident with the Ladakh stand-off, aimed to shift attention away from the negative media coverage and the public discussions in India and internationally, of China's slow and shoddy handling—by default or design—of the COVID-19 virus outbreak. Coupled with China's handling of the pro-democracy protests in Hong Kong in early 2020, the Chinese leadership looked hopeless in the eyes of its people—those with access to global news and their vast diaspora across the world. Thus, as a ploy to deflect bad press, the CPC leadership first resorted to some muscle-flexing in the South China Sea, although that angered the Trump administration enough to send in three aircraft carrier groups around China's coast. Beijing then ordered the PLA to intrude across the LAC to lay physical claim on the unsettled boundary with India.

Military Coercion: Historically, China uses military coercion by risking confrontation leading to conflict when it wants to advance its core territorial interests. The PLA build-up and fighting along the LAC was part of a greater Chinese design. It could be argued that China chose to up the ante in 2020, as it may have assumed that the world couldn't be bothered with a territorial conflict in the Himalayas, as all the major powers were too busy battling the fallout of the COVID-19 virus at home. On the other hand, perhaps, China's leadership may have decided that enough was enough and they needed some results because a border settlement based on dialogue per se was unlikely due to the obstinacy of both countries.

History had shown that whenever China has grabbed territory in Aksai Chin, as in the 1950s, it has retained and firmed up on it. Now with the world too busy battling COVID-19, Beijing may have assumed that this was as good a time as any and Chinese expansionism would go unnoticed. In some ways, this incursion was similar to the Chinese invasion of October-November 1962, when the world was busy with the Cuban Missile Crisis.[17]

However, Beijing's assumption that India wouldn't stand up to Chinese designs was proved wrong. In an India of 2020 with its watchful media and awareness of China's illegal occupation of Aksai Chin, it was impossible for any government to keep matters like this Chinese intrusion away from the public eye, like Nehru's government had done in the 1950s. China thus forced India to respond.[18]

India's Response

Apart from engaging China in several rounds of dialogue, at the military-to-military commanders' level on the LAC and diplomatically in Delhi and Beijing, India also chose to announce trade restrictions on Chinese goods and investors. Joining the global anger against China for the spread of the COVID-19 virus,[19] New Delhi finally woke up to China's steady encroachment into the Indian economy and just like other nations had done, reviewed its policies on FDI to 'wall off' Chinese investments into Indian companies. Even investments by entities which had Chinese nationals with 'beneficial ownership', including those being routed through Hong Kong, Singapore and South Asian countries, where there could be an indirect Chinese presence, were restricted by making government approval mandatory. Commentators on China in India welcomed this move, but it caused resentment in Beijing.

Among the several irritants for Beijing at present—ranging from India's growing military ties with the US to India being the only major country to openly oppose the Chinese Belt and Road Initiative[20]—the biggest challenge to China's strategic territorial claims has been the Modi government's call to liberate Aksai Chin following the creation of the union territory of Ladakh and India's publication of new maps of Jammu & Kashmir and Ladakh. For China, this was the challenge to what it had come to believe as the status quo.

The Indian government has also permitted the Indian Army to respond in a responsible manner to any further escalation on the front lines, like the aggressive occupation of certain heights by Indian troops around the Pangong Tso on 5 August 2020, which took China by surprise. This showed that the Indian Armed Forces weren't a pushover anymore.

For India, the Chinese intrusions in 2020 have woken up the government to heed the military's demands for modern weapon systems. It has also revived the discussion on a number of issues of national security and strategy, just when many of us thought that India's only external threat was from Pakistan and the generals in Rawalpindi who had been tamed by the IAF's air strikes on Balakot. In contrast, dealing with China would require India to respond on multiple fronts—military, diplomatic and economic—despite the brave fight by India's soldiers at Galwan Valley, or more recently the use of the aggressive tactics south of Pangong Tso and east of Chushul. It may still not stall China's aggressive designs, given the territorial significance of Aksai Chin.

Importance of Aksai Chin

Aksai Chin is strategically important for both the countries. China would eventually like to extend its Aksai Chin controlled areas further north of the Galwan Valley—where the bloody confrontations took place between Indian and Chinese troops in June 2020—towards the Karakoram Pass, which would add more depth to its important road link through Aksai Chin called Highway G219, the highest road on earth which connects Kashgar in Sinkiang to Lhasa in Tibet, which can facilitate quicker mobilisation of battle troops on the border.

For doing this, the Chinese army would need to control the Depsang plains that Indian troops currently dominate in north-east Ladakh. China had, in fact, begun work on the 1,300 kilometres long Karakoram Highway in 1959. It took two decades to complete and is now vital for Chinese designs over Gilgit-Baltistan.[21] Currently the Chinese have to take a circuitous 1,500 kilometres long road from the eastern reaches of Aksai Chin to link up with the Karakoram Pass to reach

Shaksgam Valley, an area that was ceded to China by Pakistan in 1963. If China is eventually able to link up with the Karakoram Pass, it could dominate all of Ladakh and reap the full benefits of the China Pakistan Economic Corridor (CPEC)[22] in which China has made large investments, initially of US$ 46 billion.

The CPEC is intended to pass through Pakistan-occupied Gilgit-Baltistan, the northern portion of the larger Kashmir region and a territory administered by Islamabad, but disputed between India and Pakistan which is a significant segment of China's Belt and Road Initiative. While the Pakistanis regard CPEC as a panacea for their ailing economy, the CPEC offers China several strategic benefits, from being an important land link for its Belt and Road Initiative to the Gulf region for the energy China increasingly needs, and as a tool to control Pakistan so as to use it against India.[23] The possession of this region is also essential for China to address its strategic need for water.

China had in fact begun to eye Kashmir's waters from the 1950s, and so it occupied Aksai Chin in 1954. Aksai Chin thus holds the key to China's plans for water resources in the Ladakh region as the Indus river system originates from Tibet and goes via Aksai Chin and Ladakh to Pakistan's northern areas that India calls Pakistan-occupied Kashmir (PoK).

The Chinese agenda is to have access to as much water in this region, which is home to 242 glaciers and is the world's most heavily glaciated area, as possible. China needs an abundance of water, for its nuclear plant in Lop Nor and also for the manufacture of microchips. In 2018, China had imported over $230 billion worth of microchips from the US, Japan and Taiwan that it now wants to produce. Silicon wafer production requires a lot of water (10,000 litres for 30 square centimetres) and thus China has strategically targeted the waters of the Indus river system and by melting the glaciers in the

Shaksgam Valley, access to which is provided by Pakistan to fulfil China's geostrategic and economic agenda. The Chinese have thus agreed to finance five major dams in PoK to use the waters there for making silicon wafers.[24]

China's desire to link up to the Karakoram Pass has compelled it to 'grab' as much territory as is strategic to assert greater power in this region. China has thus deployed a large number of troops for fighting, support and logistic arms in eastern Ladakh, compelling India to increase substantially its own military deployments along the LAC and further north towards the Karakoram Pass, which has only made the situation possibly more explosive, particularly in the Chushul sector, south of Pangong Tso in India's Leh district.

Marriage of Convenience

For India, stalling China's northwards movement to the Karakoram Pass is essential to prevent a China-Pakistan military encirclement of India's Leh plateau and the Siachen glacier. Thus, keeping the Chinese south of the Depsang plains would give the Indian Army the much needed depth against a Chinese invasion backed by the Sino-Pak pact.

The China-Pak nexus has been a 'marriage of convenience' as Indian geo-strategist Brahma Chellaney puts it. He states that 'slowly but surely, Pakistan is becoming China's colonial outpost, primarily aimed at checkmating India. China's machinations in the United Nations Security Council (UNSC) too highlight the fact that the long-standing Sino-Pak nexus has been cemented on the issue of Jammu and Kashmir (J&K) as China occupies one fifth of the original princely state, including the areas it had seized up to 1962 and the Trans-Karakoram tract ceded to it by Pakistan.'[25]

For India, a direct consequence of the Chinese intrusions and the events that have followed since then has been the realisation that New Delhi cannot look at the threat from Pakistan in isolation any more. India's forces are prepared for the challenge, notwithstanding the shortage of a few new weapon platforms, which New Delhi decided to make up in double quick time in the second half of 2020.

While Pakistan had seen India's military deployments as a direct threat to its existence, China decided to upgrade the bureaucrat-level boundary talks to the political level of a JWG.

Game-changer for India

The China challenge for India did away with any delusions that diplomacy itself would be enough to keep the Chinese forces at bay. Further, even though we are nowhere near as ill-prepared as in 1962, it would be prudent to take a leaf out of the experiences of our recent past. Having intruded past our boundary lines, neither China nor Pakistan have vacated the territories they have grabbed in PoK and Aksai Chin respectively since India's independence. It is now a given to assume that when any territory is not physically held by troops, especially where the claims of the two countries are disputed, it will be grabbed by a country like China as soon as an opportunity arises, as it has no respect for the status quo. Maps and political claims will not get China to relent. China's territorial ambitions are known and only a show of strength will work.

To do this, the IAF in April 2018 undertook its biggest air exercise in three decades named Gagan Shakti over an 18-day period. Later, Air Chief Marshal B.S. Dhanoa stated that Gagan Shakti had met 'more that its objectives' of sending a clear signal to China and Pakistan that despite the noises about the IAF's dwindling fighter aircraft fleet, it could still defend India's skies from a two-front threat.[26]

Even then, following the Chinese intrusions in Ladakh, there is a need for India's military commanders to go back to their drawing boards and do some redeployment of India's ground-based forces to increase the strength on the Himalayan front lines. The Indian Army needs to shift troops permanently, either from the Pakistan border to Ladakh, which earlier had only one army division of about 7,500 men guarding an over-400 kilometres frontage on the LAC, or from their locations around towns and cities to deploy three army divisions with a lot of air power in Ladakh.

Dealing with China, however, won't be limited to troops on the Himalayan front lines. It would require not one but two strike corps, one in India's east and the other in the north with each enduring a long-term cost of Rs 65,000 crores (US$ 8.6 billion) in reserves. These corps will have to be provided multiple military employment options with intelligence, surveillance and reconnaissance (ISR) capabilities, UAVs, light artillery, heavy lift helicopters and attack helicopters.[27]

However, in all likelihood, any future territorial conflict between India and China would be a limited one, like the Indo-Pak Kargil conflict of 1999. This is because India, China and even Pakistan all hold nuclear weapons. So arguably, a full-fledged 'hot war' is unlikely as the world wouldn't allow it to escalate beyond a point and neither would either side, as the fear of mutually assured destruction would act as a restraint.

In these circumstances, therefore, it is actually air and naval power that would be the game-changers and India has enhanced these capabilities over the years. In 2015–18, India purchased US-made C-130J and C-17 military transport aircrafts, CH-47 Chinook heavy lift helicopters and the AH-64 Apache attack helicopters for its army.

In 2020, India went in for a sudden buying spree of Russian fighter jets—Sukhoi-30 MKI and MiG-29s to add to its existing fleet of Russian fighters. The usual procrastination over defence deals was dumped for these fast-tracked government-to-government transactions. Also, adding punch to the Indian Navy's capabilities, the government ordered US-made Harpoon anti-ship missiles and the MH-60 Seahawk maritime helicopters, and indicated a desire to soon finalise a 30 drones deal for either the MQ-9 Reaper or the Predator-B drones.[28] Interestingly, the Indian Navy's P-81 maritime patrol aircraft was seen in Leh adding to the IAF's surveillance capabilities in the mountains!

'Regardless of the economic asymmetry between India and China, India does have the military capability to inflict unacceptable pain in retaliation for any Chinese adventurism; not only in the mountains, but also at sea', writes a former Indian Naval Chief, Admiral Arun Prakash.[29] Even though China now has the largest naval fleet in the world, the Indian Navy is no pushover, as it is 'up to NATO standards' and an important partner of the US-led Quad in the Indo-Pacific.

India's Weakness

With its strong and powerful forces, India can well fight its own battles. However, it must have a national master plan with clear goals and a commitment to strategic objectives.

'Delhi's real failure has been to not match its realpolitik words and deeds with a broader foreign policy framework where sustained engagement with China was also part of a grand strategy to emerge as a leading power in a multipolar world.'[30] The problem lies with the successive Indian governments that have never got around to formulating a national security strategy or a doctrine. 'The Indian parliament has never demanded a defence review or sought a white paper', unlike China, whose 'political leadership has since 1995, been issuing a defence white paper every two years', writes Admiral Arun Prakash.[31]

There are some well-known reasons for this: for one, the Indian politician often sees matters related to defence as irritants and not an election winning issue unless a defence or weapons deal becomes controversial and can lead to an election win or loss. The other is that India's higher defence management is completely controlled by India's politico-bureaucratic elite that have only a limited understanding of national security challenges.

For instance, when it became public knowledge in the late 1950s that Chinese troops had occupied the Aksai Chin region, and have stayed since then, Nehru's government made it known to the army that India's only threat came from Pakistan! China, it said, could be handled with diplomacy. This was the belief even in South Block until May 2020. Only the recent clashes in the Galwan region woke up India's establishment about the limits of Indian diplomacy.

Thus when faced with a conflict situation on the LAC, the routine explanations are 'surprise' and 'intelligence failure'. Worse still, the people responsible for it are allowed to escape, most with just a warning! This happened two decades ago in the events that led to the Indo-Pak conflict in the heights around Kargil in 1999.[32] Many events, as they unfolded in the 2020 stand-off between China and India, had echoes of the past. That is India's biggest weakness.

Today, any hopes that Chinese will withdraw to the accepted LAC appear misplaced. India must be prepared for the long haul, like the Doklam stand-off of seventy-two days or even more as New Delhi's diplomatic approach of going through talks and peace-making is a model that hasn't got us anywhere on the matter of settling the boundary line, especially on the Ladakh front. Due to differing perceptions, there is no meeting ground on the LAC issue. Will it be the LAC as agreed in 1993? Or should it be the one proposed by the British in Simla in 1914? Or the Johnson Line? It's about time we create a new mechanism to settle the boundary as 22 rounds of talks have led us nowhere. Is the 'tough' Modi government ready to talk tough with the Chinese? Or could India face another Kargil-like conflict with China? That is not quite off the table as yet. How much is each side prepared?

A SWOT Analysis

Given a thumb rule of mountain warfare, China has more disadvantages, even if it moves in more forces because each defending Indian division requires at least six Chinese divisions to push them out of their defensive lines. The defender in the mountains needs far lesser troops compared with the attacker, if deployed on heights as Indian troops are now. Thus, India currently has an adequate number of soldiers deployed on the LAC.

Although China could deploy more artillery fire units than India, there is no mathematical equation available for how much an attacker would need. Moreover, to make a substantial dent on Indian Army's Himalayan defences, China would need at least 45 if not 50 army divisions. China can rapidly deploy up to 36 divisions across India's frontiers, but in fair weather, not in the winters. Even with its well-developed road network across Tibet, China can deploy its fighting divisions only if it faces no other threat along its vast frontiers. China shares its borders with fourteen countries, but sustains territorial disputes with many more. There are at least three US aircraft carrier groups, made up of hundreds of frigates, ships and submarines armed to their teeth, that were operating along China's maritime front around the end of 2020.

So, the PLA's best face-saving bet is to try another Galwan-type encroachment along the LAC, without troops opening fire, which could give a further blow to the Chinese army's reputation as India's soldiers are now ready and waiting!

Almost all Indian Army infantry units of about 700 men have a 'Ghatak' platoon of 36 men. These men, hardened after years of battling terrorism in Jammu & Kashmir are chosen and punishingly trained to kill with their bare hands, as they did during the Galwan clashes. The Chinese army, on the other hand, looks impressive in ceremonial parades and in doctored videos, but unlike the Indian Army it has virtually no battlefield experience and is barely able to cope with the harsh Himalayan winter. Besides, with China's one-child policy, its soldiers are unwilling to die.

The only edge China has is with rocket forces, which could cause considerable damage to the airfields—not aircrafts—in Leh and Daulat Beg Oldi.[33] India's air armada would be flying from airfields far away in Srinagar, Pathankot, Agra, Bareilly, Siliguri and Tezpur. All these airfields allow fighter aircraft to load the full bomb and fuel payloads unlike the high-altitude Chinese airfields on the Tibetan plateau, which restrict air operational capabilities and take-off for their missions. Besides carrying restrictive fuel and ammunition loads, the Chinese air force (PLAAF) pilots have little experience of battlefield situations as they rarely exercise with other forces; unlike IAF pilots who regularly train with US, France and Russian air forces. Further, China's inventory of aircrafts including the J-20 Chengdu doesn't give it an edge over the IAF that can currently be an effective match for the PLAAF. So, hopefully, if push comes to shove, India will not hesitate to use the IAF. Recent history has also shown that in the event of escalation, like in the Kargil conflict when action by the IAF became a game-changer, the use of air power cannot be ruled out.

As for China's maritime claims with its stated aim to have the largest navy in the near future, the Chinese navy is indeed fast expanding at present, but it has its limitations if it were to operate near India's coastline. Its aircraft carriers are new and the Chinese navy is no match against those of the US, and its nuclear submarines are known to be inconsistent with their underwater capabilities.[34] The US not only has the largest and most experienced aircraft carrier groups (over 11 carriers with 80 fighter aircrafts each in 2020) but the total carrier deck space of US carriers in operation is over twice that of all other nations combined! The Chinese, on the other hand, had two aircraft carriers in 2020—with plans for two more—but its naval aviators are still struggling to get their act together.[35] The Chinese navy, however, has a longer history of acquiring and building a submarine fleet, that by 2030 could expand to 60 diesel subs and 16 nuclear attack submarines; more than the current US total of 52 submarines, and only half of these are for the US Pacific Fleet, with 'drone subs' being adopted to mitigate the challenge. But the technological edge of the US plus the combined fleet of its allies is still tremendous.[36]

India's navy, on the other hand, enjoys a considerable edge over the Chinese in these waters. With the Indian Navy's ability to project maritime power beyond India's coastline, for instance, by blocking Chinese ships from passing through the Straits of Malacca—a waterway near Singapore, between Malaysia and Sumatra—could throttle Chinese supply lines and send a strong message to Beijing. This can be a major pressure point against any long-term Chinese military campaign against India. Incidentally, Indian Navy ships in the Asian waters now operate closely with the US navy that respects the might and professionalism of the Indian Navy. This is China's 'Malacca dilemma' and as a counter, China has made considerable investments in the Gwadar port in Pakistan and the CPEC.

The CPEC, however, is neither ready to help China move

its oil and trade products through Pakistan from and to the Gulf region and even Africa, nor is Pakistan likely to get into a full-fledged war with India in support of Chinese ambitions. The reasons are primarily two: for one, the Indian armed forces are matched adequately against Pakistan despite the Chinese threat; and the other is that during Indo-Pak wars of 1965, 1971 and 1999, the absence of Chinese intervention had foiled Pakistan's plans. Can Pakistan forget being short-changed?

Pakistan, however, could be a major distraction for India if Beijing moves to take greater control of Aksai Chin and even Ladakh for the region's mineral wealth including uranium and water resources. China's desire to link up with the Karakoram Pass north of the Depsang plains to reduce the long and arduous journey towards the Shaksgam Valley that is over 1,800 kilometres, had driven Beijing to encroach onto the glacier-rich Shaksgam Valley well before the Pakistanis gave its control to the Chinese. However, any further ingress by the Chinese from Depsang plains from the LAC will be met by not just India's infantrymen in their trenches, but a mechanised force of tanks and Infantry Carrier Vehicles (ICVs) that have considerable room for military manoeuvres there. China has no doubt deployed a large mechanised force, but it needs at least three times India's mechanised force to make any gains, in mountainous terrain. In all military planning on conventional military conflicts, the attacking force is required to be at least three times larger than the defender, and to ensure further success in mountains, it may need to be five times larger.

Some former Indian Army commanders who have served in Leh question how many of the Chinese tanks are actually operational and not dummies and do they all have enough fuel and ammunition? Indian troops certainly do have an operational force, having been there since General Sundarji decided to move mechanised units of ICVs to Ladakh. His wisdom was questioned then, but certainly not now with the Chinese looking for gaps in India's defence to exploit.

Even though stocking of food and ammunition for winters has been done, despite the additionally large numbers of troops deployed along the LAC, there is a crying need for round-the-year supply lines to Ladakh. That is a big challenge that India must address in whatever manner possible, as it could be the decisive factor in the event of a Sino-Indian war.

The two major mountain passes—Zoji La and Rohtang—are of little use from November to April. So, whatever is required by the troops not just at the LAC, but in Siachen and Kargil too, is pushed through by the end of October. The Rohtang Pass now has the Atal Tunnel, but Zoji La Pass doesn't. This, along with activating the Chushul airfield, is essential. The move of the Indian Special Frontier Force (SFF)—a specialised force in mountain warfare made up of Tibetans and Ladakhis that occupied the heights around Pangong Tso—was perhaps intended for this purpose and took China by surprise. Airlifts of essentials are the only lifeline for the troops in the freezing front lines. Thus, there is now the need to speed up work on the Chushul airfield, which was ignored all these years.

India's biggest disadvantage against Chinese capabilities is its lack of satellite capacity and inputs. Apparently, of the total number of satellites in the skies, the US and China have 45 per cent while the rest belong to other countries of which India's share is miniscule. So, if we require satellite inputs, which we will in the event of a conflict, our sources for now would be the US and Israel, and possibly Russia and France.

Interestingly, some useful data is available for a price from private companies in the West. But India may be reluctant to use their inputs as this could give away India's intent. Satellite inputs apart, today's battlefield has a number of information providers from troops on the front, UAVs, helicopters and

AWACs. However, a 30 square centimetres satellite photo isn't helpful in giving the correct status of the enemy's troops. Hence, we shouldn't dismiss the role of local spies, who are often the nation's eyes on the ground.

Some American analysts have expressed fears that a military escalation around the Jammu & Kashmir and Ladakh region could be the spark for a bigger Sino-US conflict and even possibly the Third World War. Beijing, however, is between the 'devil and the deep sea', surrounded as it is by American naval task forces and facing India's tough stand against its territorial incursions. There is near unanimity among 'pundits' of wars and conflicts that a conventional conflict between two nuclear armed countries has the possibility of a military stalemate leading to the aggressor threatening to use nuclear weapons—escalating from tactical to strategic nuclear weapons—to achieve victory. But it would create a global crisis, and in turn draw in the entire world against the aggressor. It is also believed that the only deterrence that would work in stalling the aggressor's designs is either the threat of 'mutually assured destruction'—in this case by India to China—or from a more powerful nuclear adversary, i.e, the US to China. And if the assertions of India's leadership can be taken seriously, then India seems to be up for a fight, this time!

If Beijing decides to raise the level and threaten with the use of nuclear weapons, it must know that India can also respond. It isn't the numbers of missiles and warheads that matter once it comes to a nuclear stand-off, but if and when it points to a war between two nuclear weapon states, then it is most likely to lead to 'mutually assured destruction', or what strategists call MAD. However, signs of a Chinese-led escalation would provide the US the 'Pearl Harbour' moment as reports say, the US has been waiting for. But it is hard to tell if it could lead to US actions that'll put the brakes on China's muscle flexing.

CHINA'S BOUNDARY POLICY ON THE HIMALAYAS: AN AFTERWORD

A defining event in Sino-Indian relations in the past few decades were the clashes that took place between the Indian and Chinese troops near the Galwan River Valley in Eastern Ladakh, close to the Line of Actual Control (LAC). It may have been a coincidence that 15 June 2020, a day when Chinese troops clashed with Indian troops at Galwan, happened to be Xi Jinping's birth anniversary. The People's Liberation Army (PLA) leadership may have been looking to impress their Supreme Commander with news of beating Indians and capturing critical areas on the LAC. The first report—of the Chinese hacking to death over a dozen Indian soldiers—would have been exciting for the Chinese president, but what ensued may have turned his 67th birthday perhaps his worst. The following day, the Indian Army counterattacked the same Chinese unit with ghatak (commando platoons) and killed, according to initial reports, five Chinese soldiers. Later, as matters started unfolding, heavy casualties were reported on the Chinese side, with some reports putting the number at up to five dozen. Like the Indians, the Chinese soldiers too were killed in a hand-to-hand fight.

It is known that the Chinese military was building combined arms brigades (CABS) close to the LAC at the beginning of the season and the frequency of patrol clashes was on the rise. However, what made headlines at Galwan was the intensity of the clash and the fact that it resulted in the killing of soldiers without either side firing a bullet. The last time Indian soldiers lost their lives in a border dispute with China was in 1975.

China's 'Three Warfare' Strategy

Within weeks of the clash, the PLA appeared to mobilise troops up to a four-division strength (30,000 plus soldiers) on the LAC. Usually, it takes several months for a military build-up of this size. Considering the speed at which China moved its troops to certain tactically advantageous positions across the entire stretch of the LAC, it was apparent that they had a deliberate plan to occupy commanding heights and choke points on earmarked terrain features.

To justify their actions, the Chinese have a great tact for attributing blame to their opponent, by turning things around with a play of words and the use of terminologies, as part of their 'three warfare' strategy. China aims at gaining control over a situation by acting first, thus making information a potent tool with strategic implications. It focuses on enmeshing psychological and armed attacks, simultaneous offence and defence moves with offence on priority, and artificially using multiple forms of forces.[1] It disguises offensive action as defensive, by calling it 'active defence', which conventionally in military parlance is defined as 'counterattack'. As part of this strategy, the Chinese first force a situation on the adversary, which propels the adversary to act. With the adversary now perceived as an aggressor, China addresses its attack on the adversary as being defensive.

Similar designs were at play in 2017 and 2020. Chinese military and diplomatic circles put the blame for the Doklam and Galwan clashes on 'provocative and planned' military operations by the Indian troops and highlighted India's infrastructure build-up as a means of creating new tensions.[2] Some have explicitly described India's construction of new roads near the Sino-Indian boundary as akin to inciting a war, while delineating China's motive as being to create wealth, by stating that 'roads can be the path to wealth or the way to war'.[3]

It was clear to India that, under the garb of a military exercise, China had already positioned its forces close to the LAC in April 2020. Their reconnaissance ostensibly started earlier, with a newly inducted PLA unit establishing a tent post near the Galwan River Junction on the LAC in proximity to patrolling point (PP) 14. Galwan Nala or rivulet is a tributary of River Shyok along which Indian infrastructure is being built. The purpose of this force was to keep the Galwan Valley under surveillance, where the Indian Army was rapidly building an operational track as part of forward infrastructure development. Galwan is also the nearest point from where the Chinese can threaten the DS-DBO (Darbuk-Skyok-Daulet Beg Oldie), a 255-kilometre strategic road recently built by India to perennially connect Sub-Sector North (SSN) at DBO.

Notwithstanding the wider politics, in the last ten years, several road and rail projects along the border have been announced by India and fast-tracked by the current Modi government, and multiple advanced landing grounds have been operationalised (and revived) near the LAC. One of the most important triggers for Sino-India tension has been the construction of the all-weather Darbuk-Shyok-DBO road, which played a key role in the Galwan Valley clash. The road took about twenty years to complete (2000–19) and gives military access to a section of the Tibet and Xinjiang region, inciting tensions since the conflict in the nearby Depsang in 2013.[4]

The domination of the Galwan area would have given an advantage to the Chinese forces from where they could interdict and cut off the supply routes to the sensitive SSN. This case is similar to the Kargil conflict when Pakistani forces occupied heights overlooking NH 1A to interdict the Srinagar–Leh Highway. This was unacceptable to the Indian Army.

Early in 2020, Coronavirus spread like wildfire from China, causing the global COVID-19 pandemic. China was being squarely blamed for deliberately allowing the biological virus to spread, and there were reports that the virus had infected some Indian Army personnel in Ladakh too. In line with their three-warfare concept, the Chinese took the world by surprise. No country in the world had prepared for a biological disaster of this scale. Besides the biological attack, at the peak of the pandemic, the Chinese were simultaneously advancing their military to the forward areas opposite Ladakh along the LAC.

The disputes about Aksai Chin (in Eastern Ladakh), which India claims, and Tawang (in Arunachal Pradesh), which China claims, have kept the two countries militarily active on the land borders ever since the countries came into existence in their current forms. On the McMahon line, the Chinese have been devising imaginative strategies after the 1962 conflict, by attacking Indian posts and later claiming those territories. Somdrong Chu, northwest of Tawang, was occupied similarly in 1986. The Chinese presence in Somdrong Chu enables the PLA to influence operations in the Zimithang sector as they can keep a direct eye on Indian Army's movements behind the ThagLa Ridge. Similarly, the PLA has been sending offensive patrols to the Yangtse (Tawang sector) since 1999, after building an operational track. The clash in Yangtse on 9 December 2022 was widely reported and connected with the continuing belligerence of China.

China's Boundary Strategy

Keeping the boundary unsettled allows China to keep India under pressure. In the absence of a formal political boundary settlement, the militaries of both countries face each other—sometimes in very close proximity—on the boundary claim lines. Since the mid-1990s, twenty-two rounds of boundary talks led by special representatives have taken place between the two nations. These, however, have been without any worthwhile outcome. In Ladakh, India continues to claim the entire Aksai Chin and China claims areas along a line that is best described by India as 'the line of Chinese perception'.

The LAC has neither been surveyed nor marked on the ground. Certain pockets have been identified as 'areas of differing perceptions', based on which the lines have been drawn for patrolling protocols. In many cases, these lines are drawn with a thick pen on the map, which translates into the boundary lines being as thick as 100 metres or more on the ground. A tent pitched a few metres this way or that way along this line can create serious trouble. Since 1993, many agreements have been signed between the two countries to resolve such matters peacefully and according to laid-out protocols. The agreement of 1996 mentions that military means shall not be used while dealing with such border situations.[5]

In the absence of any boundary settlement, both sides have come face-to-face several times, resulting in clashes, with recent ones from 2013 to 2015 in Depsang, Demchok and Chumar (all three pockets identified as areas of differing perceptions) in Eastern Ladakh. The 2020 incident in Galwan (not considered a pocket of differing perceptions) was a flashpoint of the worst kind in recent times. While the militaries of both nations fought there in 1962, Galwan has never been an active area of patrol clashes ever since. The clash of this intensity has serious ramifications with both nations having large conventional forces backed by nuclear weapons.

The China–Pakistan Nexus

Under the shadow of the agreements and protocols that the two countries are expected to respect, China has been making attempts at salami slicing the Indian territory for years. As salami is usually cut into thin slices, 'salami slicing' tactics refer to the practice of using a series of many small military actions against a much larger action that would be difficult, even unlawful, to perform in one go. On India's western borders, Pakistan, a collusive state of China, has devised a strategy of 'bleeding India by inflicting a thousand cuts.'[6] Both nations use information as a tool.

Our adversaries have created another dimension. Exploiting India's fault lines, they trigger internal strife and foster trouble in the border states of India. This results in the need for the deployment of India's security forces and military units in these states. Other than its two military fronts with China and Pakistan, India has to engage on this front, which is referred to as the 'half front'. Pakistan and China are heavily invested in engaging India in a 'proxy war'. They do this by providing support to terrorists and creating divides in Indian society, resulting in a hybrid war. This is what is collectively making India face the 'two and a half fronts' scenarios—short of a hot war—with regular forces deployed on the LOC and LAC, and Pakistan-sponsored terror groups operating in the Kashmir Valley and PLA-supported groups operating in Northeast India. Both China and Pakistan have not settled border disputes with India as they want the pot to keep boiling and yet do not allow the lid to be blown off. This aims at keeping the threshold of violence below the level of hot war, as these three countries, all armed with nuclear weapons, cannot afford to fight a conventional war. China also hopes that by building pressure on the northern borders India would remain diverted away from investing in the Indian

Ocean Region, which would allow China free play in the Indian Ocean and the countries around it.

While continuing to salami slice, China expects India to respect protocols that require both sides to exercise military restraint and dominate the LAC only through peacefully coordinated patrols. In the case of any dispute or face-off, the patrols are supposed to carry out banner drills (showing banners to indicate that both patrols should turn back without being shadowed). While Indian troops have been careful in executing these drills, the Chinese often seek opportunities, through 'talk, walk and shove', resulting in shoulder pushes and sometimes violent hand scuffles. Disputes are meant to be reported through hotline messages exchanged through phone calls between the designated border personnel meeting (BPM) points. The infrastructure of BPM is built at five places along the northern borders: two in the Ladakh sector, one in Sikkim and two along the McMahon line in Arunachal Pradesh sector.

In Ladakh, the main meeting is held inside the huts specially built at the Chushul–Moldo posts. (The Chushul post is on the Indian side and opposite it, on the Chinese side, is the Moldo post.) This is the location where meetings at the level of Corps Commander take place to solve military situations. Despite such protocols, the Chinese have continued to build modern infrastructure very close to the LAC. When India was engaged in the Kargil conflict with Pakistan in 1999, China rapidly built roads and tracks right up to the LAC so their patrolling vehicles could move on these tracks and they could dominate the area more frequently. In certain cases, China went beyond the claimed areas to push constructed tracks into disputed areas. Two prominent tracks built in 1999 were a road built along the northern banks of Lake Pangong Tso up to Finger 4 (a spur rolling down to the lake) in Eastern Ladakh,[7] and a motorable track built in the Yangtse sub-sector in the Kameng district in

Arunachal Pradesh. In both these locations, the PLA has been aggressive in pushing motorised patrols.

China's Aggressive Tactics

In the years before the Galwan skirmish that began in 2020, the Chinese had been incrementally making incursions. The incursions had become more pronounced since 2013. While the Doklam crisis involved a stand-off of seventy-two days in 2017, it was perceived that the Chinese would continue activities in Eastern Ladakh through salami slicing, to create new situations by opening more friction points on the borders.

We believe that the Galwan Valley clash was more a Chinese military response to the Doklam stand-off of 2017, which the PLA perceived as a moral loss. It was equally perpetuated by India's construction of the Daulat Beg Oldi (DBO) road.[8]

Furthermore, the connection between the Tawang clash of December 2022 and India's construction of the frontier highway in Arunachal Pradesh must be made along these lines. China now argues that Indian action along the border is limited to 'three axes': attempting to build military power, strengthening control over the area via legislation, and carrying out infrastructure construction.[9] Perhaps a trigger for the Chinese to initiate the clash in the Galwan Valley could be India's decision to change the status of Ladakh to a union territory (thereby placing it under tighter control of New Delhi), by amending its Constitution. Beijing called the act a unilateral attempt to undermine 'China's territorial sovereignty'.[10] From the Indian perspective, this decision revolves around the Kashmir issue. However, China viewed this Indian domestic administrative decision as an 'unlawful and void' move affecting areas under its control.

During the Doklam stand-off of 2017, China did not deny

that the building of the road was the cause. Instead, it argued that the road was within the Chinese territory, and not in Bhutanese territory, as claimed by India. It further held that India violated the 1890 treaty between China and Great Britain by entering Doklam.[11] In 2020, China's foreign and defence ministries again blamed Indian border troops and the road and bridge construction at the LAC in the Galwan Valley for the altercation. On 20 January 2020, the PLA opened up a new front by attacking the Indian troops after intruding the border at Naku La in the Sikkim sector where there has been no traditional dispute or claims by the Chinese. A study of the brief history of certain prominent intrusions and India's face-off with the Chinese in Eastern Ladakh shows how the two sides dealt with the border clashes between 2013 and 2015.[12]

Chinese Intrusions before the Galwan Clash

On 15 April 2013, around fifty soldiers from the PLA crossed the LAC at the northern edge of Ladakh and pitched tents at Raki Nala in the Depsang Bulge, at an altitude of about 5,000 metres. The Indian Army responded to the Chinese presence by establishing a camp 300 metres away. The PLA was on the Indian side of the LAC and thus in violation of the 1996 confidence-building agreement between India and China. According to Article II of the agreement, until the boundary question is resolved '[n]o activities of either side shall overstep the line of actual control'. With the status quo altered, both sides entered into a stand-off. Negotiations between China and India lasted nearly three weeks. Since the Chinese were far away from their base, they were supplied by trucks and supported by helicopters. The dispute was resolved in the following month, after which both sides withdrew.

Following this, on 23 October 2013, India's PM Manmohan

Singh met with China's Li Keqiang in Beijing to sign the Border Defence Cooperation Agreement (BDCA) aimed at maintaining peace along the LAC. While it was an addition to the existing border management instruments, certain terms of the agreement were specifically directed towards enhancing communication and minimising misperceptions between the two border forces. At the tactical level, troops were instructed not to tail patrols of the other side and to exercise maximum self-restraint should the two sides come face-to-face in areas where the LAC is unclear. Among other instructions, the BDCA directed border troops on both sides to hold regular flag meetings across the sectors of the LAC, conduct joint operations to tackle the smuggling of arms and contraband, and undertake small-scale tactical exercises.

Notwithstanding the new agreement, on 10 September 2014, nearly eleven months after the BDCA came into effect, the PLA patrols transgressed the borders at the southern tip of Eastern Ladakh, in Chumar (an area of differing perceptions). With President Xi's visit scheduled for India on 17 September, the Indian Army was instructed to be cautious not to create friction at this sensitive point as the Chinese are known to shift the blame to embarrass India.

By 14 September, the Indian Army units were also camping at Chumar. Indian patrols discovered that Chinese troops had deployed heavy machinery to build a road in Indian territory. Chumar is the last village in Ladakh, bordering Himachal Pradesh. This small village has been a bone of contention as it offers a vantage point at the apex of a ridge, which gives the Indian troops a clear view of Chinese movements.[13]

With only three days left for President Xi Jinping's maiden visit to India, consultations with the Ministry of External Affairs and the National Security Adviser (NSA) began in earnest. The border meetings were held between local commanders at the BPM point in Chushul-Moldo. As President Xi and his wife arrived in Ahmedabad on 17 September, a thousand more PLA troops arrived in Chumar. The Chinese side wanted India to vacate the height and claim the Tible-Mane area. While at a private dinner with President Xi in Ahmedabad and again during one-to-one talks at Hyderabad House in New Delhi, PM Modi is said to have expressed his concerns about events unfolding along the frontier.

The prime minister's official statement said that he had 'raised serious concern over repeated incidents along the border' and requested that the process of clarifying the LAC be resumed. President Xi assured PM Modi that the PLA troops would retreat to their original positions. However, when the troops didn't withdraw even after twenty-four hours, PM Modi told his guest that 'a little toothache can paralyze the entire body',[14] demonstrating that the border incidents underscored a fundamental tension in the bilateral relations between the two countries.

Scholars have argued that using the summit to publicly complain to China was a sign of India's 'stiffening attitude' towards the border dispute. The statement also challenged Beijing's long-standing assertion that the border question should be left to future generations. The stand-off continued even when PM Narendra Modi and President Xi Jinping signed twelve bilateral agreements. Finally, after twenty days, the PLA troops withdrew to their pre-September position. There were two parallel thoughts by experts: some felt the PLA had disobeyed and embarrassed President Xi while others were of the view that it was a case of deliberate posturing during the meeting to unbalance India. I go with the latter view.

Around September 2015, India and China were locked in another confrontation in the Burtse area of the Depsang plains in Ladakh. Indian satellite imagery showed a PLA installation close to India's side of the LAC. Burtse lies at the southern end of the Depsang plains. Not far from the site of the 2013 border stand-off, the Chinese had constructed a new surveillance tower. However, since it was close to a mutually agreed-upon patrolling line, Indian troops destroyed it. This prompted the PLA to call for reinforcements in the region. Indian forces responded with additional deployments. Following the procedure laid down in the 2005 confidence-building measures, India displayed banners in Chinese asking the PLA to return to its side. The crisis was defused after a series of meetings between Chinese and Indian commanders. Indian troops also seized their camera and other materials and refused to return them till the PLA soldiers had retreated to their original positions. The stand-off was thus ended within a week by the local army units and, unlike the previous two instances, did not require any political intervention.

The 2020 incursions were different, rather unique, as the year was first marked by lockdowns necessitated by the COVID-19 pandemic and then later that year China's national day celebrations were upcoming. Amidst social distancing and lockdown practices that were changing human behaviour, the Chinese may have assumed that the Indian troops would not dare to come near the purportedly diseased PLA soldiers, should the PLA advance. The CPC was to commemorate seventy years of Communist rule in China, and the year China established diplomatic relations with India. It was seventy years ago that the PLA marched into Tibet and then gradually annexed it. The following year, in 2021, the Chinese were preparing to celebrate a hundred years of the establishment of the CPC. Unfortunately, for the Chinese authorities, there was nothing significant to rejoice about during these events while President Xi Jinping desired to see his popularity rise and be celebrated. On the contrary, the Chinese were carrying the blemish of being the originators of the COVID-19 pandemic, and their internal situation was worsening with the need for constant lockdowns. Even the pet projects of President Xi, like the Belt and Road Initiative (BRI), were headed nowhere. To top it, Operation Juniper, lately conducted by India to block the Chinese at Doklam, had been repeatedly reported by Indian media as a great Indian achievement.

Chinese Military Tactics

As Sun Tsu says, 'In the midst of chaos, there is also opportunity.' The Chinese perhaps felt the need to show their might by making quick military gains. And so, using the global pain and gloom of the pandemic as an appropriate smokescreen, China resorted to aggressive tactics that included the construction of outposts and other infrastructure close to areas that Beijing considers as Chinese territory. Moreover, Xi Jinping started making public appearances in military uniforms while presiding over large ceremonial military parades. President Xi has augmented his influence and rigorously centralised decision-making power across all policy areas, especially in military matters. Thus, China not only opened up the Indian front by militarising the LAC and encroaching territory but also stirred up tension in South China Sea with PLAN's vigorous sea-domination manoeuvres.

Some military experts feel that the Galwan incident could have been averted and settled tactically as this part of LAC was not considered disputed. That may be true. However, given the geopolitical climate and Chinese compulsion, the trigger could have been at any other place. Clearly, China's intent was to embarrass India and the larger die had been cast. It is noticed that as soon as Xi Jinping came to power, the frequency of border clashes rose—Depsang in 2013, Chumar in 2014 during President Xi's India visit, Doklam in 2017 and Galwan Valley in 2020—with the intensity (and length) growing with each stand-off.[15]

The Chinese way of salami-slicing for years has been orchestrated as a well-coordinated military, diplomatic and political ensemble, to achieve surprise at any opportunity. The Chumar incident of 2014 during President Xi's visit may have looked disjointed to the straight thinker, but this is what one has to understand about the Chinese chequers. In sum, China seems to be increasingly promoting tactical cooperation in the economic sphere and multilateral forums while employing intimidation tactics (both psychological and military) to prevent India from coalescing with the Western-led security architecture.

With the Chinese, some handshakes are clearly and symbolically hand-squeezing moments. The Chinese have a body language of their own that one has to take cognizance of. They know various techniques to 'unfriend' India after any visible or overt act of 'friendship'. There have been a series of incidents where the Chinese have played up 'reverse diplomacy', such as publishing maps that show the complete state of Arunachal Pradesh as part of China to build a case of claim of 90,000 square kilometres. Issuing stapled visas or assigning Chinese names to places within Indian territories is another such Chinese ploy. Even as the Doklam border issue was at its peak in 2017, the Chinese were very keen on creating a new situation in Eastern Ladakh.

In a heated exchange of words, a senior colonel of PLA told our officer that India was also sitting in a third country (referring to Ladakh). The Chinese send hotline messages to instigate Indian troops to react offensively. In one such instance, a hotline message carried disparaging language, with abuses directed at India's leadership and at me as the Corps Commander. They would have expected India to react offensively and to retaliate, but I decided to handle the message differently. I asked my General Staff not to forward the message up the Indian ladder. Instead, I asked them to send a return message to the Chinese next morning (quote not verbatim): 'India and China are both mature countries with responsible leadership. Your message under reference seems to be a handiwork of a disgruntled PLA officer. Please confirm that the content of the hotline message is approved at the Western Theatre Command, PLA or/and the Central Military Commission. Response is awaited.' I got my message repeated twice during the day. As expected, I did not get any response.

Around the same time, in 2017, based on the behaviour pattern of the Chinese and the ground realities, I had made an assessment that China could build up and advance its troops in the coming years, and that it would do so in the month of April. When posted in Ladakh, I realised that the terrain and the weather conditions on the Chinese side during the April–June period are far better compared to the Indian side, where the snow levels are at their peak and all passes are closed. While Indian passes over the Manali and Srinagar routes only open by June every year, there is no snow in Tibet, and weather and terrain conditions are far better.

With supply routes for logistics and manpower induction closed on the Indian side, the months of April and May are the weakest and most vulnerable for India. Considering this, the period could be exploited by the PLA. I also assessed that the PLA with two army divisions (of 9,000 to 10,000 troops each) deployed opposite us in Eastern Ladakh (a division north of Pangong Tso and a division south of Pangong Tso) is better poised against our one division facing them on such a large frontage. The Chinese infrastructure makes it possible for the PLA to use centrally heated vehicles and light tanks for a speedy build-up.

The Indian hierarchy at that time was inclined to act differently. We had just stalled the Chinese moves at Doklam in the Sikkim sector and did not want to spoil the 'Wuhan spirit'. Moreover, after the well-publicised surgical strikes in Pakistan,

India had the more important task of being alert on its western borders, which reflected our constant obsession with Pakistan. At a war game, when it comes to field formations, we have found that India could be surprised due to the earlier stated reasons. There have, in fact, been earlier instances when Indian military formations had been surprised. What was observed is that while our officers do make brilliant assessments, the top leadership in Delhi looks for intelligence reports to back them up. But there were no reports that the Chinese would attack us.

The Clashes at Galwan Valley

The Galwan clash led to mayhem and the follow-up actions along the entire LAC of Eastern Ladakh were nearly simultaneous. It took a few days to know that India had lost twenty soldiers. Those killed included the commanding officer, Colonel Santosh Babu of 16 Bihar Regiment. We are told that the casualties on the Chinese side were three times more—close to sixty plus. Though an even higher number was reported, it was denied by the Chinese media. The Sino-Indian hotlines went unanswered and there was a complete breakdown of military and diplomatic channels. The PLA quickly moved troops into areas claimed by them in Depsang and deployed troops at bottleneck, blocking access of Indian patrols to PP 10, PP 11, PP 11A and PP 12 (all along the limit of patrolling in Depsang Bulge).

Along the north bank of Pangong Tso, the PLA moved in vehicles to Finger 4 using the track made by them earlier. They also occupied the historic hot spring (where the CRPF was ambushed by the Chinese in 1959) and Gogra, blocking Indian patrols' access to PP 15 and PP 16. At Demchok, they increased their strength at the hot water spring area and occupied the CNN (Charding La). They adopted an aggressive stance and the objective seemed clear: to forcibly occupy areas up to China's claim lines and, in certain areas, also occupy additional buffer grounds.

The Chinese army also beefed up its strength in certain areas on their side to cater for any reinforcements that may be needed. The PLA boats were in support of the operation from the lake. The Chinese also occupied higher ridge lines overlooking Lake Pangong Tso from the north and came down to areas that overlooked the Dhan Singh Thapa post (Finger 3) held by India. By doing so, they blocked India's access to Finger 8, which India claims. The hook routes that could take the Indian Army to threaten Finger 8 were also blocked from the ridgeline in the north or by water using the boats from the south.

The Indian troops were quick to rejoice about the news of the counterattack by the Indian ghataks at Galwan, and the Indian media went to town declaring an Indian victory, with maps and satellite pictures being shared on television. It was certainly a proud moment for India and it needed to be reported. The negatives, the positives and the unfiltered views of veterans came up for debate. Media anchors seeking inputs from the veterans on the military options and plans made one thing clear—our nation understood little about China!

Maroof Raza has done well by explaining this in his book. Another aspect that comes out is the Indian mindset—we love to celebrate but do little to understand the background of the issue. It needs to be understood that we have an unresolved boundary dispute at hand and the frontline is being managed jointly by the ITBP (formally) and the Indian Army with evolving command and control structures. There are too many stakeholders and layers managing borders, many protocols and procedures, and there are many lines on the borders that need to be understood.

To complicate matters further, we know little about Chinese culture, behaviour and language (even though both sides hold up banners). It is interesting to hear soldiers from the two sides bellowing at each other! At Galwan, the news of soldiers from both sides fighting with sticks and clubs in the twenty-first century was considered primitive and raised the question: why had soldiers from both sides not exchanged fire, even when they carried weapons on themselves?

A great deal of understanding is needed for soldiers to interpret or translate the boundary agreements and protocols on the ground. Although no weapons were used as per the 1996 and 2005 agreements—which disallow the use of firearms (including 'blast operations' or explosives) within two kilometres of the LAC—primitive weaponry like nail-studded iron rods were used to bloody effect.[16]

With China occupying Indian areas after the Galwan clashes, India was left with no option but to go ahead with a quid pro quo approach. India's media went berserk with defence experts suggesting multiple possibilities. The option involving the Kailash range, now no more confidential, was a 'Brahamastra' and was laid wide open for execution. The Chinese did not occupy the range as they had not made claims in that area and had few patrols earmarked that would visit these heights periodically. This option had been talked about in most discussions, but Indian troops had not practised the occupation of the Kailash range, which lies south of Pangong Tso and around Lake Spangur.

The Kailash range dominates the Chinese Moldo garrison from the west and south. When Indian troops executed this plan brilliantly about six weeks later, it was hoped that it would work as a lever to release PLA pressure from all areas they had occupied. The Indian Army had by now built up a specialised mountain strike corps, commanded by an experienced Corps

Commander, Lt Gen. Savneet Singh, who was familiar with this area and had served as my Divisional Commander in 2017 in the same area. Indian troops quickly occupied the Black Top area south of Pangong Tso and immediately extended their presence towards the Kailash range to include Mukhpari, Magar and Gurung Hills and down Richen and Rezang La, where India had fought pitched battles in 1962. This operation was supported with tanks, completely taking the Chinese by surprise. By occupying these ridgelines, the Indian riposte not only blocked out the Chinese threat to Chushul but also threatened the Moldo garrison of the PLA.

During my tenure as a Corps Commander, I had practised the use of tanks to occupy and fight from the heights rather than on the valley floor as had been the practice till then. After having tightened the noose on the Chinese, it was expected that Indian strategists would factor in the sensitivity of this one-time option, which meant keeping the noose tightened till all conditions of achieving the status quo ante of April 2020 were met, that is, all positions occupied by the Chinese in 2020 vacated. I am sure there must have been compulsions that made India's decision-makers give up this advantage prematurely, though these were not made public. One clear reciprocal exchange of giving up the heights of the Kailash range was that the PLA left the ridgelines north of Pangong Tso, declaring the area between Finger 3 to Finger 8 as a 'no patrol zone'.

The Chinese gradually vacated the Gogra and hot springs area. This was certainly the outcome of the sustained effort by the corps and divisional commanders of both sides. A total of nineteen meetings between the corps commanders were held at Chushul–Moldo till August 2023. Simultaneously, several meetings were also held at the political and diplomatic levels. Two years later, while the disengagement process has remained stalled, reports suggest that the PLA has not completely withdrawn from its forward location in the Kongka La region in Eastern Ladakh, and problems with patrols in Depsang and Demchok have not yet been fully resolved.[17] The Chinese are still occupying the bottleneck in Depsang and CNN junctions at Demchok.

Negotiations seem unlikely to bear fruit in the future as well, as is highlighted by Chinese foreign minister Wang Yi's repeated appeals to sidestep the border issue and continue bilateral ties as they were before the 2020 stand-off.[18] Furthermore, the Chinese strategic community has presented the 2017 Doklam stand-off as a 'peaceful resolution', but one that has 'emboldened' India.[19]

Overall, in Eastern Ladakh, even though the Chinese had two army divisions (of over 16,000 troops) deployed against one of ours (with more than 7,500), at the beginning of the conflict, China had a marginal disadvantage. Its two divisions were separated by Lake Pangong Tso, which acted like a wedge and prevented them from being able to support each other.

Pangong Tso is a narrow lake with an east-to-west lie. The Chinese have the main disadvantage as 90 kilometres of the 135-kilometre-long lake lies in the Chinese territory and only 45 kilometres on the Indian side. The Chinese troops deployed on either side had to take longer detours to support their other unit, if reserves had to move between north and south. The Chinese have now overcome this disadvantage by building a bridge over the lake on their side to move troops. The occupation of the Kailash range by Indian troops made the Chinese largely isolated at Moldo as this garrison was located at the tip of Spangur, another lake running south of Pangong Tso. The garrison is maintained by a narrow 40-kilometre-long operational road. The supplies came from Rodok (close to highway G219), which was connected by the slender forward supply route lying along the south of Lake Spangur.

On Lake Pangong Tso, Chinese and Indian troops also deployed fast patrol boats to dominate the water gap that is disputed as the ground claim lines also extend through the water. Like the ground patrols, both sides routinely send boat patrols. These patrols have also clashed in dog fights and had frequent physical push matches. The aim is to prevent the other side from getting a deeper look inside and to defend the claimed territories that extend into the water. These boats can transport small bodies of troops but cannot be used for major reinforcements across the lake to switch forces. Boats of the PLA are located at Sirijap near Finger 8 and have been used in tandem with their land patrols to touch points up to and beyond Finger 8. Both sides have recently upgraded to faster and heavier-duty performance boats and can now carry troops for quick redeployment. Both sides are equally vulnerable to long-range weapons while moving on water. Similarly, a bridge built by the Chinese astride the lake is vulnerable to observed artillery fire by Indian troops.

Challenges of High-altitude Warfare

Warfare is only one of the things that make Ladakh challenging for the soldiers. The troops have to fight the terrain and weather conditions on a daily basis, causing physical and medical difficulties. The 'area of responsibility' of Indian Army's 14 Corps is approximately 1,00,000 square kilometres. It comprises super-high–altitude areas, including the Kargil sector/sub-sector Hanif going beyond 18,000 feet, Siachen glacier (22,000 feet), Sub-sector North (17,500 feet) and Eastern Ladakh (14,000–17,000 feet). The temperature range is also exceptional—going up as high as 35 degrees in Leh in summers and as low as -60 degrees in the Siachen glacier in winters. The humidity is extremely low, oxygen levels go down by 50–60 per cent in areas with altitude above 18,000 feet. High wind-chill along with rare atmosphere makes it extremely challenging to survive. The Corps Zone remains landlocked during winters, as the winter cuts off posts for five months, leaving a big psychological impact on troops, in addition to combat and altitude load. The helicopters often fly at their extreme technical limits or even beyond the design parameters.

I have seen Indian pilots operating their helicopters with numb hands and feet. Siachen glacier remains a main challenge for the troops. Cases of cerebral vein thrombosis (CVT) and deep vein thrombosis (DVT) have been of serious concern, and even those who do not show any signs of sickness could be facing potential danger with haemoglobin count rising above 20 g/dl. At least 10–12 per cent of the troops posted in Siachen suffer from some medical issue. The distribution of ailments is as follows: chilblains, which is controllable with drill and discipline, is seen in 30–50 per cent of those reported sick; approximately 50 per cent have acute mountain sickness in first month; and high altitude pulmonary oedema (HAPO) and high altitude cerebral oedema (HACO) are noticed in 15–20 per cent of the sick. Moreover, there are between two to four cases of myocardial infarction annually. Operational casualties in avalanches are also high. Sepoy Hanamanthappa of 19 Madras became a hero, as he was found after six days from under nearly 30 feet of avalanche ice. However, he died at the hospital, suffering from severe dehydration, hypothermia, hypoxia, hypoglycemia and shock.

India's Himalayan Neighbours

Beyond Eastern Ladakh, the entire stretch of the India–China border lies in high-altitude areas. China has not only restricted militarisation of the borders with Ladakh and Arunachal Pradesh, it has expanded the points of dispute, not limiting to its borders with India. China's approach is to disturb the equilibrium in our neighbourhood with its encirclement strategy. Instead of Tibet as a territorial question, President Xi, like Mao, has concentrated on the other 'five fingers' of the Tibetan Plateau, which include the northeastern Indian states of Arunachal Pradesh and Sikkim, the Indian territory of Ladakh, and the countries of Bhutan and Nepal. China has been attempting to extend its reach into Nepal and Bhutan, countries with which India has deep cultural linkages.

Both Himalayan kingdoms have had treaties of open borders with India, allowing citizens to travel without visas. There is a deep business and marital connect between Indians and the peoples of these two countries. The inhabitants of the Terai region of Nepal have strong ethnic linkages with people of the Indo-Gangetic plains. Nepali Gurkhas have served the Indian Army with utmost loyalty and the chiefs of both armies are reciprocal honorary chiefs. There are many Nepalese people residing in India, and a large number of Gurkhas from Nepal are serving in the Indian Army and armed police forces. Moreover, as many as three times that number have served in the Indian Army in the past and now enjoy the status, privileges and pensions accorded to ex-servicemen of the Indian Army.

China managed to push Nepal to join its cartographic war agenda against India, with the release of a new map by Nepal's Communist PM, which showed Lipulekh, Kalapani and Limpiyadura as Nepalese territory. This not only alters the claims of Nepal on Indian territory but also changes the trijunction between the borders with China, making China a direct stakeholder. Nepal's new map shows part of Indian territory as Nepalese, and blocks the road built by India along River Mahakali. This was the only access to the Hindu holy land of Kailash Mansarovar by road. With this denial, all routes to the holy Mount Kailash stand blocked, others being from Chumbi Valley (with a heavy PLA presence) near Sikkim and from Demchok (with PLA occupying CNN), via Eastern Ladakh.

China insidiously also lays claims on a few villages of Nepal, seeking strategic advantages, citing historical accounts. The Chinese have clearly not stopped at the annexation of Tibet and have decided to continue with cartographic trickery to usurp their neighbour's territories incrementally. China has BRI projects being pushed not only with the rail and road network to Nepal but also has local Nepalese corporate houses now embedded with Chinese advisors.

The Chinese have been desperate for widening the narrow Chumbi Valley, near Doklam. The Chinese territory of Chumbi Valley is hemmed between Sikkim and Western Bhutan. Traditionally, there has been no dispute on the Indian border along Sikkim. However, in 2020, the Chinese patrols attempted to create a new dispute at Naku La on the stable Sikkim borders, laying claims on the pass. The Chinese have also been claiming areas that are part of Western Bhutan, to deepen the Chumbi Valley southwards so they can threaten India's Siliguri corridor, the only lifeline connecting India's northeastern states to the rest of India.

The Chinese apprehend that India and its close ally Bhutan could jointly pose a threat to them in the Chumbi corridor. Therefore, the Chinese have tried to woo the Bhutanese into their camp, asking them to establish diplomatic relations and settle their borders through a package deal where Bhutan should yield Doklam and Western Bhutan ridgelines to China in exchange for concessions on their northern borders. Apparently, the new regime in Bhutan has not taken a stiff position against this offer. Any concession given to the Chinese by the Bhutanese would create a confrontation between the PLA and the Indian Army. This could create friction between the long-standing friends India and Bhutan, an outcome desired by China.

In August 2023, China and Bhutan held the first meeting of the newly set up joint technical team on the delimitation of their disputed boundary, as officials from both sides met for four days in China and agreed to speed up a boundary resolution.[20] A joint press release from Beijing and Thimphu on the 13th Expert Group Meeting (EGM) described as an 'important outcome' the setting up of a Joint Technical Team on the Delimitation of the China–Bhutan Boundary, which held its first meeting along the sidelines of the EGM. Both sides shall be holding the 14th round[21] as soon as possible. The two nations met in Beijing on 23 October 2023 for the 25th round of boundary talks and agreed to 'build on the positive momentum'.[22] Any deal between Beijing and Thimphu that accedes to a 'swap arrangement' between areas to the north (Jamparlung and Pasamlung valleys) with Doklam to the west would be of concern to India, given the proximity to India's narrow Siliguri corridor that connects its northeastern states with the rest of the country.[23]

Chinese analysts have admitted that India 'stands in the way' of China's outreach to Bhutan due to India's long-standing historical, cultural, diplomatic and defence ties with the country.[24] In recent years, India's ties with its neighbours Nepal, Bangladesh and Bhutan, with whom it has traditionally had favourable ties, have become strained as these countries have shown a tilt towards China.[25] At the same time, Chinese experts recognise that India's concerns about its vulnerable 'chicken's neck', or the Siliguri corridor—control of which would allow China to isolate northeast India from the rest of the country in the event of a war—were a prime motive for the escalated reaction.[26]

India's Management of LAC and Borders

The management of LAC needs special mention. How to deal with the Chinese in the ambiguous geopolitical environment where political, diplomatic and military coordination within the country becomes critical is a cause of dilemma. While the issue of the ramifications for national security is handled at the highest level, the role of India's Cabinet Committee on Security becomes central where the CDS, after its creation, has a role. Functionally, India's tri-service decisions are taken by the Chiefs of Staff Committee (COSC) presided over by the CDS as its permanent Chairman. However, in the case of China, the traditional role of the China Study Group (CSG) is still significant.

For a long time, India neglected the roads along the Sino-Indian LAC in the hope that it would stall or at least slow down easy access of the Chinese into Indian territory and delay a large-scale invasion. This view that India came to hold in the 1960s prevailed for a few decades. This stance created hindrances in military transportation and mobilisation for the Indian side to respond to smaller incursions and limited conflicts. However, as India sought to remedy its lack of border infrastructure, China grew uneasy, and its actions in the ensuing years have been tactical considerations undoubtedly moved by the top leadership.

Border surveillance and policing during peacetime are globally the responsibility of the Ministry of Interior (India's

Ministry of Home Affairs [MHA]). Protection of borders from surprise incursions is the responsibility of the forces guarding the borders, which primarily includes the Central Armed Police Forces (CAPFs). These forces use conventional means of carrying surveillance across borders. India's MHA, under the concept of 'One Border-One Force' has raised several forces. The Indo-Tibetan Border Police (ITBP) has the responsibility for the northern borders (Indo-Tibetan borders) and the Seema Suraksha Bal (SSB) has been given the responsibility of India's borders with Nepal and Bhutan. Similarly, the Assam Rifles is responsible for India's border with Myanmar. Under the 'Single Point Control' concept of the MHA, the responsibility for the conduct and coordination of any activity or operations to be carried out on a particular border would be under the authority of that designated force. However, the activities on the LOC and the LAC are under dual responsibility, with the Army being the primary responder to what are considered military threats.

This area remains a cause of concern due to the dual agency issue of coordination. The involvement of the Ministry of Defence (MoD) and the military is secondary during times of peace. The Union War Book contains the provisions that would dictate the activities to be undertaken on the declaration of war and serves as the guiding document for the Government of India. Under these provisions, once invoked, all forces guarding the borders and the designated police forces of the country are placed under the operational control of the Army. The military formations and units take over the responsibility of any activity on the borders in the defence of the nation and, by implication, the responsibility of guarding the borders and the nation's defence gets transferred to the MoD. Similarly, on the Chinese side, the People Armed Police (PAP) is responsible for border policing. However, it is the PLA that is responsible for guarding China's borders. Lately, the National People's Congress has passed a new law whereby the PLA and the citizens would have a role in protecting their borders, making the PLA a direct stakeholder. The PLA units are already connected to the digital wall created by the Chinese for surveillance.

Chinese Build-up along the Himalayas

The Chinese have gradually built roads and infrastructure that connect all the forward military outposts, whereas on the Indian side, the connectivity is basically up to formation/Unit HQs and gradually expanding to connect the forward posts. Both sides carry out regular patrolling of the passes from where crossing the boundary is possible. However, many other open areas also exist where vehicle-mounted patrols carry out area domination. The PLA has built a digital wall all along their side, comprising Radomes, day and night electro-optical cameras, and digital sensors connected with OFC-5G terrestrial and non-terrestrial networks. These walls provide a constant EW and surveillance grid that alerts the forward posts and the commanders, in case of any significant activity that may be of concern to them. The PLA troops not only react to the information received with physical action but also use this data for analysis and add it to institutional memory.

Over the last three decades, China has been following a process of digitisation and referring to it as 'fighting under the conditions of informatisation'. However, the emphasis is not solely on quantity but on deploying cutting-edge military technologies and equipment, including advanced aircraft, helicopters, UAVs, missile systems, and anti-missile defence systems. These developments underscore China's heightened combat-readiness in the region, signalling a significant shift in military capabilities.

China has worked towards a long-term strategy. The slogan

of Hindi-Chini Bhai-Bhai (Indians and Chinese are brothers) was a pill coined to lull India into complacency; a pill that was swallowed by the politico-diplomatic corps, and nearly got India to disband its military in the 1960s. But China not only attacked India in 1962, it later blocked most resolutions in the UN that could favour India. Pakistan was nudged to attack India soon after the 1962 war, as a long-term strategy of collusion. Pakistan rewarded China by gifting them 5,180 square kilometres of Sakshgam Valley in 1963. Since then, China has used trade and terror as policies of expansion, using Pakistan and North Korea on its two flanks and making these terror hubs immune by positioning their nuclear arsenals.

The current impasse on the borders has caused militarisation of India's borders in places where Chinese and Indian troops had never come so close to each other in such numbers, after 1962. China's strategy of establishing dual-purpose airports is gaining momentum. The expansion of housing infrastructure in military cantonments and broader villages indicates a significant increase in population compared to the period before the stand-off.

Since the confrontations between India and China in both 2017 and 2022, there has been a noticeable strengthening of the presence of China's People's Liberation Army Air Force (PLAAF) in the strategically important places of Tibet and Xinjiang provinces, which are situated in close proximity of the Indian territory.[27] This enhancement has primarily focused on bolstering air defence capabilities and power projection, including constructing new airbases and heliports, and China has made substantial investments in improving existing infrastructure. China's Western Theatre Command has operational responsibility for the Sino-Indian border and is by far the most important and high-priority theatre for Xi Jinping.

Western Theatre Command of the PLA is the largest of China's five theatre commands, controlling the country's frontiers with Afghanistan, Pakistan, India, Nepal and Myanmar. The Chinese personnel and property along the China–Pakistan Economic Corridor are among the targets of its duties. Many of these airbases in Tibet and Xinjiang serve dual civilian and military purposes. These upgrades encompass lengthening runways and enhancing defence systems to ensure heightened operational efficiency.

The events of the 20th National Congress of the CPC, held in October 2022, further underscored the party's heightened attention on the Sino-Indian border dispute and the importance of the Western Theatre Command. Further, the CPC-elected PLA commander Qi Fabao, who was reportedly injured in the skirmishes with Indian soldiers in the Galwan Valley clash in 2020, was one of the Western Theatre Command's delegates. The party also played a video clip from the clash at the meeting to showcase the victories of the PLA in the conflict,[28] further signifying the growing importance of the role played by the boundary dispute in President Xi's strategic and political reckonings.

In Eastern Ladakh, the Chinese troops have blocked Indian troops from patrolling Depsang Bulge and have almost reached their claim line. Demchok is the closest point to highway G219, which is the main lifeline of the Chinese, through Aksai Chin. They have deployed adequate military assets and have occupied CNN in Demchok to prevent Indian access to the LAC. The intrusion in Depsang is a major concern for Indians as it brings the Chinese troops very close to DSDBO in the Burtse area. This threatens the sensitive DBO in SSN. The Chinese are occupying areas that can easily interdict DS-DBO road with short-range artillery gunfire. The DS-DBO link is the major infrastructure built to connect DBO. The Chinese may not vacate these areas at all or at least not in a hurry. The rapid pace of construction by China and its use of cutting-edge technology indicate its commitment to maintaining long-term presence in the region.

The Territory Swap Proposal

At the strategic level, the Chinese have been offering a package deal of swapping Aksai Chin with Tawang. They are laying claims on 90,000 square kilometres of Arunachal Pradesh to operationalise this 'package deal'. Their leadership has indicated a desire to settle these matters only through swap arrangements and they seem to be in no hurry to offer another alternative. They have put away boundary discussions to another day—an issue that maybe the future generations can deliberate upon. However, this status quo has not been helpful and is resulting in incremental use of force, certainly detrimental to both nations, taking us to a no-win situation. While the rest of the world is trying to decouple from China, the fact is that there are interdependencies of trade and technologies that would not allow countries to make a clean break from China.

The West is not likely to confront China directly. They would want proxies to dent China and do their job. For this, ASEAN in general and nations like India and Taiwan in particular are clear contenders. Moreover, the recognition of India's leadership role in the Indian Ocean by the US only weakens China's influence (and even severely challenges it) in the region and the world at large, while encouraging Japan, Australia and other Indo-Pacific countries to forge stronger ties with New Delhi.[29]

Meanwhile, China has been wanting India as a hedge against the regional strategy and initiatives of the US. These efforts were supported by China's neighbourhood diplomacy policy and the 'developmental partnership' outlined by the Xi and Modi administrations in 2014. However, China's outlook on its border conflict with India has swung sharply in the past decade, with Beijing attempting to unilaterally impose its land claims, thereby raising tensions between the two countries. This pivot can be attributed to two key factors: first, the changing security environment and the great-power politics that China has faced; and second, China's changing perception of India, with the latter becoming an increasingly assertive voice in regional geopolitics as an Indo-Pacific power. This policy is underpinned by the Mao Zedong–era fears of India attempting to undermine Chinese influence in the region and desiring to weaken China's hold on Tibet by leveraging the Dalai Lama's ties with India.

This wary perception towards India has been deep-seated in China's decision-making process for decades and is bound to persist until the succession of the 14th Dalai Lama is settled. The writing is on the wall: India shall not be allowed to practise strategic autonomy for long. While it is the purpose of the military to prepare for the next war, the political and diplomatic constituency must work towards avoiding confrontation and getting into the crosshairs of superpowers.

Lt Gen. P.J.S. Pannu,
PVSM, AVSM, VSM (Retd)
Former Indian Commander of
Army's 14 Corps, in Ladakh

NOTES

Author's Note

1. Neville Maxwell: *India's China War*, updated edition (Natraj Publishers, 2015, p. xii)
2. Ibid., p. xiii.
3. Iqbal Malhotra, *Red Fear: The China Threat* (Bloomsbury, 2020), pp. 70–90.
4. J.P. Dalvi, *Himalayan Blunder* (Thacker, 1969), p. 372.
5. Maroof Raza, '2020 is not 1962', *OPEN* (New Delhi), 18 September 2020.
6. Kanti Bajpai, 'The incompatibles: Four reasons why India and China are not friend', *OPEN* (New Delhi) 28 June 2021

1. Defining the Boundaries

1. Ladakh, earlier a part of the Indian state of Jammu and Kashmir, became a Union Territory—a federal territory governed, in part or in whole, by the Central Government of India—on 31 October 2019.
2. Mao Zedong, also known as Mao Tse-tung or Chairman Mao, was a Chinese Communist revolutionary and founder of the People's Republic of China from 1949 until his death in 1976.
3. Iqbal Malhotra, *Red Fear*, op. cit.; Kunal Verma, *1962: The War That Wasn't* (Aleph Book Company, New Delhi, 2016).
4. Alok Bansal, 'India-China Boundary Dispute in Ladakh', in

Shakti Sinha (ed.), *One Mountain Two Tigers* (Pentagon Press, India, 2020), pp. 50–51; Krishnan Srinivasan, 'India, China, Tibet', *The Statesman* (India), 19 September 2020.

5. Krishnan Srinivasan, 'India, China, Tibet', op. cit. Also see, Iqbal Malhotra and Maroof Raza, *Kashmir's Untold Story: Declassified* (Bloomsbury, 2019), p. 112.
6. Alok Bansal, 'India-China Boundary Dispute in Ladakh', op. cit., pp. 55–57.
7. Ibid, pp. 55–56; Iqbal Malhotra, *Red Fear*, op. cit., p. 9.
8. Alok Bansal, 'India-China Boundary Dispute in Ladakh', op. cit., pp. 55–57.
9. Sinkiang was renamed Xinjiang in 1884 when the area was conquered by the Qing dynasty of China. Today, it is part of the People's Republic of China.
10. Alok Bansal, 'India-China Boundary Dispute in Ladakh', op. cit., p. 56.
11. Ibid. Also see 'China takes 1959 line on perception of LAC', *Hindustan Times* (New Delhi), 29 September 2020, front page.
12. Phunchok Stobdan, *The Great Game in the Buddhist Himalayas: India and China's Quest for Strategic Dominance* (Penguin India, 2020), pp. 54–55.
13. Ibid., p. 62.
14. J.J. Singh, *The McMahon Line: A Century of Discord* (HarperCollins, 2019), pp. 98–102.
15. *The Economist*, 18 November 1950, cited in Rajesh Kadian, *Tibet, India, China* (Vision Books, 1999), pp. 119–120.
16. J.J. Singh, *The McMahon Line*, op. cit., pp. 163–167.
17. Phunchok Stobdan, *The Great Game in the Buddhist Himalayas*, op. cit., p. 56.
18. Rajesh Kadian, *Tibet, India, China*, op. cit., pp. 71–77.
19. J.J. Singh, *The McMahon Line*, op. cit., pp. 166–167.
20. Ibid., pp. 168–170.
21. Ibid., pp. 78–79; Phunchok Stobdan, *The Great Game in the Buddhist Himalayas*, op. cit., p. 62.
22. J.J. Singh, *The McMahon Line*, op. cit., pp. 177–178
23. Ibid., p. 178.

24. Ibid., pp. 178–79, 186–88.
25. Ibid., pp. 188–192.
26. Ibid., pp. 192–194.
27. Ibid., p. 196.
28. Ibid., p. 197.
29. Ibid., pp. 198–99; Rajesh Kadian, *Tibet, India, China*, op. cit., p. 78.
30. Rajesh Kadian, *Tibet, India, China*, op. cit., p. 78.
31. J.J. Singh, *The McMahon Line*, op. cit., pp. 202–203.
32. Lt Gen. Baljit Singh, 'Tibet and trail blazing the McMahon Line in 1913', *SALUTE*, 16 January 2020, https://salute.co.in/tibet-and-trail-blazing-the-mcmahon-line-in-1913/
33. J.J. Singh, *The McMahon Line*, op. cit. pp. 204–205.
34. Ibid., pp. 209, 218.

2. China on the World Stage

1. Kuomintang or KMT, referred to in English as the National People's Party, was a major political party that governed mainland China from 1928 to 1949 under Chiang Kai-shek and his successors.
2. Phunchok Stobdan, *The Great Game in the Buddhist Himalayas: India and China's Quest for Strategic Dominance* (Vintage Books, 2019), pp. 57–59.
3. The Beiyang Army was a western-style Imperial Chinese Army established by the Qing dynasty that was divided into military cliques or factions, controlled by warlords, known as the Beiyang Clique.
4. Iqbal Malhotra, *Red Fear: The China Threat* (Bloomsbury, 2020), p. 136.
5. The Chinese Civil War was fought between the Kuomintang-led government of the Republic of China and the forces of the CPC between 1927 and 1949 that started when the CPC launched an uprising in Nanking. This conflict led to the creation of the Red Army of Mao Zedong.

6. Sinkiang province was then ruled by a succession of warlords from Tihwa, present-day Urumchi or Wushi and the capital of the Xinjiang Uygur Autonomous Region in the far northwest of the People's Republic of China.
7. Iqbal Malhotra, *Red Fear*, op. cit., p. 147.
8. Ibid.
9. Ibid., pp. 147–48; Sheng Shicai's memoir, *Red Failure in Sinkiang*, was published in 1958.
10. The region of Gilgit-Baltistan, north of Kashmir region and an administrative territory of Pakistan today, was historically a part of western Tibet. Bordered with Afghanistan to its north and Sinkiang to its northeast, it has Jammu & Kashmir and Ladakh to its southeast.
11. Iqbal Malhotra, *Red Fear*, op. cit., p. 144.
12. The NKVD or People's Commissariat for Internal Affairs was a government department and law-enforcement agency of the Soviet Union that underwent many structural changes in its organisation between 1938 and 1939.
13. Iqbal Malhotra, *Red Fear*, op. cit., p. 147; Mark Dickens, *The Soviets in Xinjiang 1911–1949* (Oxus Communications, 1990).
14. Iqbal Malhotra, *Red Fear*, op. cit., p. 148
15. Ibid.
16. Qinghai is a landlocked province in the northwest of the People's Republic of China.
17. Iqbal Malhotra, *Red Fear*, op. cit., pp. 149, 158–159.

18 This entire allied plan has been explained in good detail by Iqbal Malhotra in *Red Fear*, op. cit., pp. 150–156.

19. Iqbal Malhotra, *Red Fear*, op. cit., pp. 154–156; David Holloway, *Stalin and the Bomb: The Soviet Union and Atomic Energy, 1939-1956* (Yale University Press, 1994).
20. Iqbal Malhotra, *Red Fear*, op. cit., pp. 166–167.
21. Ibid., p. 163.
22. Ibid.
23. Ibid.
24. Ibid., pp. 177–180.
25. Ibid., pp. 174–175.

26. Ibid., p. 193; also see Dieter Heinzig, *The Soviet Union and Communist China, 1945–1950: The Arduous Road to the Alliance* (M.E. Sharpe, 1998; Routledge, 2015).
27. The 38th parallel north is a circle of latitude that is 38 degrees north of the Earth's equatorial plane and formed the border between North and South Korea prior to the Korean War.
28. Iqbal Malhotra, *Red Fear*, op. cit., pp. 182–183.
29. Michael Dillon, *Xinjiang and the Expansion of Chinese Communist Power* (Routledge, 2015).
30. Iqbal Malhotra, *Red Fear*, op. cit., p. 202.
31. Rajesh Kadian, *Tibet, India, China* (Vision Books, 1999), p. 120. Zhou Enlai was then known as Chou En-Lai.
32. Ibid. *The Economist* dated 18 November 1950 quoted on Suzerainty of Tibet.
33. Phunchok Stobdan, *The Great Game in the Buddhist Himalayas*, op. cit., pp. 57, 85–87.
34. Ibid., p. 68.

3. An Ambitious Adversary

1. Iqbal Malhotra, *Red Fear: The China Threat* (Bloomsbury, 2020), pp. 70–90.
2. Ibid., p. 174.
3. Ibid, p. 178.
4. Ibid, pp. 199, 215, 225.
5. Ibid, pp. 205–206.
6. Ibid.; Phunchok Stobdan, *The Great Game in the Buddhist Himalayas: India and China's Quest for Strategic Dominance* (Penguin India, 2020), p. 86.
7. Assam was then a vast state that covered most of India's northeast, except the North East Frontier Agency, which is primarily present-day Arunachal Pradesh.
8. Iqbal Malhotra, *Red Fear*, op. cit., p. 208.
9. Ibid., pp. 210–211; The Chinese advance on the Bumla axis, would lead to the fall of Tawang in the 1962 conflict.

10. Ibid.; Malhotra's detailed account of Major Khathing's operation is based on accounts by historian Claude Arpi and Lt Col H. Bhushan Singh.
11. Ibid., pp. 212, 219.
12. Ibid., pp. 219–220.
13. Ibid., pp. 215–218.
14. Shantanu K. Bansal, 'Why Report on Captain Rajendra Nath's 1952 Expedition to Aksai Chin is Classified to This Day', Indian Aerospace Defence News (IADN), 17 October 2020, https://newsiadn.wordpress.com/2020/10/17/why-report-on-capt-rajendra-naths-1952-expedition-to-aksai-chin-is-classified-to-this-day/.
15. Claude Arpi, 'The Panchsheel Agreement', *Indian Defence Review*, 5 August 2015, http://www.indiandefencereview.com/spotlights/the-panchsheel-agreement/.
16. An expert in Sinology, the study of China primarily through Chinese philosophy, language, literature, culture and society.
17. Iqbal Malhotra, *Red Fear*, op. cit., pp. 221–222, 226–227; Claude Arpi, 'The Indian Village in Tibet', *Indian Defence Review*, 8 December 2017, http://www.indiandefencereview.com/the-indian-village-in-tibet/.
18. Iqbal Malhotra, *Red Fear*, op. cit., p. 228; Rajesh Kadian, *Tibet, India, China* (Vision Books, New Delhi, 1999), p. 126.
19. Iqbal Malhotra, *Red Fear*, op. cit., pp. 230–231.
20. Ibid., pp. 229–230; Michael S. Minor, 'China's Nuclear Development Program', *Asian Survey*, Vol. 16, No. 6 (June 1976).
21. Iqbal Malhotra, *Red Fear*, op. cit., p. 231.
22. Ibid., p. 204; Phunchok Stobdan, *The Great Game in the Buddhist Himalayas*, op. cit., p. 86.
23. Phunchok Stobdan, *The Great Game in the Buddhist Himalayas*, op. cit., pp. 86–89; Iqbal Malhotra, *Red Fear*, op. cit., p. 234.
24. Kenneth Conboy and James Morrison, *The CIA's Secret War in Tibet* (University Press of Kansas, 2002); 'Anti-Communist Activities, Tibet 2. Chinese Communist Activities, Tibet', General

CIA Records (31 December 1952), https://www.cia.gov/library/readingroom/docs/CIA-RDP82-00457R015700080003-1.pdf.

25. Iqbal Malhotra, *Red Fear,* op.cit., p. 235.
26. Rajesh Kadian, *Tibet, India, China*, op. cit., pp. 119–120, 125–128.

4. Prelude to a Conflict

1. Giri Deshingkar, *The Nehru Years Revisited* (1998), quoted in Phunchok Stobdan, *The Great Game in the Buddhist Himalayas: India and China's Quest for Strategic Dominance* (Penguin India, 2020), pp. 88–89.
2. Rajesh Kadian, *Tibet, India, China* (Vision Books, New Delhi, 1999), p. 131.
3. Mikel Dunham, *Buddha's Warriors* (Penguin, 2004); Joe F. Leeker's essay in www.utdallas.ed, quoted in Phunchok Stobdan, *The Great Game in the Buddhist Himalayas*, op. cit., p. 100.
4. Phunchok Stobdan, *The Great Game in the Buddhist Himalayas*, op. cit., p. 10.
5. Rajesh Kadian, *Tibet, India, China*, op. cit., p. 120.
6. Phunchok Stobdan, *The Great Game in the Buddhist Himalayas*, op. cit., p. 95.
7. Iqbal Malhotra, *Red Fear: The China Threat* (Bloomsbury, 2020), pp. 243–246.
8. Rajesh Kadian, *Tibet, India, China*, op. cit., pp. 132–133.
9. Iqbal Malhotra, *Red Fear*, op. cit., pp. 246–247; Phunchok Stobdan, *The Great Game in the Buddhist Himalayas*, op. cit., pp. 84, 89.
10. Rajesh Kadian, *Tibet, India, China*, op. cit., pp. 132, 134.
11. Phunchok Stobdan, *The Great Game in the Buddhist Himalayas*, op. cit., p. 91
12. 'The Great Game' refers to the intense political rivalry between the British and the Russian empires for dominance and control over Afghanistan and neighbouring territories in Central and South Asia that existed for most of the nineteenth century.

13. Phunchok Stobdan, *The Great Game in the Buddhist Himalayas*, op. cit., p. 86.
14. Rajesh Kadian, *Tibet, India, China*, op. cit., p. 136; Phunchok Stobdan, *The Great Game in the Buddhist Himalayas*, op. cit., p. 96.
15. Phunchok Stobdan, *The Great Game in the Buddhist Himalayas*, op. cit., pp. 119, 136.
16. Rajesh Kadian, *Tibet, India, China*, op. cit., pp. 119–120.
17. Ibid., p. 125.
18. Phunchok Stobdan, *The Great Game in the Buddhist Himalayas*, op. cit., p. 92.
19. Ibid.; Rajesh Kadian, *Tibet, India, China*, op. cit., p. 135.
20. Benjamin Zachariah, *Nehru* (London: Routledge, 2004), cited by Phunchok Stobdan, *The Great Game in the Buddhist Himalayas*, op. cit., pp. 87–88.
21. S. Gopal, *Jawaharlal Nehru: A Biography*, vol. 3 (Jonathan Cape, 1984), p. 122, quoted in Phunchok Stobdan, *The Great Game in the Buddhist Himalayas*, op. cit., p. 87.
22. Giri Deshingkar, *The Nehru Years Revisited*, op. cit., p. 88.
23. Phunchok Stobdan, *The Great Game in the Buddhist Himalayas*, op. cit., pp. 88–89; B.N. Mullik, *My Years with Nehru: The Chinese Betrayal* (Allied Publishers, 1971).
24. Kunal Verma, *1962: The War That Wasn't* (Aleph Book Company, New Delhi, 2016), p. 22.
25. Paramilitary forces are presently under the Home Ministry.
26. Kunal Verma, *1962: The War That Wasn't*, op cit., p. 26.
27. Ibid., pp. 26–27.
28. Ibid, pp. 30–31.
29. Ibid., pp. 38–42.
30. K. Subramanyam quoted by Kunal Verma, *1962: The War That Wasn't*, op. cit., p. 44.
31. K. Subramanyam quoted by Kunal Verma, *1962: The War That Wasn't*, op. cit., p. 46.
32. Arun Shourie, *Self Deception: India's China Policies* (HarperCollins India, 2013), pp. 261–263.
33. Kunal Verma, *1962: The War That Wasn't*, op. cit., pp. 50–57.

5. The Confrontation

1. Great Leap Forward, Britannica, https://www.britannica.com/event/Great-Leap-Forward.
2. Gautam Das, *China Tibet India: The 1962 War and the Strategic Military Future* (HarAnand Publishers, New Delhi, 2009), pp. 106, 118; John Garver, quoted in Gautam Das, op. cit., pp. 152–153.
3. John W. Garver, 'China's Decision for War with India in 1962', in Alastair Iain Johnston and Robert S. Ross (eds), *New Directions in the Study of China's Foreign Policy* (Stanford University Press, 2006).
4. From Li's research findings, see website article titled: 'Suppressing Rebellion in Tibet and the China-India Border War' reported by Ajai Shukla in *Business Standard*, 8 December 2017.
5. 'India–China War of 1962: How it started and what happened later', *India Today*, 21 November 2016, https://www.indiatoday.in/education-today/gk-current-affairs/story/india-china-war-of-1962-839077-2016-11-21.
6. https://www.rediff.com/news/column/india-is-in-a-timidity-trap-with-china/20140402.htm). Also see Ajay Singh, 'The Shadow of 1962', in Shakti Sinha (ed.), *One Mountain Two Tigers* (Pentagon Press, 2020), pp. 66–68.
7. Iqbal Malhotra, *Red Fear: The China Threat* (Bloomsbury, 2020); Kunal Verma, *1962: The War That Wasn't* (Aleph Book Company, New Delhi, 2016), p. 272, https://www.indiatoday.in/education-today/gk-current-affairs/story/india-china-war-of-1962-839077-2016-11-21.
8. James B. Galvin, quoted in Gautam Das, *China Tibet India*, op. cit., p. 152.
9. Ajay Singh, 'The Shadow of 1962', op. cit., pp. 68–69.
10. Kunal Verma, *1962: The War That Wasn't*, op. cit., pp. 44, 113; Gautam Das, *China Tibet India*, op. cit., p. 163.
11. Kunal Verma, *1962: The War That Wasn't*, op. cit., pp 122–123.
12. A military corps is a battlefield formation made up of two or more divisions and typically commanded by a lieutenant general.

13. Ajay Singh, 'The Shadow of 1962', op. cit., p. 68; Brig. John Dalvi, quoted in Gautam Das, *China Tibet India,* op. cit., p. 163.
14. Kunal Verma, *1962: The War That Wasn't,* op. cit., p. 117; Ajay Singh, 'The Shadow of 1962', op. cit., pp. 68–69.
15. Ministry of Defence (annexure 1-A) No: 11987/JS(G)/62 COAS of 22-9-1962 (22 September 1962), quoted in Kunal Verma, *1962: The War That Wasn't,* op. cit., p. 122.
16. Kunal Verma, *1962: The War That Wasn't,* op. cit., pp. 121, 127–128.
17. Ibid., pp. 113, 129.
18. Brig. J.P. Dalvi, *Himalayan Blunder: The Curtain Raiser to the Sino-Indian War of 1962* (Natraj Publishers, 2021); Kunal Verma, *1962: The War That Wasn't,* op. cit., pp 129–132.
19. Kunal Verma, *1962: The War That Wasn't,* op. cit., pp. 134–135, 146–149, 188.
20. Gautam Das, *China Tibet India,* op. cit., pp. 174–175.
21. Kunal Verma, *1962: The War That Wasn't,* op. cit., p. 164; Gautam Das, *China Tibet India,* op. cit., p. 176.
22. Kunal Verma, *1962: The War That Wasn't,* op. cit., pp. 202–204.
23. Ibid.
24. Ibid., pp. 203–204.
25. Ibid., pp. 201, 212.
26. Ibid., op. cit., pp. 44, 46, 325.
27. Ibid., op. cit., pp. 332–362.
28. Ibid., pp. 380–382.
29. See interview of Wg Cdr JM Nath with historian Claude Arpi, https://www.rediff.com/news/interview/what-if-nehru-had-used-the-iaf-in-1962/20190301.htm.
30. Ibid.
31. Kunal Verma, *1962: The War That Wasn't,* op. cit., pp. 382–383.
32. Gautam Das, *China Tibet India,* op. cit., p. 202; Kunal Verma, *1962: The War That Wasn't,* op. cit.
33. Ajay Singh, 'The Shadow of 1962', op. cit., pp. 70–71.
34. Kunal Verma, *1962: The War That Wasn't,* op. cit. pp 367–368, 371; the Government of India, both in Nehru's tenure and then even Prime Minister L.B. Shastri's, denied that two letters were

sent to J.F. Kennedy, but these were later accessed by Inder Malhotra once declassified.

35. Kunal Verma, *1962: The War That Wasn't*, op. cit., pp. 391–393.
36. Gautam Das, *China Tibet India*, op. cit., pp. 200–201.
37. Iqbal Malhotra, *Red Fear*, op. cit., pp. 268–271, 277–278.
38. Ibid., p. 273.
39. Ibid., pp. 174, 268, 271, 276–277.
40. Ibid., p. 274. His claim is based on a book by Jung Chang and Jon Halliday, *Mao: The Unknown Story* (Random House, UK, 2007).
41. Iqbal Malhotra argues this in his *Red Fear*, op. cit.

6. The Post-war Report

1. Dunkirk is a French seaport from where nearly 3.5 lakh Allied troops were evacuated to England in mid-1940 during the Second World War.
2. *The Statesman*, 28 November 1962, quoted in Neville Maxwell, *India's China War*, revised edition (Natraj Publishers, India, 2021).
3. Kunal Verma, *1962: The War That Wasn't* (Aleph Book Company, New Delhi, 2016), pp. 365, 366, 374.
4. Ibid., p. 375.
5. Neville Maxwell, *India's China War*, op. cit., pp. 498–500.
6. Gautam Das, *China Tibet India: The 1962 War and the Strategic Military Future* (HarAnand Publishers, New Delhi, 2009), p. 317; Neville Maxwell, *India's China War*, op. cit., quoted in *Mint*, 13 July 2014.
7. Claude Arpi, '50 years later, what has the GoI got to hide?' https://www.rediff.com/news/special/fifty-years-what-has-the-government-got-to-hide/20120808.htm; also see, R.D. Pradhan, *Beyond Expectations: Tale of a Civil Servant In and Out of Office* (Ingram Publishers, 2016).
8. Neville Maxwell, quoted in Gautam Das, *China Tibet India*, op. cit. pp. 320–321.

9. Kunal Verma, *The War That Wasn't*, op. cit., p. 375.
10. Claude Arpi, '50 years later, what has the GoI got to hide?', op. cit.
11. These excerpts are from: Claude Arpi, '50 years later, what has the GoI got to hide?', op. cit.
12. Ashok Malik, 'Jaitley's U-Turn on the Henderson Brooks Report is Problematic', ndtv.com, 16 Septtember 2014; 'Henderson-Brooks Report: Hidden truths of a forgotten debacle', *Mint*, 13 July 2014.
13. Gautam Das, *China Tibet India*, op. cit., p. 320.
14. Claude Arpi, '50 years later, what has the GoI got to hide?', op. cit.
15. Ibid.
16. Ibid.
17. Ibid.
18. Ibid.
19. Kunal Verma, *The War That Wasn't*, op. cit., p. 56.
20. Claude Arpi, '50 years later, what has the GoI got to hide?', op. cit.
21. Ibid.
22. Ibid.
23. Ram Madhav, 'Brooks Report: Four failures that led to the 1962 debacle', 21 March 2014, https://www.rediff.com/news/column/brooks-report-four-failures-that-led-to-the-1962-debacle/20140321.htm.
24. Ibid.
25. Ibid.
26. Ibid.
27. Ibid.

7. A Forgotten Victory

1. Major General Randhir Sinh, 'Nathula 1967: A Lesson from History', *Fauji India* (October 2017).
2. Iqbal Malhotra, *Red Fear: The China Threat* (Bloomsbury,

2020); Kunal Verma, *1962: The War That Wasn't* (Aleph Book Company, New Delhi, 2016), p. 310.

3. Vandana Menon and Nayanika Chatterjee, 'Remembering the war we forgot: 51 years ago, how India gave China a bloody nose', *The Print*, 1 October 2018, https://theprint.in/defence/remembering-the-war-we-forgot-51-years-ago-how-india-gave-china-a-bloody-nose/127356/.
4. CIA report, Declassified in Part, approved for Release 2011/11/25: CIA- RDP85T00875R0010000010027-7, cited in Vandana Menon and Nayanika Chatterjee, 'Remembering the war we forgot', op. cit.
5. Vandana Menon and Nayanika Chatterjee, 'Remembering the war we forgot', op. cit.
6. Ibid.
7. An Indian Army division is intermediate between a corps and a brigade. Each division is headed by a General Officer Commanding (GOC) holding the rank of major general. An Infantry division has around 7,000 combat soldiers and over 2,000 combat support and logistics troops.
8. Major General Randhir Sinh, 'Nathula 1967', op. cit.; Iqbal Malhotra, *Red Fear*, op. cit., p. 309.
9. Ibid.; http://www.indiandefensenews.in/2017/09/skirmish-1967-revisited-bit-of.html.
10. Major Chandrakant Singh, VrC, 'Tibet abandoned and the lessons from Nathu La 1967', *SALUTE*, Vol. 9, Issue 9 (June–July 2017), pp. 14–17.
11. Sushant Singh, 'India-China border dispute: What happened in Nathu La in 1967?' *Indian Express*, 18 June 2020, https://indianexpress.com/article/explained/explained-what-happened-in-nathu-la-in-1967-india-china-border-dispute-6462532/.
12. Ibid.; Major Chandrakant Singh, VrC, 'Tibet abandoned and the lessons from Nathu La 1967', op. cit.
13. Intermediate between a company and section, a platoon is headed by a Captain or Lieutenant, and has a total strength of about 32 troops.

14. A company headed by a Major or Captain contains three to five platoons and around 120 soldiers.
15. Major General Randhir Sinh, 'Nathula 1967', op. cit.
16. http://www.indiandefensenews.in/2018/03/inside-story-of-how-india-gave-china.html
17. http://www.indiandefensenews.in/2018/03/inside-story-of-how-india-gave-china.html
18. Major General Randhir Sinh, 'Nathula 1967', op. cit.
19. Ibid.
20. Major General V.K. Singh, 'Lieutenant General Sagat Singh, PVSM: India's Finest Combat Leader', in *Leadership in Indian Army* (Sage, 2015).
21. Gautam Das, op. cit.,p. 216.
22. Major General Randhir Singh, *A Talent for War: The Military Biography of Lt Gen Sagat Singh* (VIJ Books, 2013); Major General V.K. Singh, 'Lieutenant General Sagat Singh, PVSM: India's Finest Combat Leader', op. cit.
23. http://www.indiandefensenews.in/2018/03/inside-story-of-how-india-gave-china.html.
24. Major Chandrakant Singh, VrC, 'Tibet abandoned and the lessons from Nathu La 1967', op. cit.
25. Gautam Das, *China Tibet India: The 1962 War and the Strategic Military Future* (HarAnand Publishers, New Delhi, 2009), p. 216; Major General Sheru Thapliyal, 'When Chinese were given a bloody nose', *Indian Defence Review*, 22 February 2018.
26. Probal Das Gupta, *Watershed 1967: India's Forgotten Victory over China* (Juggernaut Books, New Delhi, 2020).
27. http://www.indiandefensenews.in/2020/02/1967-when-india-fought-china-to-restore.html.

8. China's Strategic Intrusions

1. Zorawar Daulet Singh, 'Twists and turns in the India-China border saga', *Outlook India*, 26 May 2015, https://www.outlookindia.com/website/story/twists-and-turns-in-the-india-china-border-saga/294406.

2. J.J. Singh, *The McMahon Line: A Century of Discord* (HarperCollins, 2019).
3. Gautam Das, *China Tibet India: The 1962 War and the Strategic Military Future* (HarAnand Publishers, New Delhi, 2009), pp. 129–130.
4. Iqbal Malhotra, *Red Fear: The China Threat* (Bloomsbury, 2020), pp. 208–11.
5. V. Natarajan, 'The Somdorong Chu incident', *Bharat* Rakshak, 12 October 2006, https://www.bharat-rakshak.com/ARMY/history/siachen/286-Sumdorong-Incident.html.
6. Col. A.K. Jayachandran (retd), 'When Chinese troops came into Somdorong Chu and the Wangdung incident – 1986', *SALUTE*, Sept–Oct 2020, https://salute.co.in/when-chinese-troops-came-into-somdorong-chu-and-the-wangdung-incident-1986/.
7. V. Natarajan, 'The Somdorong Chu incident', op. cit.
8. https://idsa.in/idsacomments/CurrentChineseincursionLessonsfromSomdurongChuIncident_msingh_260413); Manoj Joshi, 'Operation Falcon', *The Quint*, 3 July 2017; Gautam Das, *China Tibet India*, op. cit., p. 217.
9. China Report , compilation of news reports in Vol. 23, Nos 1 & 3, 1987, published by The Centre for the Study of Developing Societies, New Delhi; Iqbal Malhotra, *Red Fear*, op. cit., pp. 328–329.
10. V. Natarajan, 'The Somdorong Chu incident', op. cit.
11. This author was then in service in the Indian Army, in the armoured division, and has known General Sundarji personally. Some of these operational scenarios were similar to those spelt out in Ravi Rikhye, *Fourth Round: Indo-Pak War 1984* (ABC Publishing House, 1982); also see Ravi Rikhye, *Militarization of Mother India* (Chanakya Publications, 1990).
12. Col. A.K. Jayachandran (retd), 'When Chinese troops came into Somdorong Chu and the Wangdung incident – 1986', op. cit.
13. Ibid.; Manoj Joshi, 'Operation Falcon', op. cit.; Gautam Das, *China Tibet India*, op. cit., p. 217.
14. V. Natarajan, 'The Somdorong Chu incident', op. cit.
15. Manoj Joshi, 'Operation Falcon', op. cit. This event was

explained by General Sundarji to this author at a private dinner in Washington in April 1995, at the residence of Dr Rajesh Kadian, the author of *Tibet, India, China* (Vision Books, India, 1999).

16. Manoj Joshi, 'Operation Falcon', op. cit. Indeed, the stand that General Sundarji took has been confirmed by other sources too.
17. Ibid.
18. https://idsa.in/idsacomments/CurrentChineseincursionLessonsfromSomdurongChuIncident_msingh_260413.
19. Ibid.; Manoj Joshi, 'Operation Falcon', op. cit.
20. *India Today* (15 May 1988) has a detailed analysis on General Sundarji's military career.
21. V. Natarajan, 'The Somdorong Chu incident', op. cit.; https://www.orfonline.org/research/operation-falcon-when-general-sundarji-took-the-chinese-by-surprise/.
22. R.S. Kalha, *India-China Boundary Issues: Quest for Settlement* (Indian Council for World Affairs, 2014), p. 211.
23. Manoj Joshi, 'Sino-Indian Border Deadlock: Time to Rewrite India Playbook', ORF Occasional Paper 269 (2020), p. 19.
24. Ibid., p. 11.
25. Ibid., p. 20
26. Ibid, p. 21.
27. Zorawar Dalaut Singh, *Power Shift* (Macmillan, 2021), pp. 107–108.
28. Manoj Joshi, 'Sino-Indian Border Deadlock', op. cit.
29. Ibid., p. 21
30. Ibid., p. 23.
31. Shivshankar Menon, *Choices: Inside the Making of India's Foreign Policy* (New Delhi: Penguin/Allen Lane, 2016).
32. Shyam Saran, *How India Sees the World: Kautilya to the 21st Century* (New Delhi: Juggernaut, 2017); Manoj Joshi, 'Sino-Indian Border Deadlock', op. cit.
33. V. Natarajan, 'The Somdorong Chu incident', op. cit.
34. Doklam is part of the Chumbi Valley that lies primarily in Tibet. On the western edge of the Doklam plateau is Doka La, a mountain pass that either connects the Indian state of Sikkim with Tibet in China or links Sikkim and western Bhutan.

35. http://www.xinhuanet.com/english/2017-08/02/c_136494625_7.htm.
36. http://indianexpress.com/article/opinion/india-china-stand-off-bhutan-clash-trijunction-eyeball-to-eyeball-in-the-himalayas-region-4728629/.
37. Apoorva Goel, 'India China standoff: How and why', *SALUTE*, June–July 2017, p. 10, https://salute.co.in/read-salute-pdf/salute-june-july-2017.pdf.
38. Col. (retd) Anil Bhat, in the chapter on Doklam stand-off in *China Bloodies Bullet-less Border* (Pentagon Press, Delhi, 2021).
39. Ibid.
40. Ibid.
41. https://timesofindia.indiatimes.com/india/differences-should-not-become-disputes-sitharaman-tells-chinese-defence-minister/articleshow/63899297.cms.
42. https://www.foreignaffairs.com/articles/asia/2017-09-07/what-were-chinas-objectives-doklam-dispute.
43. http://www.globaltimes.cn/content/982843.shtml.
44. http://www.thehindu.com/news/international/us-envoys-arunachal-is-part-of-india-remark-irks-china/article8556158.ece.
45. Col. (retd) Anil Bhat, in the chapter on Doklam stand-off in *China Bloodies Bullet-less Border*, op. cit.
46. Ibid.; http://www.globaltimes.cn/content/1057440.shtm.
47. Ibid.; Col. (retd) Anil Bhat, in the chapter on Doklam stand-off in *China Bloodies Bullet-less Border*, op. cit.
48. https://www.livemint.com/Politics/cZgraaRn8WS5ZAY9qiM1KJ/China-says-infrastructure-in-Doklam-aimed-at-improving-lives.html.
49. https://www.linkedin.com/pulse/china-lies-india-believes-road-ahead-lt-gen-p-g-kamath/.
50. http://indianexpress.com/article/india/gen-v-p-malik-calls-for-full-review-of-ties-with-china-diplomatically-economically-militarily-4801780/.
51. Ibid.

9. LAC: 2020 Was Not 1962

1. Ajay Singh, 'The Shadow of 1962', in Shakti Sinha (ed.), *One Mountain Two Tigers* (Pentagon Press, 2020), p. 66.
2. *Hindustan Times*, 30 September 2020, front page.
3. Zorawar Daulet Singh, *Power Shift: India-China Relations in a Multipolar World* (PanMacmillan, New Delhi, 2020), p. 114.
4. Ibid., pp. 107–108.
5. Ibid., pp. 113, 114, 106.
6. Gen. J.J. Singh, on 'Latitude', a television show of Maroof Raza, 21 August 2019.
7. See Wikipedia on 'Five Fingers of Tibet' and several references on it; also explained by Suhasini Haider, *The Hindu*, 18 June 2020.
8. Zorawar Daulet Singh in *Hindustan Times*, 24 November 2020.
9. Government of India's press releases of 2018 and 2019, quoted in Manoj Joshi, 'Sino-Indian Border Deadlock: Time to Rewrite India Playbook', ORF Occasional Paper 269 (2020), p. 32.
10. Sujan R. Chenoy, *Indian Express* (Ideas Page), 13 January 2021.
11. Vinod Bhatia, 'Post Galwan: Deter China's Aggressive Behaviour', in Shakti Sinha (ed.), *One Mountain Two Tigers* (Pentagon, 2020), pp. 109, 112.
12. *Hindustan Times*, Editorial, 18 October 2020.
13. M.K. Rasgotra, 'Beijing aims to humiliate New Delhi: Counter it', *Hindustan Times* (Opinion page), 24 October 2020.
14. Vinod Bhatia, 'Post Galwan', op. cit., p. 107.
15. Soumya Bhowmick, 'Chinese investments in Indian startups: Trends and Controversies', 5 June 2021, orfonline.org; Prabhash K. Dutta, 'How much Chinese money is there in Indian economy', *India Today*, 18 June 2020.
16. Details published in 'Finally calling China's bluff', *Outlook*, 19 April 2020; *Economic Times*, 23 April 2020.
17. Iqbal Malhotra, *Red Fear: The China Threat* (Bloomsbury, 2020), pp. 284–285.
18. Ajay Singh, 'The Shadow of 1962', op. cit., p. 66.

19. 'Is it laboratory born', *OPEN*, 3 April 2020.
20. The Belt and Road Initiative is President Xi's strategy to strengthen China's economic leadership through vast infrastructure building throughout China's neighbouring regions to connect Asia with Africa and Europe via land and maritime networks.
21. Iqbal Malhotra and Maroof Raza, *Kashmir's Untold Story: Declassified* (Bloomsbury, 2019), pp. 153–158.
22. The China–Pakistan Economic Corridor (CPEC) is a collection of infrastructure projects that are under construction throughout Pakistan since 2013 that are intended to transform Pakistan's economy by modernising its road, rail, air and energy transportation systems and to connect the deep-sea Pakistani ports of Gwadar and Karachi to China's Xinjiang province and beyond by overland routes. https://www.britannica.com/topic/China-Pakistan-Economic-Corridor.
23. For a detailed account on the CPEC, see Andrew Small, *The China Pakistan Axis* (Penguin Vintage, 2015), pp. 188–200; Sujan Chenoy on CPEC, *Hindustan Times* (Edit page), 20 January 2021.
24. Iqbal Malhotra and Maroof Raza, *Kashmir's Untold Story*, op. cit., p. 154
25. Brahma Chellaney, *Times of India*, Editorial (Ideas) page, 21 August 2019.
26. *Indian Express*, 24 April 2018.
27. Vinod Bhatia, 'Post Galwan', op. cit., pp. 112–113.
28. 'List of 10 latest defence deals of India in 2020', https://m.jagranjosh.com (1 July 2020); also see defencenews.in (6 July 2020).
29. Admiral Arun Prakash, 'A maritime awakening', *Indian Express* (Editorial page), 15 September 2020.
30. Zorawar D. Singh, *Power Shift*, op. cit., p. 115.
31. Ibid., essay by Admiral Arun Prakash.
32. *The Kargil Review Committee Report* (Sage Publications, New Delhi, 2000).
33. The Daulat Beg Oldi road connects Leh to the base of the Karakoram Pass and runs almost parallel to the border separating Ladakh from China's Sinkiang province. The road, which

has been two decades in the making, would allow the rapid deployment of Indian troops to the disputed area and has become a flashpoint between India and China.

34. YouTube report on *Defence Updates* in mid-2020
35. Kyle Mizokami, 'Here's every aircraft carrier in the world', *Popular Mechanics*, 16 December 2020.
36. David Axe, 'China's submarine fleet is huge. The US plans to whittle away at it with mines', https://www.forbes.com/sites/davidaxe/2021/06/08/chinas-submarine-fleet-is-huge-the-us-navy-plans-to-whittle-away-at-it-with-mines/?sh=5f38e052297a, 8 June 2021; H.I. Sutton, 'Chinese navy steps closer to new generation of nuclear submarines', https://www.forbes.com/sites/hisutton/2020/06/19/chinese-navy-gets-closer-to-new-generation-of-nuclear-submarines/?sh=7c6ac57d229e, 19 June 2020.

China's Boundary Policy on the Himalayas: An Afterword

1. Col. Birendra Roy, China Study Forum, CDM 2019.
2. Foreign Ministry Spokesperson Zhao Lijian's Regular Press Conference, Ministry of Foreign Affairs (PRC), Press Release, 17 June 2020, https://www.fmprc.gov.cn/ce/cgmb/eng/fyrth/t1789509.htm.
3. Zhao Xiaozhuo, 'Why Is India Sensitive to China's Road Building?' *China Daily*, 26 July 2017, https://www.chinadaily.com.cn/opinion/2017-07/26/content_30247528.htm; Liu Lin, 'India-China Doklam Standoff: A Chinese Perspective', *Diplomat*, 27 July 2017, https://thediplomat. com/2017/07/india-china-doklam-standoff-a-chinese-perspective.
4. Prem Shankar Jha, 'Are China and India Going Back to 1962?' *The Wire*, 29 May 2020, https:// thewire.in/diplomacy/china-india-border-tensions-1962; Nirupama Subramanian, 'The Strategic Road to DBO', *Indian Express*, 16 June 2020, https://indianexpress.com/article/explained/lac-stand-off-india-china-darbuk-shyok-daulat-beg-oldie-dsdbo-road-6452997.
5. P.J.S. Pannu, *Hindustan Times*, 20 June 2020.

6. Lt Gen. Hamid Gul, ex-DG, ISI, quoted in Peter Chalk and Christine C. Fair, 'Lashkar-e-Tayyiba Leads the Kashmir Insurgency', *Jane's Intelligence Review*, Vol. 14, No. 11 (November 2002).
7. This was observed by Indian military units, under HQ 14 Corps, including myself, in Ladakh.
8. 'From Doklam to Galwan Valley: Be Wary of Three Changes on the Sino-Indian Border Issue', Institute of Regional and Country Studies, Peking University, 29 August 2020, https://m.thepaper.cn/baijiahao_8911416.
9. Zhang Zhaozhong, 'The Indian Army Crossed the Sino-Indian Border to Provoke Zhang Zhaozhong: Were They Trying to Avenge a Past Defeat?', *Sina*, 22 May 2020, https://mil.news.sina.com.cn/jssd/2020-05-22/doc-iircuyvi4432817.shtml.
10. 'Foreign Ministry Spokesperson Hua Chunying's Remarks on the Indian Government's Announcement of the Establishment of the Ladakh Union Territory Which Involves Chinese Territory', Ministry of Foreign Affairs (PRC), 6 August 2019, https://www.fmprc.gov.cn/mfa_eng/xwfw_665399/s2510_665401/2535_665405/201908/t20190806_696969.html.
11. 'Full Text of Facts and China's Position Concerning Indian Border Troops' Crossing of China-India Boundary', *China Daily*, 3 August 2017, https://www.chinadaily.com.cn/world/2017-08/03/ content_30341027.htm.
12. Shibani Mehta, Impasse at the LAC, Carnegie India, 31 August 2023.
13. Ibid.
14. TNN, 'Chinese Incursion in Ladakh: A Little Toothache Can Paralyze Entire Body, Modi Tells Xi Jinping', *The Times of India*, 20 September 2014, https://timesofindia.indiatimes.com/india/chinese-incursion-in-ladakh-a-little-toothache-can-paralyze-entire-body-modi-tells-xi-jinping/articleshow/42940337.cms.
15. Ashley J. Tellis, 'Hustling in the Himalayas: The Sino-Indian Border Confrontation', Carnegie Endowment for International Peace, 4 June 2020, https://carnegieendowment.org/2020/06/04/hustling-in-himalayas-sino-indian-border-confrontation-pub-81979.

16. 'Agreement between the Government of the Republic of India and the Government of the People's Republic of China on Confidence-building Measures in the Military Field along the Line of Actual Control in the India-China Border Areas', *UN Peacemaker*, 29 November 1996, https://peacemaker.un.org/sites/peacemaker.un.org/files/CN%20IN_961129_Agreement%20between%20China%20 and%20India.pdf; 'Galwan Valley: Image Appears to Show Nail-studded Rods Used in India-China Brawl', BBC News, 18 June 2020, https://www.bbc.com/news/world-asia-india-53089037.
17. Shishir Gupta, 'Two Years after Galwan, De-escalation Still to Take Place on Ladakh LAC', *Hindustan Times*, 5 May 2022, https://www.hindustantimes.com/india-news/two-years-after-galwan-de-escalation-still-to-take-place-on-ladakh-lac-101651719113285.html.
18. 'Wang Yi Holds Talks with Indian External Affairs Minister Subrahmanyam Jaishankar', Ministry of Foreign Affairs (PRC), Press Release, 25 March 2022, https://www.fmprc.gov.cn/mfa_eng/topics_665678/kjgzbdfyyq/202203/t20220326_10656097.html.
19. Zongyi Liu, 'Boundary Standoff and China-India Relations: A Chinese Scholar's Perspective', *China Quarterly of International Strategic Studies*, Vol. 6, No. 2 (2020): 223–48.
20. Ananth Krishnan and Suhasini Haidar, *The Hindu*, 25 August 2023.
21. Press Trust of India, published by *Indian Today*, 25 August 2023.
22. Ministry of Foreign Affairs of the People's Republic of China, 24 October 2023.
23. Ibid.
24. Wang Qi, 'China, Bhutan Agree to Maintain Border Peace and Stability', *Global Times*, 9 April 2021, https://www.globaltimes.cn/page/202104/1220652.shtml.
25. Jagannath Panda, 'China's Projection and Pursuit of Power in South Asia: Implications for India', testimony before the U.S.-China Economic and Security Review Commission,

Washington, D.C., 12 May 2022, https://www.uscc.gov/sites/default/files/2022-05/Jagannath_Panda_Testimony.pdf.

26. Liu Lin, 'India-China Doklam Standoff: A Chinese Perspective', *The Diplomat*, 27 July 2017, https://thediplomat.com/2017/07/india-china-doklam-standoff-a-chinese-perspective/.
27. Dr NIthiyanandam, 'Rapid Military Infrastructure Expansion in Tibet: A Satellite Imagery Analysis', *Geospatial Bulletin*, Takshashila Institution.
28. 'At Communist Party Congress, China Plays Galwan Valley Video', *Daily Guardian*, 17 October 2022, https://thedailyguardian.com/at-communist-party-congress-china-plays-galwan-valley-video.
29. Jagannath Panda, 'Beijing's Asian NATO Maximon QuadIs Structural', Pacific Forum, *PacNet*, No. 61, 22 November 2019, https://idsa.in/system/files/news/PacNet-Commentary-Beijing.pdf.

INDEX